MEN OF FIRE

MEN OF FIRE

TORCHBEARERS OF THE GOSPEL

BY WALTER RUSSELL BOWIE

Harper & Row · Publishers · New York · Evanston · London

To the men of the Virginia Seminary
who for many generations have carried the gospel fire

Contents

Foreword

"I came to cast fire upon the earth; and would that it were already kindled!"

So Jesus said to his disciples; and the fire indeed was kindled. It would be a fire of affliction in which their courage would be tested, as gold in the furnace is tried; a fire on the altar of sacrifice where fear and selfishness could be burned away. It would also be like the light of a lamp to illumine their minds and consciences; and a flame within their hearts to burn there as unquenchable devotion.

In all these ways the fire which their Lord and Master made to blaze has come down through the centuries in generation after generation of those who have learned what loyalty to him could mean. No one can presume to write the roll of that long succession: a roll which includes not only the great according to men's recognition, but also humble souls known only to God. But the following chapters tell the continuing story of some of those who as torchbearers of the gospel from the beginning until now have been Men of Fire.

W. R. B.

MEN OF FIRE

❧ I ❧

Peter

The wonder of the Christian gospel is that its message from God
came through a life lived among men. The gospel was not first
read in a book; it was seen and known in Jesus. For the disciples,
their faith was built upon "that . . . which we have heard, which
we have seen with our eyes, which we have looked upon and
touched with our hands, concerning the word of life" (I John
1:1).

And as the gospel came through a living figure, so it was to be
transmitted through other lives. "You shall be my witnesses,"
said Jesus to the men who followed him; and it was by what
those men were and what they did that the spirit of Christ has
been passed on like a flame from generation to generation. It is
good to look back and to remember who some of those were that
began the great succession.

The first name that comes instinctively to mind is that of
Simon Peter; and there is immediate suggestion in that doubling
of his name. At first he was only Simon, a fisherman on the
Lake of Galilee. Then one day—according to the Gospel of
John—when Simon and Andrew his brother had gone down to
the Jordan River where John the Baptist was preaching, they encountered Jesus. When Jesus looked at Simon he saw in him a
possibility which few if any of Simon's acquaintances might
have recognized. He said to Simon that from that day forward
he should have a new name, Cephas—from the Aramaic, *Kepha*.
Sometimes in the Gospels he is called Cephas, but more often by

the Greek translation of *Kepha*, which is *Petros*, and in its English form is Peter. And Peter, like Cephas, means "a Rock."

Peter's history after that is the gradual story of how he grew toward the reality which Jesus had foreshadowed in the name he gave.

The accounts in the Gospels make plain the fact that Peter was no rocklike character to begin with. One of the great features of the Gospels is the honesty of their description of the disciples. These men might ultimately be remembered as "Saint" so-and-so, but the Gospels show them in their first ordinariness before the power of Christ had worked in them the elements of sainthood. Simon in the beginning was no hero. He had a mingled strength and weakness which were very human.

What then specifically were his characteristics, insofar as we can discern them?

He must have been a virile person. Fishing on the Lake of Galilee, with its sudden and treacherous winds, was rough work. A man had to be a man to measure up to it. And there is nothing in the Gospels to suggest anything other than that Simon was in the fullness of a young man's strength. For some reason, Christian art traditionally pictures Peter as an oldish man, although the most conspicuous facts about him suggest exactly the reverse of the kind of quieting down that comes with middle age. He had the vehemence and impulsiveness that belong to the years when a man's early energies are still at their flood tide.

It was his impulsiveness and his vehemence that made Peter lovable, but also led him into trouble. He could follow his emotions quickly, but he did not always follow through.

In regard to that double fact, consider first the positive side. In any group and in any circumstances, Peter was nearly always the first to act. On the day when Jesus came along the shore of the Lake of Galilee and saw some men in their fishing boats and said to them, "Follow me," it was Peter, with Andrew his brother, who first responded. On a day after that when the disciples were caught on the Lake in a storm and suddenly they saw Jesus, it was Peter—according to the Gospel of Matthew—who cried out, "Lord, . . . bid me come to you on the water."

At Caesarea Philippi when Jesus gathered the disciples round him and asked them what the people were saying about him, and then who *they* thought he was, it was Peter who burst out with the exclamation, "You are the Christ!" And at the Last Supper, when Jesus warned of the coming dangers which might make them all desert, it was Peter who declared passionately, "I will never fall away. . . . Even if I must die with you, I will not deny you." (Matt. 26:33-34).

But he did! And in the earlier instances also his impulses had come short. When he tried to go to Jesus on the water, his faith failed and he began to sink. When he made his great confession of Jesus as the Christ, he then went on into a blundering effort to tell his Master what sort of Christ he ought to be. In the Garden of Gethsemane when Jesus had to ask his disciples, "Could you not watch with me one hour?" Peter had fallen asleep like the rest. And following on presently to the house of Caiaphas where Jesus was arraigned, Peter had cowered before the questions of a servant girl and denied with an oath that he had had anything to do with Jesus.

Then when Jesus turned and looked at him, there swept over Peter the awful realization of what he had done; and he went out and wept bitterly. It seemed a wretched business that all he could do now was to cry his heart out. But at least his emotions were alive, and there was cleansing in them. Even in the depths of his shame that he had denied his Master, he knew that the love of Jesus would not let him go. He might have hanged himself, like Judas, but something stronger held him back. However much he had failed, the purpose of Jesus for him must not fail.

So, after the crucifixion and the resurrection, there is a different Peter. Not a finished Peter, for he would never be fully that. Not a man without flaws, but a man who had come through the furnace where some of the slag in him had been burned away and the metal refined. Although he was not a Rock yet, he was at least a great deal nearer to being one than he had been before.

Part of the story of Peter's subsequent career is in the book of Acts, and part of it in the traditions and legends of the early church. Old weaknesses have not disappeared, but the dominant picture of Peter now is that of a man in whom a tremendous change has been wrought. The former impulsiveness has been steadied by a new power which had come to him from trust in his risen and living Lord. He is the leader now not merely in being the first to say something, but in being the first to do something that would also be dependable. He was the center of the little group that gathered together in Jerusalem after Jesus was no longer with them, and on Pentecost he went out and preached to the crowds in the city streets that "God has made him both Lord and Christ, this Jesus whom you crucified" (Acts 2:36). When he and John had been arrested for healing a lame man in the name of Jesus, the ruling Council before whom they were arraigned took knowledge of their "boldness"; and when they were threatened and ordered not to preach again concerning Jesus, it was Peter who dared to answer, "Whether it is right in the sight of God to listen to you rather than to God, you must judge; for we cannot but speak of what we have seen and heard" (Acts 4:19-20).

As one who had been born a Jew and lived with the thought of the Jews' religious separateness, Peter supposed that no Gentiles belonged within the fellowship that would be gathered when the Messiah came. When he called Jesus "the Christ," he was calling him the Messiah by another name; he would be the Savior of "the Chosen People" of Israel, but those outside Israel could have no claim upon him. That apparently was what Peter believed when he had the vision which is described in the tenth chapter of Acts. One day he went up on the flat roof of the house of a man whose guest he was, and there in a trance he saw something like a great sheet let down from heaven; and in it were all kinds of animals and reptiles and wild birds—of the sort that the rules about decent food would prohibit any faithful Jew to eat. There came a voice to Peter which told him to rise up and to kill and eat.

"No!" he answered. "I have never eaten anything that is common or unclean."

But the voice spoke a second time: "What God has cleansed you must not call common." Three times that happened; and then the sheet seemed to be taken up again into heaven, leaving Peter perplexed as to what the vision he had seen might mean.

He was soon to learn. For in the city of Caesarea there was a Roman centurion named Cornelius, "a devout man who feared God with all his household." In his prayer, Cornelius was given an awareness that in the city of Joppa there was a man named Peter who would have a message from God for him. So he sent one of his soldiers and two servants to look for Peter and to ask him to come to Caesarea. They found Peter and gave him Cornelius' message; and Peter went with them to Caesarea and to Cornelius' house, where the Roman awaited him, together with his kinsmen and close friends, whom he had called together.

"You yourselves know," said Peter, "how unlawful it is for a Jew to associate with or to visit anyone of another nation, but God has shown me that I should not call any man common or unclean. So when I was sent for, I came without objection. I ask, then, why you sent for me."

The climax of this same chapter of Acts is the account of how Peter, at Cornelius' desire, told of Jesus: of his life that had been filled by God "with the Holy Spirit and with power," and of his death and his resurrection. And when Cornelius and his company were greatly moved, Peter recognized what to him was the sign of God that these Gentiles should be baptized into the fellowship of Christ. So he did baptize them.

When Peter next went to Jerusalem, he found that the news of what he had done in Caesarea had gone before him. Some of the apostles and the other brethren were much disturbed. "Why did you go to uncircumcised men and eat with them?" they demanded.

Then Peter told them the whole story: of his vision on the housetop at Joppa, of Cornelius' message, of his going to Cornelius' house, and of how it seemed that the Holy Spirit came upon Cornelius and his family and friends as they heard of Jesus. "If then God gave the same gift to them as he gave to us when we believed in the Lord Jesus Christ," said Peter, "who was I that I could withstand God?"

So the words of Peter prevailed; and the account in Acts con-

cludes with the description of the disciples in Jerusalem glorify-
ing God and saying, "Then to the Gentiles also God has granted
repentance unto life."

Thus Peter had moved over from the conservative to what
would become the liberal conception of the Christian church.
For the most part, he would stand with those who wanted the
doors of welcome open to the Gentiles—for the most part, but
not quite always. Sometimes, as in the old days, he fell short of
dependability. In Paul's letter to the Galatians (2:11-21) there is
a reference to what Peter did once in Antioch when a new little
Christian congregation was being gathered in that non-Jewish
city. The question was whether those who had been born into
the supposed special spiritual privilege of being Jews should sit
down to eat with Gentile Christians. Peter was inclined at first
to do so, but when some of those he knew best came from Jerusalem to Antioch and wanted to have nothing to do with Gentiles
there, Peter did not want his friends to criticize him—any more
than he had wanted the maidservant in Caiaphas' court to point
an accusing finger at him; so he shifted his ground, and said that
he would not eat with Gentiles either, which made Paul say, "I
opposed him to his face." But, after that, Peter came back to the
more generous and courageous attitude which he had had when
he responded to the call of Cornelius. In the fifteenth chapter of
Acts is the account of a Council of all the apostles and elders in
Jerusalem assembled to hear from Paul and Barnabas how they
had preached Christ among the Gentile peoples of Asia Minor.
The question was whether the converts there ought to be cir-
cumcised and made obedient to all the Mosaic laws. Some insisted that they should be, but Peter came to the defense of the
larger freedom which Paul and Barnabas believed in. Why should
the Council, he said, "make trial of God by putting a yoke upon
the neck of the disciples which neither our fathers nor we have
been able to bear? . . . We believe that we shall be saved through
the grace of the Lord Jesus, just as they will."

After that reference to him at the Council of Jerusalem, no
more is told of Peter in the entire book of Acts. In the beginning,
Peter had been the most vivid and conspicuous figure among the

disciples, and after the crucifixion and the resurrection he was obviously the one looked up to as the head of the church which was gathering in Jerusalem. But it is equally plain that at the Council described in Acts 15 he was not the official head; it was James, the brother of Jesus, who was presiding. Apparently Peter now was the apostle who would help shepherd those churches beyond Jerusalem which were made up mostly of persons who had been Jews. That may have been why he was in Antioch at the time, described by Paul, when he hesitated about having full fellowship with Gentile converts because he was deterred by men who "came from James." Traditions which have come down from the early church say that he went later to Rome; that in Rome he and the young John Mark came together, and that Peter told him part of what Mark later wrote in his Gospel; and that ultimately, in Rome, Peter died a martyr's death. With these traditions which may rest on solid fact there is also a beautiful, though unsupported, legend. According to it, Peter who had been in Rome, was fleeing in fear from the persecution which had broken out within the city. On the road he met a stranger coming in, and when he looked again he saw that it was Christ. *"Quo vadis, Domine?"* he said; "Where are you going, Lord?" The answer came, "I go to Rome to suffer in your place." Then Peter, moved again to a devotion greater than his fear, turned back to Rome and was crucified, like his Lord.

In the New Testament itself there is no statement of Peter having been in Rome—as, on the contrary, there is the explicit description in Acts of Paul's arrival there; and the traditions concerning his connection with the city must be sifted so as to distinguish between the facts and the elaborations which have been woven round them. In Christian writers of the second century, there begin to be references to the tradition that the church in Rome was founded by Peter and Paul: a manifest error, inasmuch as Paul's epistle to the Romans makes unmistakably plain that he was writing to a church which already existed and which he had never seen. If Paul was thus certainly not one of the founders of the church in Rome, there may be an equal error in the tradition that Peter founded it. It may have begun instead by the witness of humble disciples whose names, "known only to God," have long since disappeared from human memory, like the men and women equally unknown who created the church at Antioch. But that Peter did come later to Rome rests on stronger evidence; and there is good reason to believe that both Peter and Paul were in Rome at the time of the persecution of the Christians in the reign of Nero, that they were put to death and buried somewhere there; and furthermore, that they may have been betrayed to the persecutors by fanatical Jewish-born disciples who resented the part that Peter, as well as Paul, had played in letting Gentiles into the church.

The Roman Catholic Church, as is well known, has built a great superstructure of dogmatic claims upon what is supposed to have been the divinely given primacy of Peter. It asserts that Jesus himself gave Peter authority over the rest of the original apostles, that Peter founded the church in Rome, that he was the first bishop of the church there in the imperial city, that he transmitted his supreme spiritual authority to his successors in that bishopric, and that thus what has grown into the Roman papacy represents the continuing purpose which has come down unbrokenly from Christ himself. Who was it but to Peter, the Roman Catholic advocates ask, that according to Matthew 16:18, Jesus said, "You are Peter, and on this rock I will build my church, and the powers of death shall not prevail against it"?

No other passage in the whole New Testament has given rise to such debate and such conflicting judgments as have centered round those words. The Roman Church links them with its claim—for which the New Testament gives no evidence—that Peter was the first Bishop of the Church in Rome, and that he handed on to an unbroken line of his successors a supreme spiritual authority which Christ had given explicitly to him; conclusions which, for non-Roman thought, are only dogmas which a right interpretation of the facts can never justify.

There is uncertainty, in the first place, as to the words "on this rock . . . ," which appear in Matthew's Gospel only, and have no parallel in the Gospels of Mark and Luke. Many New Testament scholars believe that in the reference to "my church,"

the words concern a period later than that of the earthly life
of Jesus, and that therefore in the form in which Matthew gives
them they did not come directly from Jesus' lips. But suppose
they did. There remains then the vital question: What do they
mean?

In the mind of Jesus, what is "this rock" on which "I will
build my church"? Said Chrysostom: the rock means the faith
confessed. Said Augustine: the rock is Christ. And Martin Luther
believed that this is what Jesus would have Peter hear and understand: "You are . . . the rock man, for you have recognized the
true man who is the true Rock, and you have named him as the
scripture names him, which is Christ."[1]

Oscar Cullman, one of the contemporary New Testament
scholars who stands in the highest rank for learning and sobriety
of judgment, in his profound book *Peter: Disciple, Apostle, Martyr* defends the genuineness of the words in Matthew's Gospel;
and then he reads in them a meaning much like that which Luther
saw. Simon Peter *was* the rock which Christ would make the
special foundation for the early church. Peter had been the leading figure among those who were the companions of Jesus during his earthly ministry; Peter—according to I Corinthians 15:5
—was the first to whom the risen Lord appeared. He, out of his
own knowledge, and out of his experience of weakness gradually
lifted by Jesus into strength, could pre-eminently "hand on the
news that Jesus, who lived and died on earth, died and rose for
the salvation of the world." And if it be asked, "How can the
church today still be founded upon the historical person of the
Apostle Peter?" the answer is, "Without apostles we would have
no New Testament, no knowledge at all of Jesus the Risen One.
Everything that we know of him we owe to them. And this is
true of Peter in a special way. Papias tells that the Gospel of
Mark was written according to the sermons of the apostle Peter,
and so rests upon his testimony. If this report is correct, then it
is also historical to say that the oral tradition lying behind the
written Gospels goes back in the first instance to the apostle
Peter, especially if we, in agreement with recent study, regard
the Gospel of Mark as the oldest Gospel. When we read the

Gospels, we are thus in contact with the person of the apostles and the rock apostle."[2] And through the witness to the power of Christ which comes to us through him the church is forever builded and renewed.

Thus Cullman, the Protestant scholar, magnifies the importance of Peter who belongs to all Christendom and not to one division of it. At the same time, with devastating thoroughness, he shows that Jesus' promise of the part that Peter would play and did play in furnishing the foundation of spiritual faith on which the early church in Jerusalem was built, had nothing to do with what might happen to the church in Rome. "Neither from Scripture nor from the history of the ancient Church can a divine right for the primacy of Rome be derived. . . . Ancient tradition . . . knows nothing of a government of the Church at large from Rome by Peter, and also knows nothing of a transfer of his succession to the Roman Bishops."[3]

When all is said and done, it is a twisted and unreal representation of the eager and loving but often stumbling and fallible and altogether human Simon Peter to turn him into the alleged foundation for a huge and supposedly infallible legal structure. Of truer insight are the words about Peter in Dean Charles R. Brown's book *These Twelve*. It is "upon first-hand knowledge of spiritual reality gained by personal experience of the divine help . . . that God will build his church. Upon that personal experience of divine help which changes weakness into strength, God will establish that kingdom which is an everlasting kingdom."[4]

So it is not Peter the alleged first pope, but the struggling, stumbling, yet achieving Peter of the New Testament record, who is a permanent inspiration. Besides the accounts of Peter in the Gospels and in Acts, the New Testament includes the brief but precious book which according to early and confident testimony of Clement of Rome, Polycarp, and Irenaeus, has come to us as the message of the apostle himself, the First Letter of Peter. Reading that letter is as though we heard again the real voice of the man who loved his Lord, denied him once and failed him, but then was saved into great and lifelong devotion by the love

that would not let him go: "Blessed be the God and Father of our
Lord Jesus Christ! By his great mercy we have been born anew
to a living hope through the resurrection of Jesus Christ. . . .
He himself bore our sins in his body on the tree, that we might
die to sin and live to righteousness. By his wounds you have been
healed" (I Pet. 1:3; 2:24).

II

Paul

Certainly the greatest and most influential of all the servants of Christ was the man who in his spiritual self-abasement called himself "the least of the apostles": Saul of Tarsus, who became the dedicated Paul.

In his famous book, *The Varieties of Religious Experience*, William James distinguished between the "once-born" and the "twice-born" human souls. The "once-born" are those whose religious life seems to develop without crisis. Their awareness of God and their response to him seems like the growth and unfolding of the seed into the flower. But the experience of the "twice-born" as they strive toward God is very different. For them "there are two lives, the natural and the spiritual, and we must lose the one before we can participate in the other,"[1] and the process may be one of crisis and of agony. That was true of Saul of Tarsus, turned into Paul. And because he was of the "twice-born" type, the story of his religious life is a drama which has always gripped the imagination of Christians who try to understand it.

The main facts of his life are clear. He belonged to the Jews of the Dispersion, that great number of the people of Israel who were scattered through many provinces of the Roman world, but bound together by common blood and by unbreakable loyalty to their ancestral faith. They had their local synagogues, but their devotion turned also toward Jerusalem, the Holy City. They paid their taxes for the Temple, and thousands of them went to worship at Passover and other great festivals of the Jewish year. In

Jerusalem, also, were the chief centers for the study and teaching of the law.

Saul went as a young man from Tarsus to Palestine. According to Acts, he was a student in the rabbinical school, at Jerusalem, of the famous expounder of the law, Gamaliel. If so, he may have been in the city in that Passover week of passionate events when Jesus of Nazareth came in with the little group of men who followed him from Galilee, taught in the Temple, purged it of the traders whose greedy traffic was corrupting it, then was arrested, tried, and crucified.

Did Saul of Tarsus see him? There is no evidence that he did. But what is certain is that not long after the crucifixion, Saul encountered the fact of Jesus as a disturbing influence in Jerusalem. There were men and women in the city who believed and said that this man of Nazareth who had been crucified had risen from the dead, and that he was now the living Lord who fulfilled the age-long hope of Israel for a Redeemer.

From that idea Saul of Tarsus recoiled as from intolerable blasphemy. He would stop its spread, and stamp it out if he could. So when he first appears on the stage of history it is as a persecutor of the people who were presently to be called "the Christians."

The impulse that moved him, and the reasons for it, are not hard to understand.

First of all, it must have seemed to him that the proud hopes of Israel were being turned into ignominy. Down through many centuries, and straight to Saul himself, had come the faith that the glory which God destined for Israel would some day be revealed and vindicated among the nations of the earth. When the one anointed by God to be Messiah should appear with the clouds of heaven, then there would be given to him "an everlasting dominion, which shall not pass away, and his kingdom one that shall not be destroyed" (Dan. 7:14). What was it then but subversive falsehood to say that a man crucified on a Roman cross was meant to be the Christ? With the angry patriotism which was to him a religious passion, Saul would avenge that insult to his people's expectation.

And the covenant on which Israel's hope depended had been

put in danger. To the Chosen People, God had given his promise through Abraham, and through Moses he had given them his law. The promise of salvation depended upon obedience to the law. *That* had been the divinely appointed lamp for Israel's feet and the light upon its path. Righteousness meant behavior that followed the strict pathway of the law, and careless departure from it was apostasy. But this Jesus of Nazareth—what had the law meant to him? The law that was ordained to keep the Sabbath holy, the law of fasting, the law of aloofness from sinners and the unregenerate crowd—which of these had he not violated? And should *this* man be allowed now to become a center of devotion?

Furthermore, Saul knew that he was not alone in what he felt about Jesus. The authorities of the Jewish church had condemned him. Rejection of Jesus meant orthodoxy, and agreement with every responsible and respectable religious group.

So it seemed that Saul was a man completely sure of himself. Who could have seen in him the hidden man that would break through in crucial change?

But new potentials were there. Underneath the surface of his vehement assertions, Saul was restless and dissatisfied. He did not show it then; he would not have admitted it to himself; but his inner being was split by a deep frustration whose tremors he was powerless to keep from his unwilling consciousness. Religion to him was a matter of intense and desperate importance. He wanted to be sure of his acceptance in the sight of God, and all his training had taught him that what God desired was faithful observance of the law. Therefore, he had been "as to the law a Pharisee," and he had done his utmost to attain such a point of faithfulness that he could be accounted "as to righteousness under the law blameless." But as he was afterward to write in his letter to the Romans, "I find it to be a law that when I want to do right, evil lies close at hand. For I delight in the law of God, in my inmost self, but I see in my members another law at war with the law of my mind and making me captive to the law of sin . . ." (7:21-23). Thus he had begun to be like a man who tries to climb toward heaven on stairs that move under him in a treadmill, so that every attempted step of goodness upward was brought to nothing by the drag that pulled him back. How then by his own strength would he ever come close to what he thought was the goal of God's demands? And what verdict could he expect except of failure when he stood before the divine judgment which must reckon a man's worth implacably according to his deeds? Therefore, in Saul the persecutor, outwardly so aggressive, so single of purpose and fanatically sure, already there was the smothered cry which later he was to put into words, "Wretched man that I am!"

But, to his astonishment, the followers of Jesus whom he was arresting were not wretched. The conditions surrounding them might be described by that word, but no such word could be applied to *them*. He saw in their faces a light and a courage which he could not understand. The first of them to die, Stephen the deacon, whose stoning he himself had witnessed, had cried out as he was dying, "Lord Jesus, receive my spirit." This "Lord Jesus" who had been crucified was the one who had been called "a friend of tax collectors and sinners," and who had said once that he had not come for the sake of the righteous but in order to call sinners to repentance. He had told a parable in which the hero was not a priest or a Levite or even a Jew, but one of the despised race of the Samaritans; and he had dared to say that many—including even the harlots—might be brought into the kingdom of God before the men who supposed themselves to be pious.

What did it all mean, then? Could it be that what he had been trained to think fell short of the truth? Did the ways of God go beyond the human calculations? Were men brought nearer to God by Jesus on the cross than by Moses on Mount Sinai with the Commandments of the law? Was the Father in heaven not so much a God concerned with the righteous—and the self-righteous—as a love that reached out toward those who knew that they still were sinners and trusted in his mercy alone?

Questions such as these must have been stirring in Saul's soul on what was to prove his crucial day. Then on the road to Damascus the stifled intuitions of a new truth burst through his repressions. He recognized the living reality which he had seen reflected in the faces of some of the followers of Jesus. Jesus himself as the risen Christ appeared to him in an overwhelming vision. *This* figure whom he thought he could despise, this man who had come not to be ministered unto but to minister, this servant of the love of God who had reversed all the proud considerations which for him had been controlling—this one now became the master of his life. Henceforth, Saul not only had a new name, he was a new man—Paul the Apostle who would carry across the Roman world his gospel of "Christ the power of God and the wisdom of God."

Most of our knowledge of Paul's activities—where he went and what he did—derives from Acts: his evangelistic work in Asia Minor, his founding of churches in Macedonia, in Corinth and in Athens, and in great Ephesus; his being assaulted by a mob in Jerusalem when he had gone there at the time of Pentecost; his protective arrest by the Roman authorities; his hearing before a Roman governor in Caesarea; and his being sent a prisoner under escort across the Mediterranean for review of his case at the imperial court in Rome. There the narrative in Acts ends—to be supplemented by statements in the writings of early church fathers that at the end of what was perhaps a second imprisonment at Rome, Paul was put to death as part of the general vengeance against Christians in the evil reign of Nero.

More important than the book of Acts, however, is our possession of Paul's own letters which make up now so large a part of the New Testament. Even the greatest fact, when it has been a long time familiar, may be regarded casually as though it were a matter of course; and so we do not stop to marvel at the immeasurable enrichment for our thinking which belongs to us because Paul's letters do exist. But suppose no trace of them had come down through the early centuries, except a dim tradition that there *were* letters once, which had disappeared. And then suppose that in some forgotten cave, such as that in which the Dead Sea Scrolls were found by an Arab herding his goats, someone discovered ancient manuscripts which, when they were deciphered, turned out to be the nineteen-centuries-old letters of

Paul! A great wave of excitement would sweep through all the world of scholarship and of religion. The substance for that excitement we do have in the less spectacular but no less important fact that from century to century, and from one language to another, the contents of those very letters have been handed down. In those letters, which any one of us can take up and read, there comes no secondhand account of Paul, but such an outpouring of his thought and his emotions as makes his whole personality come alive. Here are his hopes and his disappointments, his messages of affection and his flashes of anger, his discouragements and his triumphs, and above all the revelation of the faith and the devotion which had set his soul on fire.

How, then, shall we think of him as we read what he has written of himself?

First of all, that he was what James Stewart of Scotland has described him as being in the title of one of the most inspiring of all books about Paul, *A Man in Christ.* No average Christian can fully understand or express all that Paul meant when he spoke of being "in Christ," but certainly the fact of it was this: The living influence of Christ so pervaded Paul's whole thought and purpose that he could say, as he did say to the Galatians, "It is no longer I who live, but Christ who lives in me; and the life I now live in the flesh I live by faith in the Son of God, who loved me and gave himself for me" (Gal. 2:20). The power of Christ was the new atmosphere in which he existed; and as he breathed it, so also it was in him. "Therefore, if any one is in Christ, he is a new creation," he wrote to the Corinthians, and he asked them, "Do you not realize that Jesus Christ is in you?" (II Cor. 5:17; 13:5.)

Because he was thus "a man in Christ," it is no wonder that Paul had what Christians always are entitled to have, and which the world sorely needs in the critical present time; namely, a lift of spirit which comes from something bigger than uninspired human beings know. Therefore Paul could be the forerunner of those great—though few!—Christians in every generation who have been transfigured by an inner light, and of whom their times could say:

Beacons of hope, ye appear!
Languor is not in your heart,
Weakness is not in your word,
Weariness not on your brow.[2]

When that brilliant leader in the twentieth-century church,
Henry Sloane Coffin, died, passages from some of his sermons
and many of his prayers were gathered from among his manuscripts. What should the title be for a book in which they would
be published? His wife, the one who knew him closest, gave the
immediate right answer. It should be the words from the epistle
to the Romans, *Joy in Believing*. That was the note which characterized his glad and gallant Christian living, as it had characterized the great apostle from whom those words first came. And
the glory of Paul's spirit is never grasped until we remember
how vibrant his essential spirit was. Theological specialists and
laborious commentators have often done him a grave injustice
even when they were meaning to pay him tribute. In trying to
show the profundity of his thought, they have sometimes made
an image of him as though he had been a somber figure wrestling
with gloomy dogmas in a half-lighted room. They have transferred their heaviness to him. But the truth is that Paul was above
all else intensely and ardently alive. He was most himself not as
the speculative theologian, nor as the builder of a system, nor as
the administrator of church affairs—although he was all these
things. No, he was most of all the man—the man possessed by the
love of Christ and going out in eagerness to help other men and
women know the wonder and power of what had laid hold on
him. And this he did in no gray or lukewarm spirit. Read his
letters—the first one he wrote, that to the Thessalonians; or one
of the last, that to the Philippians—and see how they are starred
again and again with "joy" and with "rejoice." The wider gamut
of the reality of life is there, its evil as well as its good, its darkness as well as its light; but there is a great note of exultancy
which runs throughout, and like the motif of a symphony binds
all its lesser chords together.

The lift of spirit which came to Paul as "a man in Christ" was
not a matter only of emotions. It gave him reinforcement for the

demands that would have appalled most men and drained their energies dry. Apparently Paul was not a man who was constitutionally rugged. He said he had "a thorn in the flesh." There has been a wide range of theories and guesses as to what sort of ailment that may have been. No one can possibly have any certain knowledge of its nature, but the one thing sure is that Paul prayed again and again to be delivered from it, and never was. The important thing is that he not only went ahead in spite of it but undertook adventures, endured hardships, and outfaced dangers which sound almost incredible as he recites them. He had gone on incessant journeys, sometimes into half-civilized regions; he had encountered bandits by land and been shipwrecked at sea; he had been arrested and scourged by provincial officials, and he had been beaten by vicious mobs. He had had to face malignant opposition from the people of his own blood who regarded him as a traitor to Israel, and he had had to endure cruel misrepresentation from men who were supposed to belong to the Christian fellowship. But he met whatever he had to meet, and he never surrendered. "Thorn in the flesh" or not, he would run his race to the end, "for the prize of the upward call of God in Christ Jesus."

In one of our American cities was a big, warmhearted man who for many years was the City Missionary for his church. His business—and his enthusiastic choice—was to be a minister to the prisoners in the State Penitentiary and the City Jail, to carry his cheerful encouragement to sick people in hospitals, to see old people in an Old People's Home, and generally to be a friend to anybody who needed one. All the while he was partly deaf, and with such poor vision that he stumbled along like a big, half-blind bear. Once there was a Healing Mission at one of the churches in the city, and someone asked him whether he was going. He said Yes, he was; and he believed God could heal him if he wanted to. He hoped there would be healing; but if God did not choose to heal him, then, he said, "I will know that what God wants with me is that I should try to show what a man can do under handicaps"—and that was what Paul the Apostle had learned long before.

The reason why that City Missionary was loved by many was

because they felt love in him; and looking at him they could believe that there was love in God. Even the prisoners in the jail could begin to trust that there was a divine mercy which reached out to them and would not let them go. And that was the supreme message which Paul—not merely a City Missionary, but a missionary to the world—carried everywhere to human hearts. It was the truth which had taken away his own frustration and his sense of inner defeat—the truth that God does not wait for men to make themselves righteous, but meets their groping desire with his reconciling love. It was what Martin Luther, agonizing over his own sense of sinfulness, was long afterward to learn, when he cried out, "Lo to me, an unworthy, condemned and contemptible creature, altogether without merit, my God of His pure and free mercy has given in Christ all the riches of righteousness and salvation, so that I am no longer in want of anything except faith to believe this is so."[3] That has been called Paul's doctrine of "justification by faith," or "salvation through grace," and sometimes the meaning of it has been so wrapped in abstract words that those who needed it most could not understand that it was meant for them. But what it says is what the self-confessed sinner who was to become St. Paul learned from his vision on the Damascus road, and sought always to proclaim: that the wounded hands of Jesus have broken down the barriers which men's guilt and fear had built between them and God, so that the way is open for every longing soul to turn again Home.

❧ III ❧

Polycarp and Justin Martyr

In the twentieth-century Western world, no one is likely to
think that he will be killed for being a Christian. The greater
likelihood is that it may seem to make no particular difference
whether he is or is not a Christian. The world will not be disturbed either way. For being a Christian may sometimes appear
to be a matter of cushioned pews, agreeable music, and comfortable sermons on Sundays—and business as usual during the
week. There is nothing stringent about it. Nobody is going to
suffer.

But there was a time when men *were* killed for being Christians. They were not expecting to be comfortable. They were
set to be courageous, whatever the consequences. If they had to
pay a heavy cost for their convictions, they would pay it; even if
this meant that they had to die.

Two such men were Polycarp and Justin, called Justin Martyr.
It can be a good thing to remember them, for to do so may make
us contemporary Christians less complacent with our soft selves.
It could show us our need for more iron in the blood.

Polycarp

Polycarp was the bishop of Smyrna, born probably in A.D.
65, a time when some persons who had known Jesus were still
alive; for we know that Irenaeus, afterward bishop of Lyons
(of whom more is to be said in the next chapter) wrote that

"Polycarp was instructed by the apostles, and was brought into contact with many who had seen Christ."

One writing affirmed by the great weight of historical scholarship to have come in its main contents, if not quite in its completeness, from the hand of that Christian of eighteen hundred years ago is *The Epistle of Polycarp to the Philippians*. It was written from Smyrna to the church in Philippi which Paul had founded and for which he had a special love.

> These things, brethren, I write to you concerning righteousness, [said Polycarp] not because I take anything upon myself, but because you have invited me to do so. For neither I, nor any other such one, can come up to the wisdom of the blessed and glorified Paul. He, when among you, accurately and stedfastly taught the word of truth in the presence of those who were then alive. And when absent from you, he wrote you a letter, which, if you carefully study, you will find to be the means of building you up in that faith which has been given you, and which, being followed by hope, and preceded by love towards God, and Christ, and our neighbor, is the mother of us all.[1]

In the way of theology, the letter has in it nothing profound or new. Rather, it is the loving pastoral message of one already grown old in the service of Christ, to the Christians in Philippi for whom he prayed that "the God and Father of our Lord Jesus Christ, and Jesus Christ Himself" might build them up "in faith and truth, and in all meekness, gentleness, patience, long-suffering, forbearance, and purity."[2] What makes the letter most significant is its constant echo of the words which we can now read in the gathered New Testament, many of the books of which Polycarp knew and by which his instinctive speech was shaped. In the passage included above concerning Paul, the final words echo the spirit of Colossians 3:12. Fifty-nine times in his not very long letter, Polycarp uses expressions directly quoting or closely recalling phrases from Paul's epistles, from I Peter, from Acts, and from the Gospels. Thus, throughout the Christian church there was already an accepted understanding of what Christian life and devotion were meant to be.

Of Polycarp's long life not many details are known, but of his death there is a shining record. When he was a very old man he went to visit Anicetus, then the bishop of Rome, to confer with him about the proper date of Easter. Returning home in A.D. 155, he was arrested. At the end of the previous century the Roman empire, which at first had supposed Christianity to be merely a sect of the tolerated religion of the Jews, had begun instead to take another attitude. The suspicion grew that Christians represented some sort of secret loyalty that might be subversive. What was this talk of a "kingdom of God," and of a Christ who would come back to earth to rule? As a symbol of the authority of the state, there were busts of the emperors set up in the temples, before which persons to be tested could be required to burn incense as a token of devotion. . . . but Christians would not do it, because to do so would seem to deny the loyalty they owed to God alone. Under the Emperor Trajan, at the beginning of the second century, Ignatius, the bishop of Antioch, had been seized on that account, taken to Rome (by way of Smyrna, where Polycarp saw him) and there in Rome thrown to the lions in the arena. Now at the mid-century, even with two of the noblest and most conscientious of the emperors, Antoninus and Marcus Aurelius, on the throne, the danger to the Christians was not less. Regardless of who or what the Christians were, the requirement of the empire for its own supposed safety was implacable. There should be no stubborn, secret disaffection. Those against whom there was any question should do reverence to Caesar, or they should die.

So it happened with Polycarp. The account of it is in *The Encyclical Epistle of the Church of Smyrna*, a letter apparently written and sent to other churches to describe a martyr's death. Part of it, as the text now exists, is made up of later elaborations, but the central facts which it describes are authenticated by other early Christians, such as Irenaeus in that same century.

Polycarp's presence in Smyrna was divulged to the authorities by a youth who was put to the torture. When those who were sent to arrest him came to the house where he was, Polycarp went down to meet them; after having offered them something to eat, he asked that he might be left alone for an hour to pray. When he was brought before the prefect in the city, he was asked, "What harm is there in saying, Lord Caesar, and in sacrificing with the other ceremonies observed on such occasions, and so make sure of safety?" But Polycarp answered, "I shall not do as you advise me."

They brought him to the arena. There the proconsul demanded, "Swear by the fortune of Caesar; repent, and reproach Christ." But Polycarp answered, "Eighty and six years have I served Him, and He never did me any injury; how then can I blaspheme my King and my Savior?" And when the proconsul again pressed him, saying, "Swear by the fortune of Caesar," he replied, "Since you are vainly urgent that, as you say, I should swear by the fortune of Caesar, and pretend not to know who and what I am, hear me declare with boldness, I am a Christian."

Then the proconsul caused a herald to proclaim in the arena, "Polycarp has confessed that he is a Christian"; and the crowd shouted, "This is the teacher of Asia, the father of the Christians, and the over-thrower of our Gods, he who has been teaching many not to sacrifice, or to worship the Gods." They clamored that Polycarp should be thrown to the lions, but the proconsul answered that the shows that included the wild beasts were finished. "Let him be burnt, then," they demanded. So they bound Polycarp to the stake, piled the fagots about him, and lit the flames.

In the letter of the church in Smyrna there was handed on the tradition of the prayer that Polycarp uttered as the flames began to rise about him—a prayer that no one could have heard and reproduced altogether in its actual words, but words which caught the essential spirit of Polcarp's last utterance:

"O Lord God Almighty, the Father of thy beloved and blessed son Jesus Christ, by whom we have received the knowledge of thee, the God of angels and powers and of every creature, and of the whole race of the righteous who live before thee, I give thee thanks that thou hast counted me worthy of this day and hour, that I should have a part in the number of thy martyrs, in the cup of Christ."³

Justin Martyr

Justin was born in or about the year A.D. 110 in Flavia Neapolis, a Roman colony in the Samaritan region of Palestine. He was a Gentile of Roman ancestry, not born a Christian. With an active and inquiring mind, he began to investigate various systems of thought which had come down from the great philosophers of Greece: Zeno the Stoic, Aristotle, Pythagoras, Plato. What the exponents of the first three had to say did not attract him; but Plato's conception of a realm of eternal ideals of truth, beauty, and goodness did fascinate his mind. One day, according to his own account, he had gone out to walk alone and to think, when he became aware of an old man of gentle dignity who was overtaking him. Half reluctantly he let the man approach and begin a conversation. Out of that conversation came results beyond anything that Justin at the moment would have imagined. For the man who had overtaken him was a Christian, and he put into Justin's thought a new and different conception.

Justin was seeking a philosophy of life? He was looking for the highest human wisdom?

Yes, that was exactly what Justin was concerned with.

Well, then, the stranger said, there was a surer way to truth. Above the speculations of human intellects there were the revelations that could come to souls attuned to God. Such, he said, had been the revelations given to the Hebrew prophets, and fulfilled in Christ. Here was the end of the search for wisdom, and here was the meaning of life.

The stranger—for Justin, silenced perhaps by the unexpectedness of what he had said, never asked the man's name—went on his way. But the new suggestion had come to Justin's mind exactly at a time when his long questionings were ripe to receive it. He began to read the Old Testament, and he began to observe Christians. Presently he became a Christian himself. The notable thing about him was that he became not the kind of Christian all

too familiar in most generations: the kind who is willing to have
it supposed that he is one, but who never says or does anything
to carry affirmative witness to his world. Justin devoted himself
completely to the vindication and the spread of the Christian
gospel. He was never ordained, but he became an indefatigable
lay evangelist, with long journeys that carried him apparently to
Ephesus and Corinth and certainly to Rome. There would be
fewer indifferent or indolent members of the church if all who
have the name of Christian could be startled by his words. For
this is what he said: "Everyone who can preach the truth and
does not preach it incurs the judgment of God."

Between the early part of Justin's life and its end not many
details can be filled in. But what he was thinking and saying to
his time is clear. He wrote much; and although some of his
writings have disappeared, others have come down through the
years, vivid records of how a man of intellectual interest tried to
interpret Christianity to the Roman world. It has been correctly
said of him that he was "the first among the fathers who may be
called a learned theologian and Christian thinker."

Among his writings which have survived, the most important
are the *Apologies* addressed to the authorities of Rome, and his
Dialogue with Trypho.

Trypho was an orthodox Jew whom Justin met in Ephesus,
and with whom he had a long debate that began unpleasantly
because of the jeers from some of Trypho's associates who were
standing round him, but which developed into a sincere and
courteous discussion when the two men sat down together. At
the beginning of the *Dialogue*, Justin told Trypho of his own
futile search for a satisfying faith through Greek philosophy, and
of his meeting with the old Christian who turned his thoughts to
the Hebrew prophets, and so to the revelation in Christ.

Then began the long debate in which Justin tried to convince
the Jew that Jesus Christ was the fulfillment of all the longings
and hopes of the Old Testament. His particular arguments were
often based on interpretations of passages in the Old Testament
which were highly allegorical and fanciful. His manner of thinking, genuine as it was to him, is outmoded now, for he had little

recognition of the actual historical setting and reference of the Old Testament books, and treated them not with primary regard for their immediate meaning, but as though they were cryptograms important only for their hidden meanings which everywhere foreshadowed Christianity. But although the form of his argument might seem in the best light of biblical knowledge to be untenable, the central themes for which he contended were part of enduring truth. For he tried to show, as Paul had done before, that there was a message from God, and a life in God, which transcended the Jewish belief in salvation by obedience to the law; and that the Christian church was the new Israel in which there had come to pass Jeremiah's prophecy:

"Behold, the days are coming, says the Lord, when I will make a new covenant with the house of Israel and the house of Judah, not like the covenant which I made with their fathers when I took them by the hand to bring them out of the land of Egypt, . . . But this is the covenant which I will make with the house of Israel after those days, says the Lord: I will put my law within them, and I will write it upon their hearts; and I will be their God, and they shall be my people" (Jer. 31:31, 33).

At the time when Justin lived and wrote there were some—most notably, Marcion—who wanted to cut Christian thinking loose entirely from acceptance of the Old Testament, as though the God of Judaism had been some false or inferior deity from whom "the God and Father of our Lord Jesus Christ" was to be wholly distinguished. Justin helped save Christian belief from what would have been the impoverishing denial of its unbroken heritage that went back to the patriarchs and the prophets. Justin was often faulty in his particular reading of the Old Testament, but he was right in his central conviction that Christian faith had its roots in the revelation of the one Eternal God who had been manifesting himself through all history, and who—although only partially understood in earlier times—was the same redeeming God whom men had seen in Jesus.

The two *Apologies* of Justin had a different objective. As the *Dialogue* was an effort to answer the objections of a Jew to Christianity, because Christianity ignored circumcision and the

Mosaic law as necessities for salvation and made the incredible claim that a man crucified on a Roman cross could be Messiah, so the *Apologies* were an effort to correct the dangerous belief in the Roman empire that Christianity was a subversive sect. The *First Apology*, written about the middle of the second century, was addressed to Emperor Antoninus Pius, and to his two adopted sons, one of whom, Marcus Aurelius, was to be his successor; the *Second Apology* was addressed to the Roman senate. There is no way of knowing whether these appeals were read by the authorities to whom they were addressed; but if they were, they failed of their immediate objective. Justin asked that Christians be considered and judged according to the facts concerning them, and not on the basis of false popular denunciations.

> When you hear that we look for a kingdom, [he wrote] you suppose without making any inquiry, that we speak of a human kingdom, whereas we speak of that which is with God. . . . And everywhere we, more readily than all men, endeavor to pay to those appointed by you the taxes both ordinary and extraordinary, as we have been taught by Christ; for at that time some came to Him and asked Him if one ought to pay tribute to Caesar; and He answered, "Tell me, whose image does the coin bear?" And they said, "Caesar's." And again He answered them, "Render therefore to Caesar the things that are Caesar's, and to God the things that are God's." Whence to God alone we render worship, but in other things we gladly serve you, acknowledging you as kings and rulers of men, and praying that with your kingly power you may be found to possess also sound judgment.[4]

But what the empire regarded as "sound judgment" would not yet conform to Justin's plea. There was the fixed opinion that the Christians were "atheists" because they refused to acknowledge the gods of the Roman pantheon, and that their loyalty could not be depended upon. Justin himself was to find—in contradiction to the *First Apology*—that it was not the fact that "no evil can be done us, unless we be convicted as evil-doers, or be proved to be wicked men; . . ."[5] Being a Christian, and that only, could lead to persecution and to death.

But if Justin's *Apologies* did not bring about the particular results he pleaded for, they are none the less of enduring value for what they reveal about the Christian church and about some aspects of Christian thinking in the middle of the second century.

In the first place, they give important evidence concerning the circulation of the Scriptures. Justin, like Polycarp, quotes not only from the Old Testament but from what was becoming the New Testament, and especially from the Gospels of Matthew and Luke, which he refers to as "Memoirs of the Apostles." For Justin himself it had been true, as he said in his *Dialogue with Trypho*, that "a flame was kindled in my soul; and a love of the prophets, and of those men who are friends of Christ, possessed me."[6]

In the *First Apology* also there are exceedingly interesting and informative references to Christian baptism, and to the bread and wine of the Lord's Supper. "And this food is called among us . . . the Eucharist, of which no one is allowed to partake but the man who believes that the things which we teach are true, and who has been washed with the washing that is for the remission of sins, and unto regeneration, and who is so living as Christ has enjoined."[7] "And on the day called Sunday," he wrote further, "all who live in cities or in the country gather together to one place, and the memoirs of the apostles or the writings of the prophets are read, as long as time permits; . . . Sunday is the day on which we all hold our common assembly, because it is the first day on which God . . . made the world; and Jesus Christ our Saviour on the same day rose from the dead."[8]

Notable in the thinking of Justin, who has been called "the broadest of all broad churchmen," was his conviction that the eternal Word of God, the logos, which the Gospel according to John proclaimed to have been made flesh in Jesus, had communicated at least partial truth to "every race of men," and that great souls, like Socrates, "who lived reasonably are Christians, even though they have been thought atheists."[9]

Thus, in his writings, Justin was a witness for Christ. But not most, or finally, in words alone. Denounced in Rome as a Christian, he was executed some ten years after the martydom of Polycarp. Of his heroic spirit it was true, as he had written, in his *First Apology*, "You can kill, but you cannot hurt. . . . If we looked for a human kingdom, we should also deny our Christ, that we might not be slain. But since our thoughts are not fixed on the present, we are not concerned when men cut us off."[10]

~ IV ~

Irenaeus

All the four whose lives have been remembered in the three chapters preceding died because of their unshaken loyalty to the Christian gospel which their world could not endure. In an age that does not often summon forth such costly loyalty they may seem too far off to find their likenesses in modern life. But the recollection of them ought at least to induce self-confrontation, and bring some wholesome challenge to a kind of Christianity which may avoid discipline and hardship. There should be something always in the human soul that will echo the words of seventeenth-century Richard Crashaw:

> Oh! that it were as it was wont to be
> When thy old friends of fire, all full of Thee
> Fought against frowns with smiles, gave glorious chase
> To persecutions, and against the face
> Of death and direst dangers durst, with brave
> And sober pace, march on to meet a grave.
> On their bold breasts about the world they bore Thee,
> And to the teeth of hell stood up to teach Thee:
> In centre of their inmost souls they wore Thee,
> Where racks and torments strived in vain to reach Thee!

Polycarp and Justin both were identified with the region toward the eastern end of the Mediterranean: Polycarp with Smyrna, Justin with Samaria as his birthplace and with Ephesus as one of the cities where he most conspicuously taught. The next memorable figure in the Christian church of the second century also was born in or near Smyrna, in A.D. 115 or not long after that. This was Irenaeus.

After the evangelistic preaching of Paul when he first set out with Barnabas from Antioch, and especially after the many months during which Paul preached and taught in the great center of Ephesus, Asia Minor became one of the strongholds of Christianity in the Roman world. Christian congregations were in cities that now are only almost forgotten names; and from Asia Minor, perhaps more surely even than from Rome, Christianity reached out into the West.

In Smyrna, as a youth Irenaeus knew Polycarp, and was greatly influenced by him. What that experience meant to him he was afterward to express so eagerly that the warm and thrilling quality of what he remembered still vibrates in his words after these nearly eighteen hundred years. Writing to Florinus who had been his friend and fellow Christian, but who had been led astray by false teaching, Irenaeus said:

> For while I was yet a boy, I saw thee in Lower Asia with Polycarp. . . . I have a more vivid recollection of what occurred at that time than of recent events (inasmuch as the experiences of childhood, keeping pace with the growth of the soul, became incorporated with it); so that I can even describe the place where the blessed Polycarp used to sit and discourse—his going out too and his coming in—his general mode of life and personal appearance, together with the discourses which he delivered to the people, also how he would speak of his familiar intercourse with John and with the rest of those who had seen the Lord, and how he would call their words to remembrance. Whatsoever things he had heard from them respecting the Lord, both with regard to His miracles and His teaching, Polycarp having thus received from the eye-witnesses of the Word of life, would recount them all in harmony with the scriptures.

These things, through God's mercy which was upon
me, I then listened to attentively and treasured them up
not on paper, but in my heart.[1]

From Smyrna to Marseilles, on the Mediterranean coast of
Gaul, now France, was a long journey, but one on which Christian missionaries had already gone. At Lyons, in the valley of the
Rhone, there were Christian churches shepherded by an aged
bishop named Pothinus. Irenaeus came there, apparently some
time after the middle of the century. His life was not destined
to end in martyrdom, as had the life of Polycarp whom he
revered and loved; but in Gaul he had abundant reason to learn
what martyrdom could be. In the empire there had been a succession of catastrophes: a flood of the Tiber, an earthquake, a
pestilence that spread all the way from Africa to Gaul. The
superstitious fears of pagan populations turned here and there
to mob-passion against the Christians, who were alleged to have
provoked the wrath of the gods they would not worship. Although the emperor was the philosopher Marcus Aurelius, whom
Gibbon in his history describes as "severe to himself, indulgent to
the imperfections of others, just and beneficent to all mankind,"
local passions broke out into persecutions of savage cruelty. In
Gaul in A.D. 177 a maiden named Blandina was tortured, and
then tangled in a net and thrown to the beasts. Pothinus, the
bishop, was abused and locked in a dungeon, where after two
days he died. Irenaeus was made bishop in his place.

For the rest of the century until his death some time around
A.D. 200, the career of Irenaeus was filled with missionary activity, so that the number of Christians greatly increased. But what
is most surely known about him is the voluminous writing in
which he sought to defend and explain the Christian faith.

Christianity could have deadly external enemies, as the persecutions in Gaul had shown, but a subtler and no less critical
danger might come from within. If Christian belief became infiltrated by false ideas, all the living power of it might be lost.
And this danger became real and immediate in the rise and spread
of the systems of thought called Gnosticism.

"Systems" rather than a single system, for Gnosticism was a wide and often confused assemblage of influences that came from many origins—from pagan myths, from Oriental mystery religions, from Hellenistic speculations—and many individual teachers shaped it into their own particular patterns. But its general character can be held to be represented in the teaching of Valentinus, born in Egypt about the beginning of the second century, educated in Alexandria, later promulgating his Gnostic ideas in Rome, in the conviction that they expressed a more enlightened Christianity. Valentinus and several other Gnostics genuinely longed to discover light on some of the ultimate mysteries that forever fascinate the human mind: man's relation to the universe, how the world and life came to be, the origin of evil and the way of deliverance from it, the quest for knowledge of God. At its highest, the impulse and desire that stirred in Gnosticism was such as that which Valentinus expressed when he wrote: "The heart is cleansed by the expulsion of every evil spirit; and when the only Father visits it, it is sanctified and gleams with light; and he who possesses such a heart is so blessed that he shall see God."

But *how* shall the heart be "cleansed," and what is the means for "the expulsion of every evil spirit"? The answer to that, according to Valentinus, was through a process so complicated that it is difficult to give an outline of it that will not seem fantastic. Two conceptions, however, which govern it emerge through the cloud of its speculations. One is the thought of the infinite God as essentially so remote that only through gradual stages can the finite world come into existence from him; and the other is the conception—made familiar in the East by Zoroastrianism—that in the universe there is the eternal division between a realm of light and a realm of darkness, that salvation for the human soul consists in being brought out of darkness into light, and that to know the meaning of this is the supreme gnosis to which the spiritually elect may attain.

So much in principle; in elaboration, the teaching of Valentinus was this:

The Father of all, or the First Cause, dwells in unity; yet in that unity there can be distinctions, which like the male and female principles, give rise to a descending succession of aeons, emanations of the Eternal Being. From the First Cause, which Valentinus calls also Bythos, the unfathomable, and Sige, silence, come Nous, the intellect, and Aletheia, truth. From them in turn come Logos, the divine Word, and Zoe, life; and from them Anthropos, the heavenly idea which is the prototype of mankind, and Ecclesia, which is the prototype of the church. From Logos and Zoe proceed other emanations, and also from Anthropos and Ecclesia. All these together make up the Pleroma of the saving forces which have come from the Absolute Being, who by an inner necessity of love chose to impart his fullness. They constitute the realm of light. But one of the aeons, Sophia, wisdom, has broken its harmony. Whether from inordinate ambition to know too much, or from being trapped by the lower world of darkness, she becomes a prisoner and produces an abortion. Then two new aeons, Christos and the Holy Spirit, are sent from the Pleroma to deliver her, and they bring back Sophia into the realm of light.

But some of the element of heavenly light is left in the world outside the Pleroma through the offspring of Sophia. Born of her is the Demiurge; and this Demiurge, a lower order of spiritual being, imagines that he is actual God. It is the Demiurge, and not the Supreme Father, who creates the world and mankind in it; and it was only the Demiurge who was known and worshiped in Old Testament times. Old Testament law and ritual are part of the bondage laid upon men by the Demiurge; but in the substance from which mankind was made there is still some element of light that had come down from the Pleroma of the higher aeons, and this light waits to be released. So, the Christos is sent from the Pleroma in the form of the human Jesus to bring mankind the mystic understanding by which it may be set free from the realm of the flesh and darkness. In some of the Gnostic speculations, the Christ spirit came into Jesus at his baptism, illuminated his teaching, and then left him before his crucifixion. In other systems, Jesus is not crucified at all, but Simon of Cyrene is crucified in his place. Thus, instead of being the Word made flesh, who entered completely into human life and brought into it a redeeming love that went all the way to the cross, Jesus becomes only the conveyor of a supposed form of mystic knowledge that is to be the password to salvation. In one of the writings of the Gnostic sect of the Naassenes, Jesus is made to say: "Father, a searching after evil on the earth makes man to wander from thy Spirit. He seeks to escape the bitter chaos, but knows not how to flee. Wherefore, send me, O Father! With the seal will I descend, travel through all Aeons, disclose all mysteries, show the forms of the gods: the secrets of the holy path which are called 'Gnosis' I will impart."[3]

In the wide range of Gnostic teaching, with its almost limitless variations, there were other and more crude conceptions which were hardly more than would-be magic. Some of these affirmed a series of planetary spheres through which a soul would have to pass if it would ascend from the realm of darkness to the light. Demons might block the entrances to these spheres; and to know the saving gnosis was to be instructed in the incantations by which the demons could be repelled, and in the names of the good angels who could be called upon to aid.

Thus Gnosticism could lead to twisted belief. It could also lead to a perversion of what ought to be Christian behavior. It was based upon a dualism which held matter and spirit to be two contradictory and forever antagonistic facts. Man as he is in the actual world was created by the Demiurge, and not by the Supreme God; and man becomes what he ought to be only when the spirit of light within him ceases to be affected by the surrounding world. From that premise, one of two different but distorting consequences followed. Some of the Gnostics preached an extreme asceticism, including complete celibacy. Others went to an opposite and much worse extreme. They maintained that the spiritual side of a man's nature is so superior to the body that nothing which has to do with the body can affect it. Therefore, let a man be as sensual as he chooses. Indeed, libertinism was sometimes an asserted virtue, on the ground that laws of moral restraint, such as the Old Testament Commandments, were an imposition of the Demiurge, and therefore the illumined man ought to reject them.

Gnostic teachings such as these spread widely in the Roman world, including Gaul. Irenaeus was bound to take account of them, and to try to defend his Christian congregations against what he saw to be their corrupting influence. Consequently, he produced his most notable work, *Against Heresies*, the original Greek text of which has largely been lost, but the substance of which has been transmitted in long quotations by later writers, and in a Latin version.

Irenaeus wrote with vehemence because—according to his indignant judgment—"certain men have set the truth aside, and bring in lying words and vain genealogies, which, as the apostle says, 'minister questions rather than godly edifying which is in faith,' and by means of their craftily constructed plausibilities draw away the minds of the inexperienced and take them captive."[4] And as his thought grew increasingly wrathful, so did his language, until he sums up his estimate of the Gnostics by saying that they had been "sewing together, as it were, a motley garment out of a heap of miserable rags."[5]

But general denunciations would not have accomplished Irenaeus' purpose. At great length and explicitly he reviews the Gnostic teachings and endeavors to show how and why and where they were a perversion of Christian truth. As against the Gnostic invention of the Demiurge, the lower deity alleged to have been the false god of the Old Testament, Irenaeus defends the great conception of biblical history as representing the unfolding purpose of the one God who is both Creator and Redeemer, and whose meaning for human life was forever revealed in the measure that men could understand. As against the Gnostic conception of a Christ whose seeming human form was only an appearance, he presents "Jesus Christ the son of God, who was crucified for us," who fasted and hungered and shared our human lot as "real and substantial man." And as against the Gnostic dualism which sometimes despised morality on the ground that the illumined spirit could not be affected one way or the other by acts in the flesh, he challenged those who "puffed up through knowledge of this kind fall away from that love which is the life of man." Although Irenaeus' form of argument is often involved and difficult, he is trying always to present a

Christian faith which he intensely believes to be the Word of life both for the learned and for the simple. "True knowledge," he wrote—not in the long *Against Heresies*, but in another one of his writings, a fragment of which has come down through the years—"consists in the understanding of Christ. . . . For the Truth is unsophisticated; and 'the word is nigh thee, in thy mouth and in thy heart,' . . . being easy of comprehension to those who are obedient. . . . For this is the affinity of the apostolical teaching and the most holy 'faith delivered unto us,' which the unlearned receive, and those of slender knowledge have taught, not 'giving heed to endless genealogies,' but studying rather [to observe] a straightforward course of life; . . . For truly the first thing is to deny one's self and to follow Christ; . . ."[6]

The Gnostic influence, against which Irenaeus contended, gradually waned, not only because of Irenaeus' particular arguments but because of its own inherent confusions and irrationalities. There was need to controvert it, for, in the words of that profound scholar, Ernest F. Scott, whenever it prevailed, "Christian ideas were hopelessly buried under a debris of mythology; the Christian morality was sacrificed or perverted; the historical facts of the Gospel were eliminated."[7] But although Gnosticism thus failed to overcome the essential Christian message, it did have powerful effect upon the church through what it forced the church to do in the process of resisting it. Under stress of organizing its defenses, the church moved toward a development both of organization and of doctrine that was more definite, which was good, but that also became increasingly rigid, which was not good. In order to have a standard for judging and controlling other teachings that might be heretical, new emphasis was given to the literal authority of those Scriptures included in the canon as inspired; the creeds were fashioned and made binding upon all believers; the importance of the episcopate was magnified; and, increasingly, the bishops assumed and tried to fulfill what they regarded as their responsibility to define and promulgate one orthodox and official faith for Christians everywhere.

To this development Irenaeus himself was thoroughly devoted. If Justin Martyr had been conspicuously the Broad Churchman, Irenaeus was the High Churchman. He wanted to create a structure for Christianity so firm and sure that no heresies could shake it. In his refutation of the heretical teachings which he believed to pervert the saving integrity of the Christian gospel, Irenaeus needed to do more than to assert his individual judgment against the words of some other individual. He needed to show that there was a divinely given authority to which sure appeal could be made. So in Book III of *Against Heresies,* thinking of the church as the possessor of all saving knowledge, he wrote: "The apostles, like a rich man depositing his money in a bank, lodged in her hands most copiously all things pertaining to the truth; so that every man, whosoever will, can draw from her the water of life."[8] He lists the Gospels of Matthew, Mark, Luke, and John as embodying "the plan of our salvation."[9] But suppose the heretics should ignorantly or willfully distort the meaning of the Gospels? Then where could the decisive voice be heard? "In the tradition of the apostles manifested throughout the whole world," Irenaeus answered; and that tradition was preserved and safeguarded, he declared, by the succession of the bishops in those churches which the apostles had established. But "since it would be very tedious," he wrote, "to reckon up the succession of all the churches," he would refer "to that tradition derived from the apostles of the very great, the very ancient, and universally known church founded and organized at Rome by the two most glorious apostles, Peter and Paul." Then Irenaeus lists what he believed to have been the continuity of bishops of Rome, from Linus, the first after the apostles, to Eleutherius, the bishop in his own time; and therefore, he argues, men who seek the truth can turn to Rome as to a center where most conspicuously and continuously the apostolic tradition has been preserved.

It is doubtful that there was in Irenaeus' mind even a far-off imagination of a fact which persons in later centuries would claim he had recognized: such an authority imputed to the Roman bishopric as would lead directly to the medieval papacy. What he believed in and wanted to assert was not the supremacy of any local church as such, but the sovereignty of the apostolic tradition as it had been "manifested throughout the world" by a living succession in many churches, of which Rome was the most vivid illustration. That he had no idea of any right vested in the bishop of Rome to overrule other bishops seems evident from a letter he wrote later to Victor, then bishop of Rome, in which he pointed out that in a particular issue Victor had forgotten the example of "those presbyters who preceded thee" and had tried to make an arbitrary ruling contrary to the spirit of churches that "held fellowship with each other."[11]

So it would seem untrue to assert, as apologists for the Roman papacy do, that Irenaeus acknowledged the papacy as predestined for the church. He did not believe in that kind of rule. He did, however, intensely believe that if the Christian gospel were not to be lost in heresies there had to be an orthodox tradition, handed on through the bishops, by which all teaching should be ruled. That there was value in that is clear. If truth is to be transmitted from generation to generation, there may need to be a form within which it is safeguarded, and through which it is made known. But sometimes the deposit of the faith which once was like living water may become a static reservoir, into which no fresh conviction flows: orthodoxy a matter of tradition, the creeds an accepted form of words. Then the spirit must break through into new expressions, so that, in Irenaeus' greater words, the living truth may come "not on paper, but in my heart."[12]

❧ V ❧

Tertullian

If one looks back upon the long course of the church's history, the immense power of the medieval Roman papacy looms so large that it is difficult to believe that Rome was not always most important. But the fact is that in the early centuries the greatest influence for the shaping of Christian thought and life came from other regions of the Mediterranean world. Nearly all the work of Paul, and the founding of the churches named in the book of Acts and in Paul's epistles, took place outside Italy. It was to Asia Minor that Polycarp and Justin Martyr belonged. Irenaeus, the most creative scholar of the second century, lived in Gaul. And beginning with the second half of that century and continuing for more than two hundred years, the living forces which had most to do with determining the church's faith and practice were in yet another part of Christendom; again not in Rome or in its neighborhood, but in North Africa. From men who arose in North Africa came the thinking that not only produced much of the church's theology and the ultimate formulation of its creeds, but created also the convictions about the church's structure which have continued—sometimes with acceptance and sometimes as the cause of controversy—from their time until now.

The first of these figures to make the Christianity of North Africa significant for the whole church was Tertullian or, to give him his full name, Quintus Septimius Florens Tertullianus, who has been called "the father of the Latin theology and church

language, and one of the greatest men of Christian antiquity."
He was born about A.D. 150, the son of a centurion in a Roman
legion assigned to service under the proconsul of Africa; his
birthplace was Carthage, the city that for a hundred years had
waged its war to the death with Rome. Whether his father,
though in the Roman army, was a North African by birth and
lineage is not clear, but Tertullian himself, in the words of Philip
Schaff, "had in his constitution the tropical fervor and acerbity
of the Punic character, and that bold spirit of independence in
which his native city of Carthage once resisted . . . the rising
power of the seven-hilled city on the Tiber."[1] As he was growing up, he was given a thorough Greco-Roman education in
history, philosophy, and literature, and in the arts of rhetoric and
eloquence. Until he was thirty or more years old, he had no
contact with any religion but paganism; but then through some
influence not now known he embraced Christianity, with a burning religious acceptance and with an uncompromising morality
in the dedication of his life.

His temperament was eager and passionate. Whatever he did
and whatever he said had in it a tumultuous energy of complete
conviction and commitment. Because of that, his writings have
the stormy power of rhetorical thunder through which indignant
lightning flashes. He lived in a time when Christians might at any
moment be subject to arrest and punishment, but in his *Apology*
he condescends to no timorous plea; instead he makes his defense
of Christianity in the form of a head-on attack upon the paganism that to him was a darkness quenching the light. He denounced the persecution of Christians, which was based, he said,
on fantastic misrepresentations of what Christians really were—
misrepresentations so demonstrably false that ignorance could
not excuse them. He contrasted the loftiness of Christian belief
and the purity of Christian life with what he charged to be the
increasing corruption in the pagan society that had nothing to
look to except the decadent religion of the Roman state. He
dared to proclaim the Christian fellowship as having spread so
far and thrust its roots so deep within the Roman world that no
violence could destroy it. "We are but of yesterday," he wrote

in the *Apology*, "and we have filled every place among you: cities, islands, fortresses, towns, market-places, the very camps, tribes, companies, palace, senate, forum. We have left nothing to you but the temples of your gods."[2] "We say, and before all men we say, and torn and bleeding under your tortures we cry out, 'We worship God through Christ.' "[3]

As a theologian, Tertullian did not formulate a system as elaborate as that which presently was to be wrought out by another great North African, Origen of Alexandria; but he had emphatic beliefs and a power of vivid expression which has made much that he said unforgettable. He built his faith upon unquestioned witness of the Scriptures; the twenty-first chapter of the *Apology* is a remarkable summary of the life and work of Jesus and a burning account of the resurrection, especially as it had been recounted in the Gospel according to Matthew. It was Tertullian who, impatient with the complications in which he thought some would-be philosophers obscured religious facts, exclaimed, "*Credo quia absurdum est;* I believe because it is beyond reasoning." It was Tertullian who answered the persecutors of the church with this defiance: "The oftener we are mown down by you, the more in number we grow. The blood of Christians is seed."[4] Tertullian was the first to speak of the church as the new *ark* of salvation, an expression which would have its unending echoes in Christian imagination from that time to this. He was the first also to use the Latin word "*trinitas*" to describe the nature of the Godhead, and thus the first to give its explicit name to what would develop as the doctrine of the Trinity. Of Jesus as an example, Tertullian wrote, "Taught of God himself what goodness is, we have a perfect knowledge of it as revealed to us by a perfect Master."[5] And as to the relationship between the Incarnate Son and God the Father he wrote this: "We have been taught that He proceeds forth from God, and in that procession He is generated; so that He is the Son of God, and is called God from unity of substance with God. For God, too, is a Spirit. Even when the ray is shot forth from the sun, it is still part of the parent mass; the sun will still be in the ray, because it is a ray of the sun—there is no division of substance, but merely an extension. Thus Christ is Spirit of Spirit, and God of God, as light of light is kindled."[6]

Tertullian thus had his own expressions and comparisons by which he tried to set forth what he held to be the church's right beliefs; but through all that he wrote there ran the emphatic insistence that everything anyone taught must be subject to the authoritative tradition which had been handed down in the church from the beginning. Among his most important works were *The Prescription against Heretics* and the five long books *Against Marcion*. Before the end of the first century there had grown up the conviction that the Christian church, although it might be hurt by persecution from without, could be hurt much more by heretical ideas growing within. How could there be a saving gospel for the world if irresponsible teachers were allowed to twist it according to their own ideas? And how could irresponsibility be curbed unless there were a central standard of control? So there was conceived the need for a catholic church, a church everywhere aware of its oneness in tradition and able to ensure a stricter uniformity in the interpretation of Christian truth. Ignatius, bishop of Antioch at the beginning of the second century, first used thus the word "catholic," and he insisted that if the church were to be catholic there must be unmistakable authority. Authority, he said, had been given by Christ to the apostles. All Christian preaching and teaching, therefore, must square with what the apostles had taught; and who had the right and duty to say what the apostles did teach except the apostles' successors? That meant, said Ignatius, the bishops in the church. "Look to the bishop," he wrote, "that God also may look upon you."[7] "It becomes you to be in harmony with the mind of the bishop."[8] This emphasis which Ignatius began was echoed by Tertullian. He too believed that all preaching of the gospel must be controlled by the sure tradition which was witnessed to by the

apostolic churches, in which the very thrones of the apostles are still preeminent in their places, in which their own authentic writings are read, uttering the voice and representing the face of each of them severally. Achaia is very near you, in which you find Corinth. Since you are not far from Macedonia, you have Philippi; you have the Thessalonians. Since you are able to cross to Asia, you get Ephesus. Since, moreover, you are close upon Italy, you have Rome, from which there comes even into our own hands the very authority (of the apostles themselves). How happy is the church, on which apostles poured forth all their doctrine along with their blood! Where Peter endured a passion like his Lord's: where Paul wins his crown in a death like John's![9]

"This, therefore," wrote Tertullian, is "our rule." The truth revealed by Christ "can properly be proved in no other way than by those very churches which the apostles founded in person, by declaring the gospel to them directly themselves, both viva voce, as the phrase is, and subsequently by their epistles. If, then, these things are so, it is in the same degree manifest that all doctrine which agrees with the apostolic churches—those moulds and original sources of the faith—must be reckoned for truth, as undoubtedly containing that which the (said) churches received from the apostles, the apostles from Christ, Christ from God."[10]

Asserting thus the authority of an orthodox tradition, Tertullian gave powerful impulse to the tendency in the church to exalt the authority of those who were regarded as the guardians of that tradition. Before his time there had already developed the conception of the clergy as distinct from the laity, and Tertullian made this the more specific by being the first to claim expressly a priestly status for the ministry and to use the term "*sacerdotium*." In the government of the churches the council of all the presbyters still had a large part, but the bishops were becoming increasingly important. They were regarded as the church's spokesmen; and the urgency of Tertullian's argument that the church must have spokesmen against the heretics whom nobody could question magnified their office.

Yet, by a strange contradiction, the same Tertullian who did so much to establish the principle of authority in the church, through his own fervor of spirit broke beyond it. He who had been the assailant of all heresies never became in any essential element of the faith a heretic, but he did move off into what the majority regarded as unlawful schism; the great exponent of Catholic unity associated with a sect. The reason was that the same emotional intensity which had moved in one way in Tertullian's writing found a new channel which satisfied the emotional intensity of his life. While he had been defending the church as it was meant to be, he saw where it fell short of what his restless expectation reached for. Was it in danger of losing the fervor present in New Testament days when the Holy Spirit filled it? If that question rose in his mind, there was a movement in the church which claimed to have an answer for it. About the time of Tertullian's birth there had appeared in Asia Minor an ecstatic ex-pagan named Montanus, who now as a self-proclaimed prophet and reformer preached with fanatical zeal in the Christian church a message of rigorous demand to prepare for the approach of a new age of the Holy Spirit and of Christ's millennial reign. From the time Tertullian himself became a Christian, he was the sort of man who scorned any tame compromise, giving complete devotion to whatever he thought full Christian loyalty called for. Now at the turn of the century, perhaps in A.D. 200, he came in contact with Montanism, which had spread from Asia Minor into the West. To some within the churches it seemed to promise a new revival of the power which had first come with the tongues of fire at Pentecost.

Montanism, under that name, vanished long ago, but its essential characteristics reappear in the church again and again, including the present time, in the fringe sects which emphasize possession by the Holy Spirit, ecstatic experience as the sign of the true believer, and repudiation of whatever a new code of rigorous puritanism may list as belonging to the world and to the flesh. Narrow and fanatical though they may be, these fringe enthusiasms can make their appeal to troubled human beings who crave a sense of spiritual completeness, and who think that the established churches have grown so conventional and so dully satisfied that the fire of the Spirit no longer burns within them. Even Tertullian, with his great intellect, could be moved by that attraction; and he *was* moved, to the extent ultimately of separation from that Catholic unity which at first he had so extolled.

In the *Apology*, Tertullian had written a description of the church, than which hardly any words could have been more glowing. He said: "We are a body knit together as such by a common religious profession, by unity of discipline, and by the bond of a common hope. We meet together as an assembly and congregation, that, offering up prayer to God as with united force, we may wrestle with Him in our supplications. We assemble to read our sacred writings. . . . With the sacred words we nourish our faith, we animate our hope, we make our confidence more stedfast; and no less by inculcations of God's precepts we confirm good habits. In the same place also exhortations are made, rebukes and sacred censures are administered." And then having described how the Christian congregations gave their willing and loving help to any of their members who were sick or distressed or caught in persecutions, he declared that "a love so noble" had won instinctive recognition even among the enemies of the church. They said of the Christians, "See how they love one another."[11]

But presently Tertullian's passionate asceticism demanded a more rigorous separation from the things of the world than the church at large expressed. Montanism seemed to him to have the burning zeal which his instinct craved. Caught by its influence, Tertullian became more and more possessed by the conviction that the reality of religion must be measured by the degree of its mortification of the flesh. He wrote *On the Veiling of Women, On Exhortation to Chastity, On Modesty*, and *On Fasting*, and a letter *To His Wife*, urging her not to marry again if he should die. He began now to speak of the general body of Christians as the Psychics, by which he meant those who were governed by the natural mind; whereas the truly devoted must be the Pneumatics, those who were governed by the Holy Spirit.

"It is on this account" he wrote, "that the New Prophecies are rejected . . . not that (these prophecies) overturn any particular rule of faith or hope, but that they plainly teach more frequent fasting than marrying." "Those who would not listen to the Montanists," he said, "are constantly reproaching us with novelty"; and what some of the Montanists' particularities were are indicated in his references: "keeping our food unmoistened by any flesh; . . . not eating or drinking anything with a winey flavour; also . . . abstinence from the bath, . . ."[12] He condemned those whom he now regarded as halfway Christians because "so far as pertains to fasts" they neglect the obligations laid down in the Scriptures and "being prone to appetite, find it possible to regard as superfluous, and not so very necessary the duties of abstinence from, or diminution or delay of, food."[13]

Thus Tertullian embodied in himself the tension which may come to a Christian caught between the fact that life must be lived in this world and the imperatives of the Spirit which can be fulfilled only in the world beyond. Tertullian was one of the impetuous souls who cannot find a bearable adjustment, and was driven therefore to a rigorism which seemed to most men impossible. The common judgment counted him "unbalanced," but neither his own age nor any subsequent one could fail to honor his devotion.

In the ultimate reckoning of his career there was an ironic contrast. Because he turned away from the church's central fellowship to be a Montanist, he was considered a schismatic; but long after the man himself was gone, his writings exerted their powerful influence toward establishing the close-knit authority that many desired in the church—an authority which later and different developments were to cause to center in Rome.

❧ VI ❧

Cyprian

The somber words spoken by Mark Antony at the funeral of Julius Caesar—"The evil that men do lives after them; the good is oft interred with their bones"—are not always true. Certainly they were not true concerning Tertullian, with whom the preceding chapter has dealt. The fact that he had gone off to espouse a disturbing sect was accounted as an evil; but in spite of that, the church laid hold upon, and made continuing use of, what he had done that it found reason to consider good. His writings furnished contradiction to various heresies, and gave reasons to those who wanted to strengthen the structure of the church. Therefore it was told of Cyprian, bishop of Carthage, in the generation next after Tertullian, that when he desired, as he often did, to read Tertullian's words, he would say to his deacon, "Hand me the master."

Cyprian himself was to have even more influence than Tertullian upon the subsequent history of the church; an influence which, as we shall see, is subject to highly controversial interpretations of what he himself stood for and desired. Like Tertullian, he was not born a Christian. He was well along in middle years before he was converted. But he was a man of learning and of great force of character, and very shortly after his conversion a general demand of the Christians in Carthage made him bishop. From that time on, the church's conception of the episcopate was affected by the stamp he put upon it.

It might have looked at the beginning as though his episcopate

49

would amount to little. Within two years after he had been made bishop, a new persecution of Christians broke out under the Emperor Decius. Cyprian left Carthage and went into hiding, on the ground that his presence in Carthage would intensify the danger to the general congregation there. Inevitably some accused him of having fled only on account of cowardice—an accusation which the climax of his career would sufficiently deny. Meanwhile, there was the double fact: he was separated from the flock he was supposed to shepherd, but he nevertheless managed to keep in effective contact through his letters. After about a year in exile, he went back to Carthage.

As to the manner of man he was, the most direct indication comes from *The Life and Passion of Cyprian, Bishop and Martyr,* by Pontius the deacon.[1] This Pontius who was constantly at Cyprian's side, writes of him with the emotional fervor of a devotee, and one may discount sometimes his rhetorical praise; but the fact of his devotion is itself a witness to something big in Cyprian that called it forth. Pontius indicates that Cyprian had had large wealth, which he gave away in endless generosity wherever there was need. He tells that there broke out in Carthage "a dreadful plague, and excessive destruction of a hateful disease invaded every house. . . . All were shuddering, fleeing, shunning the contagion, impiously exposing their own friends, as if with the exclusion of the person who was sure to die of the plague, one could exclude death itself also."[2] In the midst of all the horror, Cyprian rallied his people to go to the help not only of their fellow Christians but of the non-Christians as well. "His countenance," says Pontius, "was grave and joyous. Neither was his severity gloomy, nor his affability excessive, but a mingled tempering of both, so that it might be doubted whether he most deserved to be revered or to be loved, except that he deserved both to be revered and to be loved."[3]

For ten years Cyprian was bishop. Then, in A.D. 258, he was arrested, taken before the Roman proconsul, found guilty of being a Christian and therefore, according to the emperor's decree, subversive, and condemned to be beheaded. When he heard the sentence pronounced, he answered, "Thanks be to God"; and at the place of execution he knelt in prayer, tied the bandage over his eyes with his own hands, and gave a gold piece to the executioner. So with dignity and composure he died, expressing in himself what he had expressed in words when he wrote his tract *Concerning Mortality* during the plague in Carthage: "Only above are true peace, sure repose, constant, firm and eternal security; there is our dwelling, there our home. . . . There a great multitude of beloved awaits us. . . . There is a glorious choir of apostles; there the number of exulting prophets; there the countless multitude of martyrs, crowned with victory after warfare and suffering. . . . After the earthly comes the heavenly; after the small follows the great; after perishableness, eternity."[4]

Thus the persecution brought Cyprian to his death. Also it was the persecution and the problems arising from it that called forth the acts and words that made Cyprian's career as bishop most significant.

In the persecution, many of the weaker Christians succumbed to fear. Threatened with punishment and perhaps with death, they burned incense, as demanded by the officials, before the image of the emperor, and were given certificates saying they had done so—or sometimes they twisted their consciences into thinking that they had not really lapsed by bribing officials to make out the certificates anyhow. Later these men and women who had betrayed their Christian loyalty might become remorseful and perhaps repentant, guilty and lonely outside the Christian fellowship. They wanted to return to the church. But on what terms? That was the question which began to have various answers. In Carthage, there were some among the clergy who had been resentful of Cyprian's election as bishop over the heads of many who had been in the church longer than he. They organized a faction which thought to gain strength by dealing indulgently with the lapsed. Some representatives of that faction, ready to make a travesty of all church discipline, turned to men who in the persecution had endured punishment and near martyrdom for their unshaken faithfulness, and tried to get from them letters asking that this or that unfaithful Christian should be received back into communion, for their sakes who had not lapsed. Thus there threatened to grow a sort of system of irresponsible indulgences and transfer of merit which would throw the whole moral order of the church into chaos. It had to be determined who could speak and who could not speak in the church's name. Cyprian had his emphatic answer. The one center of unity, he said, the one voice that could speak with the authority that came from Christ through the apostles, must be the bishop.

In a Council held in Carthage in 253, Cyprian read his pronouncement, *The Unity of the Catholic Church*. In it he said, "We who have put on Christ, the wisdom of God the Father, must not lack the wisdom to safeguard our salvation." He went on to show how it might be imperiled by "wily trickery and subtle deceit no less than [by] open and obvious perils." There were those who

> though they do not stand by the gospel and discipline and law of Christ, call themselves Christians. . . . Though they are walking in darkness, they think they are in the light. . . . That is what happens, my brothers, when we do not return to the font of truth, when we are not looking to the Head and keeping the doctrine taught from heaven. . . .
>
> Can one who does not keep the unity of the Church believe that he keeps the faith? Can one who resists and struggles against the Church be sure that he is in the Church? For the blessed apostle Paul gives the same teaching and declares the same mystery of unity when he says: "There is one body and one Spirit, one hope of your calling, one Lord, one faith, one baptism, one God." It is particularly incumbent upon those of us who preside over the church as bishops to uphold this unity firmly and to be its champions, so that we may prove the episcopate also to be itself one and undivided. Let no one deceive the brotherhood with lies or corrupt the true faith with faithless treachery. The episcopate is a single whole, in which each bishop's share gives him a

right to, and a responsibility for, the whole. So is the Church a single whole, though she spreads far and wide into a multitude of churches as her fertility increases. We may compare the sun, many rays but one light, or a tree, many branches but one firmly rooted trunk. When many streams flow from one spring . . . unity is preserved in the source. Pluck a ray from the body of the sun, and its unity allows no division of the light. Break a branch from the tree, and when it is broken off it will not bud. Cut a stream off from its spring, and when it is cut off it dries up. . . . If you leave the Church of Christ you will not come to Christ's rewards, you will be an alien, an outcast, an enemy. You cannot have God for your father unless you have the Church for your mother. If you could escape outside Noah's ark, you could escape outside the Church. . . . [But] to break the peace and concord of Christ is to go against Christ. To gather somewhere outside the Church is to scatter Christ's Church.[5]

Thus it is sufficiently plain that Cyprian had an exalted belief in the supreme importance and the spiritual responsibility of the bishop. This did not mean that he was selfishly aggressive or that he had haughty pride of office. He was moved instead by the profound conviction that Christ had given to the apostles the charge of the church, that the bishops were the successors of the apostles, with the awful and humbling commission to act and speak in the name of the church's Lord. Unmistakably, then, Cyprian, like Irenaeus, was a prototype of the High Churchman and of those who consider the apostolic succession essential for the true life of the church. Yet at the same time Cyprian was no narrow autocrat. He had a sensitive regard for the rights of the presbyters and took them into his counsel in all important matters. Nor did he try to arrogate to himself any superiority over other bishops. In a letter *On The Baptismal Controversy* (of which more presently) he wrote: "I do not lay down the law to anyone. I do not condemn any bishop beforehand for doing what he thinks best. He has the right to use his own judgment freely. So far as lies in me, I do not contend with my own colleagues and fellow-bishops. . . . I keep the harmony of God and the peace of the Lord with them, remembering the words of the apostle, 'If any man thinketh to be contentious, we have no such custom, neither the Church of God.' "[6]

In the service for the consecration of a bishop in the *Book of Common Prayer* there is set forth the spiritual ideal to which the one made bishop must pledge his faithfulness: "Be to the flock of Christ a shepherd, not a wolf; feed them, devour them not. Hold up the weak, heal the sick, bind up the broken, bring again the outcasts, seek the lost. Be so merciful, that you be not too remiss; so minister discipline, that you forget not mercy; that when the Chief Shepherd shall appear, you may receive the never-fading crown of glory; through Jesus Christ our Lord." According to the testimony of Pontius the deacon, Cyprian as an individual was such a bishop as is envisioned in those words.

But the importance of Cyprian in the history of the church has to do with something wider than the question of his own personal character. It has to do with the conception of the church's essential organization which he represented. In word and deed he "crowned the edifice of episcopal power. . . . If with Ignatius the bishop is the centre of Christian unity, if with Irenaeus he is the depository of apostolic tradition, with Cyprian he is the absolute vicegerent of Christ in things spiritual."[7] Thus in the long history of the church those who have reflected the convictions of Cyprian have believed that bishops, and their authoritative leadership, are essential to the life of the church. And on the other hand, of course, great numbers of Christians in the nonepiscopal churches reject the idea of apostolic succession as Cyprian maintained it, holding that the commissioning action of the Holy Spirit is not tied to any rigid system. For the sake of Christian unity, there is a growing movement toward reconciliation of these contrasting loyalties. Churches in the Reformation tradition which are episcopal and those which are nonepiscopal are moving closer to a possible reunion: a reunion which would involve on one side a less rigid assertion of the authority of bishops than that which Cyprian voiced, and on the other side a larger recognition of the function which bishops at their best can fulfill as chief shepherds of the flock of Christ.

From what has been reviewed, there can be little question how Cyprian regarded his own episcopate. But as we noted at the beginning, there is one crucial matter which is the focus of specific controversy. What did Cyprian think, or what would he afterward have thought, of the bishopric of Rome that grew into the autocratic power of the medieval papacy? Roman apologists claim him and his words as witness to the fact that the papal claim to supreme papal authority was already recognized by those who embodied the great tradition of the church. The claim rests upon expressions used by Cyprian concerning the church in Rome as having been founded by Peter and as having presumably, therefore, a primacy among the churches such as Peter seemed to have had among the original twelve disciples of the Lord. Cyprian had written, for example, in *The Unity of the Catholic Church*, concerning the need for a sure tradition as against the teachings of heretics and schismatics:

> Faith finds ready proof when the truth is stated succinctly. The Lord says to Peter: "I say unto thee that thou art Peter, and upon this rock I will build my Church; and the gates of hell shall not prevail against it. I will give unto thee the keys of the kingdom of heaven; and whatsoever thou shalt bind on earth shall be bound in heaven; and whatsoever thou shalt loose on earth shall be loosed also in heaven." He builds the Church upon one man. True, after the resurrection he assigned the like power to all the apostles, saying: "As the Father hath sent me, even so send I you. Receive ye the Holy Ghost; whosesoever sins ye remit, they shall be remitted unto him; whosoever ye retain, they shall be retained." . . . Certainly the rest of the apostles were exactly what Peter was; they were endowed with an equal share of office and power. But there was unity at the beginning, before any development, to demonstrate that the Church of Christ is One.[8]

But so far as support of the papal claims is concerned, what Cyprian wrote must be read in the light of two realities. One is the actual character of the "primacy" that belonged to Peter, and the lack of any connection between what he was in himself and any power that could allegedly be passed on from him to his supposed successors (regarding which the judgment of Oscar Cullman quoted in the chapter on Peter is significant). The other reality is the position in regard to the bishop of Rome which Cyprian actually took in the sharp difference between them concerning baptism.

What happened was this: The problem of what to do about those Christians who had denied their faith at the outbreak of persecution led to sharp divisions in the church. There was a faction headed by Novatian, whose followers claimed that they had properly elected him bishop—a faction which had opinions about treatment of the lapsed so positive that they claimed to be the only true representatives of the Catholic Church—and people here and there were drawn into their fellowship. Some of these in North Africa were afterward sorry, and they wanted to come into the communion of which Cyprian was the shepherd. Cyprian held that the Novatianists were no true part of the church. Any baptisms which they had performed therefore were no valid baptisms; and any who sought admission into the fold of Christ's real flock must be baptized as though they had had no sacrament before.

The bishop of Rome was of another opinion. According to him, any baptismal rite performed in the name of Christ was a baptism into the grace that came from Christ himself, regardless of the status of the minister who happened to be the instrument. Therefore, even baptism in a schismatical body could be valid, and the person thus baptized did not have to be rebaptized if he sought admission into the Catholic fellowship.

What the comparative theological merits were in these two positions is a matter to be discussed on another plane. What concerns us here is this: On an open question of spiritual importance Cyprian, bishop of Carthage, allowed no overruling authority to the bishop of Rome, and treated his opinion as extraneous and invalid. Rome, because of its history, might be treated with special honor; but for an ultimate decision Rome had no prerogative to impose a judgment which only a council of all the church could determine.

In *The Ante-Nicene Fathers*, Bishop A. Cleveland Coxe, the editor of the American edition, has written a summary of Cyprian's position which may well stand as the interpretation of his

> simple and elementary system of organic unity. It embodies no hierarchical assumption, no 'lordship over God's heritage.' . . . Cyprian was indeed a strenuous asserter of the responsibilities of his office; but he built upon that system universally recognized by the Great Councils, which the popes and their adherents have ever laboured to destroy. Nothing can be more delusive than the idea that the mediaeval system derives any support from Cyprian's theory of the episcopate or of Church organization. His was the system of the universal parity and community of bishops. . . . Cyprian is the patron and defender of the presbytery, and of lay co-operation, as well as of the regimen of the episcopate. His letters illustrate the Catholic system as it was known to the Nicene Fathers; but, of all the Christian Fathers, he is the most clear and comprehensive in his conception of the body of Christ as an organic whole, in which every member has honourable function.[9]

❧ VII ❧

Origen

"Thou shalt love the Lord thy God . . . with all thy mind."
That was the part of the summary of the law which was fulfilled, more nearly than by any of his contemporaries, by the
great scholar and teacher, Origen, surnamed Adamantinus.

Origen was born in Africa, probably at Alexandria, in A.D. 185,
and he lived to be seventy years old. His father, Leonides, was
not only a Christian, but one who in the persecution under the
emperor Septimius Severus in 202 was imprisoned, and whose
property was confiscated before he died. The boy Origen, for he
was then only seventeen, knew thus early in life the price that
sometimes had to be paid for Christian loyalty. When his father
was imprisoned, the son wrote to him, urging him not to sacrifice
his constancy for the sake of his family. In his own efforts to protect others who were threatened in the persecution, he roused
the fury of a mob which pursued him from house to house. He
carried out in act what the Gospel according to Luke had said
that John the Baptist commanded for those who would belong
to the kingdom of God: "He who has two coats, let him share
with him who has none." Nor was that all. He read in Matthew
19:12 the words attributed to Jesus, ". . . there are eunuchs who
have been made eunuchs by men, and there are eunuchs who
have made themselves eunuchs for the sake of the kingdom of
heaven"; and in a terrible zeal for complete commitment he took
those words literally and emasculated himself, that he might cut
away thus the temptations of the flesh.

As the years went on in that perilous century, Origen would escape actual martyrdom, but his life would move on the edge of danger and would need to be capable of great devotion. When persecution broke out again in the reign of Caracalla, he had to escape from Alexandria; and at the mid-century, when Decius was emperor, he was imprisoned and cruelly treated at Tyre, so that his death thereafter came sooner than it might otherwise have come, because of the sufferings he had undergone.

Yet it was not outward events that made Origen's career most unforgettable. It was the activity of his brilliant mind, which resulted in great influence for his teaching, and also in bitter hostility roused against him among some who would ultimately assert that there was heresy in what he taught. He had been trained by his father both in classical culture and in the Scriptures; and he lived at the time and place most fit to stimulate his eager intellect.

The city of Alexandria owed its existence to Alexander the Great who, at the flood time of the victories by which he "held the gorgeous east in fee," had conquered Egypt in 331 B.C., and determined to establish there where the Nile River flowed into the Mediterranean the provincial capital that should bear his name. Built magnificently, with a harbor sheltered from the open sea by the island of Pharos, it grew into a rich port of commerce; but, more important, it had become a center of learning that rivaled what Athens once had been. It held two great libraries and a university; and in this atmosphere had grown up the catechetical school in which Demetrius, the bishop, made Origen the master at the incredible age of eighteen.

In the early part of his life, Origen was a layman. About the year 216, he was asked by the bishops of Jerusalem and Caesarea to expound the Scriptures in a public assembly of which they were part. When his own bishop, Demetrius of Alexandria, heard of this, he was outraged. "Such an act was never either heard or done before," he declared, "that laymen should deliver discourses in the presence of bishops." He summoned Origen back to Alexandria immediately and Origen, obeying, resumed his teaching and writing in his own city. But some ten years later another event brought down on him his bishop's impulsive and unpredictable wrath. Called for some reason to Greece, and passing through Palestine on his way, Origen was received by friends, the bishops of Jerusalem and of Caesarea, and ordained by them to the priesthood. But Demetrius, who had objected before to Origen's teaching in an ecclesiastical assembly as a layman, now was equally angered because he felt that his own authority over Origen had been infringed by Origen's ordination at the hands of others than himself. He summoned two synods and influenced them to declare Origen excommunicated from the church in Alexandria and deposed from his priesthood; and when Origen left Alexandria and went to live and work henceforth in Caesarea, Demetrius started accusations of heresy which were to pursue Origen to the end of his career.

In Alexandria, a wealthy friend had given Origen the means to employ amanuenses to copy material for his use and to write at his dictation, and thereby he was able to accomplish an amount of work that sounds stupendous. It was reported that he wrote six thousand books. That seems incredible unless the "books" included, as doubtless they did, short observations and comments on subjects which momentarily engaged his mind. But whatever be the number of the manuscripts that came from him they included some of great length and of pre-eminent importance. Most notable among those that have survived—for many have been lost—are commentaries on books of the Bible, especially on the Gospels according to Matthew and to John, and on the Epistle to the Romans; his defense of Christianity against the attack made upon it in the previous century by a philosopher named Celsus; and his *De Principiis*, the most profoundly learned and original exposition of Christian theology produced by anyone in the early church. Unhappily, the original Greek text of *De Principiis* has vanished, and what has been handed down is the often crude translation into Latin, with its Latin title, by Rufinus. Here and there it obscures rather than reveals what must have been Origen's own thought, but it does transmit the substance of his beliefs.

Origen's predecessor as head of the catechetical school, and his teacher, was Clement; and Origen was greatly influenced, as

Clement had been, by the environment in which he had lived. Alexandria, more than any other city of the Roman world, was a center of philosophical learning and discussion. It had seemed to Clement that unless Christianity could be interpreted convincingly in intellectual terms, it would fail to appeal to the educated and become a religion only for the ignorant. The simple believer, Clement taught, could be saved by faith no matter how unlearned he might be; but he was convinced also that fullness of Christian understanding and communion with God could be attained only through knowledge of the deeper truths and the mysteries of the gospel which are veiled to the uninstructed multitude.

Origen's thought moved in this same channel. In the Preface to *De Principiis* he wrote: "Now it ought to be known that the holy apostles, in preaching the faith of Christ, delivered themselves with the utmost clearness on certain points which they believed to be necessary to every one, even to those who seemed somewhat dull in the investigation of divine knowledge; leaving, however, the grounds of their statements to be examined into by those who should deserve the excellent gifts of the Spirit, and who, especially by means of the Holy Spirit Himself, should obtain the gift of language, of wisdom, and of knowledge . . . those persons, I mean, who should prepare themselves to be fit and worthy receivers of wisdom."[1]

The "wisdom" that Origen sought—a wisdom that might penetrate the depths of divine truth, and deliver men from finitude of knowledge into a deathless communion with God—was based for Origen on the authority of the Gospels and of the rest of the New Testament teaching as it had been handed down in the church. This was to be the starting point. But the mind must not stop inertly there. Origen believed that it was not possible for anyone to be truly pious who did not philosophize. As a great modern scholar, A. C. McGiffert, has written concerning Origen's thought, "The materials with which the logician had to deal were to be drawn from Scripture and tradition, not from experience or observation; they were revealed by God not discovered by men, and they must be taken on trust and accepted unquestioningly. But to elucidate them, to discover their implications and draw the necessary conclusions—this was the work of human reason. Thus authority and reason were combined, and in orthodox circles the combination has remained unbroken to this day."[2]

Both Clement and Origen had a genuineness of Christian devotion which kept them from being supercilious or condescending, but they did represent a kind of aristocracy of the intellect which exalted learning. By that fact they gave a new dimension to the impact of Christianity upon their age, but they also incurred a danger. They made it clear to learned men that the Christian gospel could face all opponents in the area of the mind; the danger came in the possible suggestion that intellectual subtleties in this area are the weapons by which Christianity can prevail. Unintentionally they were opening a door for a distorted idea which from time to time has found entrance into the church: the idea that philosophy can be the same thing as religion, and that "enlightenment" equals life. Once that idea prevails, explanations of Christianity, with all the accumulated weight of formal authority, may cramp and smother the Christian faith, which ought to be a continually new experience.

The twofold Origen—Origen the devoted servant of Christ and Origen the philosopher who sometimes seems to turn Christianity into abstractions—is evident in the opening pages of *De Principiis*. The Preface begins: "All who believe and are assured that grace and truth were obtained through Jesus Christ, and who know Christ to be the truth, agreeably to His own declaration, 'I am the truth,' derive the knowledge which incites men to a good and happy life from no other source than the words and teachings of Christ."

It is interesting and significant to note in that introduction the thoughts and words which come instinctively to Origen's mind. It is on "the words and teaching" of Christ that his emphasis falls, and from these is to be derived "the knowledge which incites men to a good and happy life." But on the level of the deepest fact, the saving power of Jesus Christ came not so much from his "words and teaching" as from himself, in his life and in his sacrificial death. The original disciples did not get from

Jesus a textbook of truth which they were to learn and then expound. They got the tremendous conviction of God's grace and
power brought into immediate touch with their own lives in
him whom "we have heard, we have seen with our eyes, have
looked upon and touched with our hands." It was this Jesus, the
Master of their hearts, who became for them the Christ. He was
the Master of Origen's heart also, as his long devotion showed.
But as an interpreter of Christianity, Origen began not from the
ground of the Christian's experience but from the premises of
the philosopher; not from the disclosure in Jesus through which
men would see the nature of God, but from assumptions about
God from which metaphysical explanations of Christ then would
be deduced.

Book I, Chapter I of *De Principiis*, therefore, is "On God."
The first effort is to refute every notion which might suggest
that believers were to think of God as in any degree corporal.
Jesus said that God is Spirit, "that He might distinguish Him from
bodies; and He named Him the truth, to distinguish Him from a
shadow or an image. . . . God is not to be thought of as being
either in a body or as existing in a body, but as an uncompounded
intellectual nature. According to strict truth, God is incompre-
hensible, and incapable of being measured." How then shall God
be known? The nearest answer, Origen says, is by the analogy of
the sun known by the rays, although no human eye can look
into the awful light of the sun itself. "So, in like manner, the
works of Divine Providence and the plan of the whole world
are a sort of rays, as it were, of the nature of God, in comparison
with his real substance and being. As, therefore, our understanding is unable of itself to behold God Himself as He is, it knows
the Father of the world from the beauty of His works and the
comeliness of His creatures." From the Gospel according to
Matthew come the words of Jesus, as Origen remembers, "Blessed
are the pure in heart, for they shall see God"; and about that he
asks, "What else is seeing God in heart but understanding and
knowing Him in mind?"[3]

Thus the great Christian theologian whose trend of thought
was primarily that of the philosopher reasons about God. And it

is on the same plateau of rarefied intellectual atmosphere that he is moving when he turns to his next theme. "In the next place, let us see what is meant by the name of Christ. He is called," says Origen, "by many different names. He is termed Wisdom, according to the expression of Solomon: 'The Lord created me—the beginning of His ways, and among His works, before He made any other thing; He founded me before the ages.' . . . He is also styled First-born, as the apostle has declared, 'Who is the first-born of every creature.' . . . Finally the Apostle Paul says that 'Christ [is] the power of God and the wisdom of God.' "[4] Then Origen goes on to interpret Christ's relationship to the Father under those terms, and his contribution to Christian thinking was as long-lasting as it was profound. Particularly did his doctrine of "the eternal generation of the Son" influence the creeds which the church was presently to formulate, for he furnished terms in which men who moved within the circle of Hellenic philosophy could find rational adjustment for their faith in the timeless authority of Christ.

He was one of the rare great intellects, appearing now and then to meet the needs of a particular century, who interpret truth in the fashion necessary for their own time. But in Origen's greatness was also the inevitable limitation. Because he was controlled innately by the metaphysical interest of the Alexandrian schools and because his thought thus moved on a rarefied level, Origen's theology could make his Christ seem to a reader more the conclusion of a syllogism than a warmly apprehended Savior. The faith he expressed in the language of his age and place would need other expressions, more concrete and more vivid, in order that Christ might again be heard gladly by the common people. The philosopher made his precious contribution; but very different contributions would be made, and forever must be made, by men who speak straight to the human heart; as by a Francis of Assisi, a Martin Luther, a John Wesley. Every theological system must recognize the fact which Alfred Tennyson put into words:

> Our little systems have their day;
> They have their day and cease to be:

> They are but broken lights of thee,
> And thou, O Lord, art more than they.

But if Origen's theology may have seemed attuned only to the learned, it nevertheless had a wide sweep of imagination, and its temper was always generous. He believed that God had created a realm of spirits before he had made the material universe, and those spirits were meant to enjoy eternal communion with God their Creator; but they were free either to choose or to reject it. Some chose complete goodness and some deliberately turned to evil; these became, on the one hand, the heavenly angels, and, on the other, the Devil and his train. Some of the pre-existent spirits took a middle course, less committed to goodness than were the heavenly angels, less evil than the demons. These spirits became men; and for these human beings God created the material world where they might seek, through struggle and self-discipline, to win back their original communion of life with God. The Logos, or Son of God, became incarnate that he might be seen of men and might show them by example and by precept the way back to the heavenly state which they had lost. And it was characteristic of Origen's academic cast of mind that he thought of the work of Christ as primarily one of instruction, through which would be imparted a saving wisdom, which only the enlightened could grasp. Similarly he interpreted the Bible as having different levels of meaning. There was a literal meaning; there was an ordinary moral meaning; and there was the hidden meaning which the incarnate Logos had come to reveal. But although it would have seemed thus that the doors of salvation would open only for those who understood the mystic word, Origen actually had a great optimism. He rejected completely what seemed to him the crude conception of a thousand-year reign of the saints with Christ on the earth; but he believed in a spiritual resurrection through which not only all men, but even the fallen angels, might ultimately be brought back to life in God. It was partly this optimism which caused Origen ultimately to be denounced as a heretic. There were some in the church who thought that their proper beliefs would enroll them among the saved, and who did not want to forgo what they felt would be the satisfaction of regarding the different status of the damned.

In the two centuries following Origen's death, repeated councils of the church condemned various aspects of his teaching as heretical, and therefore Origen as an interpreter of the faith stood under a cloud. Nevertheless, he affected the thinking of many men, whether they acknowledged it or not, and some of the later declarations concerning Christ's eternal oneness with the Father go back in substance to his thought.

Nor was it only as a master in intellect that Origen affected the church's life. His bodily self-discipline that went even to the point of mutilation deepened a trend which before long would become almost irresistible. There had been thinkers both within and without the church who taught an absolute dualism of body and spirit, with the ultimate conviction that only as the desires of the body were suppressed could the spirit be set free. In the Roman empire, with its recurrent persecutions, many Christians had begun to believe that there could be no saving relationship between Christianity and the existing world. About the time of Origen's death, Anthony—later to be called St. Anthony—went out to his stark asceticism in the Egyptian desert. Some hundreds followed him; and not long afterward, when the barbarians had broken the frontiers, monasteries rose everywhere throughout what had been the Roman world, islands of spiritual life and light in a time of darkness. The long record of monasticism, representing so strangely both devotion and dereliction, nobility of purpose and the subtle corruptions of mind and of body which human nature can fall into, is another story. But the immense impact that the monastic movement had upon the life of Europe for many centuries is a fact which needs no arguing. And one of those whose conception of the Christian life helped create that fact was this same Origen whose story has been traced, and who wrote in his *Commentary* on Matthew 16:25: "If we then wish life to be saved let us lose it to the world, as those who have been crucified with Christ and have for our glorying that which is in the cross of our Lord Jesus Christ, through which the world is to be crucified unto us and we unto the world."[5]

VIII

Jerome

By the middle of the fourth century A.D., the world was experiencing what Edward Gibbon, in his great history, would eventually describe as the decline and fall of the Roman empire. The fall had not yet come to pass, but the decline had begun and was moving on its inexorable way. For many years, from north of the Danube and the Rhine, Goths, Alemanni, and Franks had been threatening the frontiers; while within the empire, the power and wealth which came from the military triumphs of the earlier centuries had bred the enervating luxury by which the old strength of the Roman spirit had been corrupted. There no longer existed the sureness of purpose and the virility that could hold together the widespread provinces which once had submitted to unquestioned Roman rule. Emperors had been set up by one division or another of the armies, to rule briefly, and in repeated instances to be assassinated and succeeded by another whom a rival faction had proclaimed. The old confidence in order and security was gone. In A.D. 378, the Emperor Valens was killed in battle against the West Goths. A few years later these same West Goths, enraged at what they thought was betrayal of an agreement to pay them money for keeping the peace, invaded and ravaged Macedonia, Illyria, and Greece. In A.D. 408, the Goths, under Alaric, marched into Italy, and in 410 captured Rome. To the shocked peoples in the wide regions of the earth where all the civilization they had ever known was identified with the rule of the imperial city, it seemed as though the end of all meaningful existence was at hand.

At the beginning of this fateful span of years there was born near the then great city of Aquileia, at the northern bend of the Adriatic Sea, Eusebius Hieronymus Sophronius—later to be known more simply as Jerome. The exact date of his birth is uncertain, but it was around A.D. 346. He was to live a long time, and to become one of the most important figures in the history of the Christian church. To an extraordinary degree he would affect the life and thinking of his time; and round that certain fact lies the larger framework of the conditions of his age, and the question how profoundly these affected him. At the time of Jerome's birth, the fall of Rome was still nearly a full lifetime in the future, but already there were tremors in the ground as of some not-yet-arrived disaster. It was as though the events of history were whispering, "The world is very evil, the times are waxing late"; and certainly it was this mood which Jerome would afterward represent.

In 312, at the climax of fierce struggle among regional commanders for supremacy, the young Constantine had won imperial power. It was said that before the decisive battle of the Milvian Bridge, he had seen in the heavens a vision of the cross, with the inscription *"In hoc signo, vinces."* Whatever the source of his decision was, after he had become emperor he espoused the cause of the Christian church; and under him and his successors Christianity, instead of being proscribed and often persecuted as it had been before, became the official religion of the empire. In 361, Christianity had its last challenge by paganism. The Emperor Julian, the last pagan who would rule, did his best to turn back the clock and re-establish the worship of the ancient gods. He failed, and after two years he was killed in battle. It seemed that Christianity now was free from further danger. So far as persecution was concerned, that would be true. But there was a subtler and more deadly danger. The church which the fires of affliction had helped to keep pure was being softened by safety, and corrupted by the disintegrating culture from which for three hundred years it had stood apart. Could there be any real Christian living in the actual world which confronted the would-be consecration of the human soul? That was the question which Jerome would presently encounter.

When he was about seventeen years old, Jerome went to Rome to study. Notwithstanding the long shadows falling across the empire, the outward magnificence of Rome seemed undimmed. As the fact was expressed in the volume on Jerome in *The Fathers for English Readers:* "The series of public buildings and monuments with which a succession of emperors and great nobles had adorned the Mistress of the World—the temples, basilicas, palaces, forums, colonnades, triumphal arches, statues, theatres, baths, and gardens—had been completed by the triumphal arch with which Constantine commemorated his victory over Maxentius: and the whole series was still uninjured by time or violence." The patrician families, who had drawn immense wealth from their own estates and from the revenues which had come to them from conquered regions, maintained their superb establishments "dignified with the busts of great ancestors, and adorned with the spoils of provinces."[1] On the fringes of the city and in the hovels where increasing numbers of the dispossessed were herded, there was only the ugly contrast of poverty and degradation. Many of the rich could be indifferent to that; but into the minds of some was creeping a new and strange unrest. Matthew Arnold used extreme language when he wrote:

> On that hard Pagan world disgust
> And secret loathing fell.
> Deep weariness and sated lust
> Made human life a hell.

But there *was* weariness, and there was satiety; and on the borders of the empire there began to be a revulsion of spirit which would presently be felt in the capital itself.

In the year 341 there had come to Rome the great bishop and theologian, Athanasius; and with him two men whose like Rome had never seen. They were anchorites from the Nitrian desert in Egypt—two of those who had renounced the world and gone out to a solitary, bare existence, with their days spent only in prayer and meditation. Their prototype was the famous Anthony, who nearly a century before gave up a rich patrimony, and went to live as a hermit in Egypt near the Red Sea. When Athanasius and his two companions came to Rome, Anthony was still living, already venerated as a saint, and having led hundreds after him into the deserts to follow his example.

Like a contagion, the will for renunciation of the world began to take hold in Rome. A number of the most high-placed and wealthy women refused marriage, went into seclusion, and turned parts of their houses into monastic refuges where others came to pray. Jerome was familiar with all this; and when he went back to Aquileia he gathered round him a group of young men who devoted themselves to ascetic living. But this did not satisfy him long. In 373, being then about twenty-six years old, he joined a priest from Antioch who was passing through Aquileia, to go with him to the East and to come into contact with the ascetic life as it was completely practiced.

After a short while in Antioch, Jerome and several others whom he had persuaded to join him went to a monastery on the border of the desert of Chalcis, some fifty miles from the city. Under the hardships of existence there, in a climate of fierce heat in the summer and bitter winds from snow-covered mountains in the winter, two of his companions died, and Jerome himself came near to death. But what he did was to go from the monastery to the still more bleak existence of the solitaries who dug holes to live in. There he could follow to the limit the kind of asceticism which Anthony had exemplified, asceticism which, as Philip Schaff defined it in his *History of the Christian Church*, is not only "moderation or restraint of the animal appetites, which is a universal Christian duty, but total abstinence from enjoyments in themselves lawful, from wine, animal food, property, and marriage, together with all kinds of penances and mortifications of the body."[2]

The vigor and vehemence of Jerome's convictions, blazing up to a fire that was almost fanatical, appear in a letter to his former companion, Heliodorus. (Jerome's letters, astonishing in number and almost incredible in length, are like an immense mirror in which the whole living man is vividly reflected.) Heliodorus

had been with Jerome in the desert, but had abandoned the
ascetic life and gone back to Aquileia. Stirred to the depths by
what he thought was Heliodorus' desertion of his first ideal,
Jerome wrote: "You have spurned my petition; perhaps you
will listen to my remonstrance. What keeps you, effeminate soldier, in your father's house? Where are your ramparts and
trenches? When have you spent a winter in the field? Lo, the
trumpet sounds from heaven! Lo, the Leader comes with clouds.
He is armed to subdue the world. . . . But as for you, what will
you do? . . . A body used to a tunic cannot endure a buckler;
a head that has worn a cap refuses a helmet; a hand made tender
by disuse is galled by a sword-hilt. Hear the proclamation of
your King: 'He that is not with me is against me, and he that
gathereth not with me scattereth. . . .' Not to aim at perfection
is itself a sin."[3]

After such a letter it might have seemed a glaring inconsistency
that Jerome himself did not stay permanently in the Syrian desert.
Later he would come back to the life of solitude and complete
self-abnegation, but first there was a different interlude. Ecclesiastical quarreling in Antioch and in Syria generally grew so
bitter that Jerome could not endure it. Leaving Syria, he went
to Constantinople, and remaining there for two years he was
present at the important Council of all the Eastern churches which
met in 381. The next year he was in Rome for a Council of the
West called by Pope Damasus. At that Council, Damasus pre-
sided; and recognizing that Jerome had become a man of excep-
tional learning when he studied in Rome before, Damasus gave
him important work to do. When the Council was over, Jerome
continued in Rome; and he renewed and deepened the association,
which he had had as a student, with the coterie of those who had
revolted from the moral laxity of Roman society and had with-
drawn more and more from what they regarded as the world's
entanglements. Some of them were men; more of them were
women, many being of noble birth and high position. Among
these was Paula, descended from the Scipios and the Gracchi,
a widow of great wealth; and her daughters, who were to play
a conspicuous part in Jerome's later life. As the most devoted

and burning advocate of the ascetic life, Jerome seemed to have before him a great and needed mission to the church in Rome. He could acknowledge that there was a moment when "all Rome resounded with my praises," and "almost every one concurred in judging me worthy of the episcopate."[4] So marked also was the favor in which he was held by Damasus that Jerome may have begun to think that he would be elected bishop of Rome when Damasus died. But at Damasus' death in 384, no such expectation was fulfilled.

Although Jerome had friends, he also had implacable enemies. Nor is it hard to understand why. With his stern passion for a life made free from the seductions of the flesh, he looked with indignant contempt upon the self-indulgence of many of the Roman clergy who catered to the rich; and there was enough of the unregenerate in him to make him resort to sharp invective. He wrote of some who

> when they have once gained admission to the houses of the high-born, and have deceived "silly women laden with sins, ever learning and never able to come to the knowledge of the truth," feign a sad mien and pretend to make long fasts while at night they feast in secret. . . . There are others . . . who seek the presbyterate and the diaconate simply that they may be able to see women with less restraint. Such men think of nothing but their dress; they use perfumes freely, and see that there are no creases in their leather shoes. Their curling hair shows traces of the tongs; their fingers glisten with rings; they walk on tiptoe across a damp road; not to splash their feet. . . . Certain persons have devoted the whole of their energies and life to the single object of knowing the names, houses, and characters of married ladies.[5]

In the career of Jerome, and in the immense influence which he exerted upon the church of his time and in the church for many centuries thereafter, two great facts were dominant. One was the asceticism which he preached and lived. The other was his rich achievement as a scholar and translator of the Bible.

In his asceticism, Jerome combined qualities which present to modern thought a startling contrast between an ideal that commands our humbled reverence and an interpretation of that ideal so harsh as to be fanatical. He did not stop with the kind of balanced self-discipline that will try to keep a pure purpose and a brave devotion in the midst of ordinary life. His conviction could not come to rest on the saying attributed by the Fourth Gospel to Jesus, that his disciples should be in the world, yet not of it. To Jerome, the Christian unquestionably must be not *of* the world, with the affections and lusts thereof; but beyond that, he must be no longer *in* the world as represented by involvement in those relationships ordinarily accepted as part of all normal human life. So he was a celibate himself; so also he would have young girls dedicate themselves to virginity, and widows never marry again. Only thus, he believed, could they give their lives in complete loyalty to Christ.

Yet, in his exhortations, Jerome instinctively used language which showed how surely the bodily senses, with their normal expression cut off, will be reflected even in the religious ecstasy which is supposed most to deny them. There can be a sublimated eroticism, which carries the symbols and suggestions of the flesh into the mystical experience. Jerome repeatedly used the Old Testament Song of Solomon, which actually is the unabashed poetry of sensuous human love, as expression of the communion of the virgin soul with Christ. In his letter to Eustochium, he speaks of her as "Christ's spouse." And urging her to keep from any worldly walk or conversation that would betray her spiritual devotion, he wrote: "Ever let the privacy of your chamber guard you; ever let the Bridegroom sport with you within. Do you pray? You speak to the Bridegroom. Do you read? He speaks to you. When sleep overtakes you, He will come behind and put His hand through the hole of the door, and your heart shall be moved for Him, and you will awake and rise up and say: 'I am sick of love.' Then he will reply: 'A garden inclosed is my sister, my spouse; a spring shut up, a fountain sealed. . . . Jesus is jealous. He does not choose that your face should be seen of others.' "[6]

Back of Jerome's asceticism were two influences special to his time. In the first place, interpretations of life which the Christian church repudiated had nevertheless seeped into the instinctive thinking of many people, Christians included. The Gnostic philosophers had taught an extreme dualism, according to which the world of spirit stood always in antagonism to the whole realm of matter. In the third century the Persian prophet, Manes, had preached detachment from all involvements of the flesh, and had become the center of a widespread heresy. Jerome called him the "infamous Manes" but, all the same, the metaphysical dualism of the Gnostics and the Manichaean hatred of the body as the prison of the spirit were reflected in his own conceptions. In addition to that influence from his contemporary world of thought, there was the pressure of appalling objective facts. For Jerome, the fall of Rome was no echo out of ancient history; it was the immediate and devastating shaking of all the foundations of his life—as fateful as it would be if merciless armies from Communist China should overrun and destroy all Western society in our own day.

Because of forces such as those, Jerome's asceticism became the more extreme. Some of his denunciations of marriage and of family life have a fierceness that sounds frantic. But it would be a cheap mistake to disparage his devotion, and to look down at him from the supposed superiority of smug well-being. There will always be something in the human spirit that feels the awful mystery of life and the solemnity of its ultimate issues, and can never be content with what William James, in *The Varieties of Religious Experience* has called "neatness, cosiness, and comfort." There is everlasting challenge in the stringent and heroic dedication which was the spiritual ideal—even though in actual working it could be distorted—in the monastic rule of poverty, chastity, and obedience. Some of its spirit might well be sought, to use again the words of William James, by those who "scramble and pant with the money-making street," that there might be achieved once more a higher dedication, "the unbribed soul, the manlier indifference, the paying our way by what we are or do and not by what we have, the right to fling away our life at any moment irresponsibly—the more athletic trim, in short, the moral fighting shape."[7]

As asceticism was one of the two great areas of Jerome's influence, the other was scholarship. In this he was one of the supreme figures in the church for many centuries; for he had wide, if not always exact, learning in both secular and biblical fields; indefatigable industry; and the gift of putting his thought into swift and clear and vivid phrase.

When Jerome was in Rome in the period from 382 to 385, Pope Damasus invited him to commence the translations which were to become his supreme work. The New Testament of course had been written in Greek. Beginning in the third century B.C., the Hebrew Scriptures of the Old Testament had been translated into the Greek version known as the Septuagint. In Rome, Greek had been the language for the church's liturgy. But in all the provinces of the West, and in North Africa, the one language prevailingly known and used was Latin. In North Africa, there had been a translation of the Scriptures into what came to be called the Old Latin Version by the latter part of the second century A.D.; and not long afterward there was another version made in Italy. In both versions there were many crudities; and, therefore, Damasus urged Jerome to make a new Latin translation of the Gospels; and also to improve the Old Latin rendering of the Psalms. This Jerome did while he was in Rome, but his monumental work was to belong to Bethlehem.

In the monastery at Bethlehem, for fifteen years from 389 to 404, Jerome wrote commentaries on many of the books of the Bible, and letters of prodigious length, some of them—such as those addressed to Rufinus and Vigilantius—being violent denunciations of any thought or conduct in the Christian church which did not conform to his rigorous ideas. But over and above these was the accomplishment of what no other man in the church of that time was equally fitted to create—a version in Latin of the whole Bible, which included a translation of the Old Testament books not from the Greek Septuagint, which was the source for the former versions of North Africa and Italy, but directly from the original Hebrew. When he first went to live among the hermits in the Syrian desert near Antioch, he began the study of Hebrew; and in the years following he possessed not only a mastery of that language but wide related learning, critical acumen, and felicity of style. The Latin Bible which he put forth gradually won its way to universal acceptance in all the countries which had once formed the Roman empire; it was the one Bible known to medieval Europe, and is the official form of the Scriptures in the Roman Catholic Church to this day. Through the centuries it has been known as the Vulgate, and in that name—from vulgus, multitude—there is a meaning which may be forgotten now when Latin seems no more than the echo of an ancient language belonging only to priests saying Mass, and not to the people. In Africa, Italy, Gaul, Spain, and Britain, for many centuries all those who could read at all read Latin, and the Vulgate therefore was the Bible from which innumerable souls gained what they had of the Bread of Life.

Ultimately Jerome was canonized, and in the calendar of the Church of Rome he ranks as one of the figures most revered. This does not mean that the man pronounced to be St. Jerome was in all respects saintly. Some of those with whom he clashed in violent controversy would have had a very different opinion concerning him. He could be arrogant in opinion and passionate, self-assertive, and sometimes unjust to his opponents. He was an illustration of the words of Paul that heavenly treasures may be contained in what are very "earthen vessels." But the great distinction of Jerome lay in the iron discipline he imposed upon his body, and in the prodigious industry of his mind and the result that this produced. As Canon Henry Fremantle of Canterbury wrote of him, "He lived and reigned for a thousand years. His writings contain the whole spirit of the church of the middle ages, its monasticism, its contrast of sacred things with profane, its credulity and superstition, its subjection to hierarchical authority, its dread of heresy, its passion for pilgrimages."[8] And concerning Jerome's Vulgate, Georg Grützmacher has said what many other scholars would echo: ". . . in that work he produced what must be numbered among the supreme achievements of the Christian mind in any age."[9]

❧ IX ❧

Aurelius Augustine

In the three centuries after the apostolic age there had been, as we have seen, great witnesses for Christ. In the middle of the fourth century there appeared another, who was to rank, in the judgment of such a historian as Adolf Harnack, as the most important figure possessed by the Christian church "between Paul the Apostle and Luther the Reformer." This was Aurelius Augustine. Not for one aspect only of his character and his career but for three will Augustine be remembered.

The first significant fact about him was the drama of his own inner life which began with long conflict between the flesh and the spirit, between the drag of the world and the impulse of a soul that was reaching toward God.

Augustine was born in A.D. 354, in Thagaste, a town in the Roman province of Numidia in North Africa. It is not easy for historical imagination now to reconstruct the world that Augustine first knew. Today one looks at the map of North Africa along the Mediterranean coast from Egypt on the east to Morocco on the west and recognizes it in its life and religion as wholly Muslim. Such indeed it has been since the seventh century when the Arab armies, with their battle cry, "There is one God, and Mahomet is his prophet," swept out of the desert to capture the great part of what had been the Roman empire. There is little in those regions now to suggest that they once belonged to Christendom. But when Augustine was born, Christian churches with their clergy and their bishops were the dominant forces in the culture of North Africa, and men like Tertullian and Origen and Cyprian and Athanasius had made the voice of North Africa more influential in Christian thinking than the voice of Rome.

Augustine's father became a member of the Christian church only when he was near death, and perhaps the conversion was only superficial. But his mother, Monica, was a Christian of intense conviction and of unbounded dedication. When Augustine was born he was signed with the cross and sprinkled with salt —but not baptized; and this which might be supposed to indicate indifference of his mother to the sacrament actually represented the almost superstitious regard for the sacrament as the one means for regeneration and remission of sins, and therefore better to be kept until later in life when there were more sins to be remitted. It was not until he was a mature man and had passed through critical experiences that Augustine came at last to baptism and to the genuine dedication which had always been his mother's passionate prayer for him.

From a boy, Augustine had an insatiate thirst for knowledge. After he had been to school in Thagaste and in a neighboring larger town, he entered the university in Carthage, the ancient and famous city which Rome had conquered and completely destroyed in 146 B.C. following a century of struggle for the mastery of the Mediterranean world, and then one hundred years later had been allowed to be rebuilt as a Roman colony. In Carthage were survivals of old pagan worship, and also new religious influences from the East. Among these was Manichaeism; and the young Augustine was captivated by its message, and for the next years he counted himself a Manichaean.

Exactly what this religion was it is impossible now to be sure. Once, its influence was wide; but as a living fact it vanished, and authentic records of its teaching also have mostly faded beyond recovery. It began with Mani (or Manes) who was born in Babylonia early in the third century A.D., and declared that he was the promised paraclete whom Jesus had said would come to lead men into larger Truth. In a third century book in Persian, the *Shapuragan*, attributed to Mani himself, it is written: "Wisdom and deeds have always from time to time been brought to mankind by the messengers of God. So in one age they have been brought by the messenger called Buddha to India, in another by Zaradusht [Zoroaster] to Persia, in another by Jesus to the West. Thereupon this revelation has come down, this prophecy in this last age, through me, Mani, the messenger of the God of truth to Babylonia."[1]

Mani taught that originally there were two limitless and un-mingled kingdoms of light above and darkness below. Out of the darkness arose Satan, who attacked God's kingdom of light. Adam and Eve, representing mankind, belonged to the realm of Satan, but in them were some of the elements from the world of light. Jesus was sent to instruct Adam concerning "the Paradises and the gods, Hell and the Devils, the earth and the Heaven"; in the Manichaean system Jesus becomes thus an abstract element in a philosophy, and the Jesus who lived among men, faced the realities of his actual world and time, and was crucified and then became the risen and living power in the church, fades out. According to the Manichaean teaching, only "the Elect" could fully comprehend the relationship of the kingdoms of darkness and light, and the means by which the light is liberated. That teaching could appeal to the unconscious arrogance of restless intellects who supposed that a religion must be the more true and the more exalted through the very fact that ordinary people would not understand it. At any rate, and for whatever reason, Augustine was caught by its attraction, and separated from his mother's Christian faith.

He studied to become a master in rhetoric, which meant something much larger than the word would suggest in modern vocabulary. It meant mastery of humane learning, plus the ability to express that knowledge with eloquence and power. When he had finished his studies at Carthage, Augustine could not be content till he had gone to test his ability as a teacher in the greater academic area of Rome. But having arrived in Rome, he learned of a post as professor of rhetoric which was open in the university supported by the imperial government in Milan; and he sought that post and won it.

Thus it seemed that in the field of his ambition, Augustine was going ahead fast and far. But all was not well within. He could not forget his mother's yearning—a yearning to which he knew the hidden depths of his own soul responded. It was not only that Manichaean ideas had swung him away from Christian thinking. Passions of the flesh had swung him away from Christian living. While he was still in Carthage he had begun an illicit relationship, and although he was never married he had a son. In Rome and in Milan the same manner of life continued. In his own self-judgment there was building up a tension demanding more and more to be resolved. Yet when he knew that the voice of God was calling him to new decisions, all he could say was, "I, convicted by the truth, had nothing at all to answer, but only those dull and frowsy words, 'Anon, anon,' 'presently;' 'leave me but a little.' But 'presently, presently' had no present, and my 'little while' went on for a long while."[2]

At length, though, the resolution came. As Saul of Tarsus was changed perhaps by the silent witness of Christians who never knew that they had affected him, so Augustine was stirred by two lives to whom had come a transformation he knew he needed. There was a noted scholar in Rome, long a skeptic, who suddenly came with the eagerness of a child to be baptized. And in Milan, Augustine met a man named Pontitianus, also from North Africa, and at that time high in the emperor's court. Pontitianus told him how not long before, in a cottage of some humble people, he had chanced upon a little book that told him of the life of Anthony, who had given himself as a hermit in the desert to prayer and meditation. Suddenly all that he was engaged in seemed to Pontitianus only the dust and ashes of this world. He turned to a friend who was with him. "Now have I broken loose," he said, "from those our hopes, and am resolved to serve God from this hour."[3]

As Augustine listened to Pontitianus, a change came over him, which he afterward described in these words:

> Thou, O Lord, while he was speaking, didst turn me round towards myself, taking me from behind my back, where I had placed me; unwilling to observe myself, and

setting me before my face, that I might see how foul I
was, crooked and defiled, bespotted and ulcerous. And I
beheld and stood aghast; and whither to flee from myself I found not. And if I sought to turn mine eye from
off myself, then again didst thou set me over against
myself, and thrustedst me before my eyes that "I might
find out mine iniquity and hate it" (Ps. 36:2). I had
known it, but made as though I saw it not, winked at it
and forgot it. . . . With what scourges of condemnation
did I not lash my soul, that it might follow me, striving
to go after thee. Yet it drew back; refused, but excused
itself.[4]

Caught in this tumult of spirit, Augustine went out into a
garden by his lodging. There he seemed to hear a voice, "Take
up and read, take up and read." He found a Bible and, opening
it, gazed at the section on which his eyes first fell. These were
the words he read: "Not in rioting and drunkenness, not in
chambering and wantonness, not in strife and envying, but put
ye on the Lord Jesus Christ, and make not provision for the flesh
to fulfil the lust thereof." Then, as Augustine told of it, "No
further would I read, nor needed I; for instantly at the end of
this sentence, by a light, as it were, of serenity infused into my
heart, all the darkness of doubt vanished away."[5]

It could be dangerous for the particular circumstances of one
soul's experience to be seized upon and made a mechanical
method which others might think they could employ. A writer in
The Fathers for English Readers, describing Augustine's conversion, adds this footnote: "It was the custom of the heathen
when in doubt to open a copy of the Aeneid of Virgil and accept the first lines upon which the eye alighted as a kind of orac-
ular solution of the doubt; this superstition was called the Sortes
Virgilianae. . . . It is not a less unreasonable superstition when
the book read is the Bible. . . . The example of even so great a
man as Augustine ought not to lead others into the same superstitious practice."[6] But this right word of caution of course does
not invalidate the fact that in the case of Augustine the words

he read, by their immediate appropriateness, did give to the higher impulses of his conscience what William James has called "that last acuteness, that touch of explosive intensity, that enables them to burst their shell, and make irruption efficaciously into life and quell the lower tendencies forever."[7]

Augustine's mother had followed him to Milan, and when he told her what had happened to him, she had the answer to her unceasing prayer. At Easter, Augustine was baptized by Ambrose, the bishop; and after that he started home to North Africa. At Ostia, on the journey, Monica fell ill and died, but with her heart now satisfied. Her son would be henceforward his generation's greatest spirit in the Christian church.

Augustine was still a layman. Dressed in ascetic garb he gathered others about him at Thagaste, where he organized a sort of monastic community for study and contemplation. But he was not allowed to remain there long. One day when he was present in the cathedral church at Hippo Regius, the congregation did what was not unfamiliar in that time; recognizing a man's conspicuous fitness, they laid hold of him and conscripted him for the church's service. Augustine was ordained a priest; and five years later, in 395, he was made bishop.

For thirty-five years, until his death in 430, Augustine lived in monastic simplicity with the group of his clergy whom he bound by rules of poverty and dedication like his own. No conspicuous outward acts were to mark these final years of his career. The diocese of which he was bishop was a relatively insignificant one. But by the greatness of his mind and soul he became the most powerful personality of his age, and an influence that would affect the thought of the Christian church unendingly.

The instrument of his influence was his writings, and that fact brings us to the second aspect of our consideration of him.

Augustine always possessed the keen desire for learning which belongs to quick and eager minds, and he acquired knowledge in many fields. But over and above the possession of knowledge he had the gift of a brilliant intellect which could bring together scattered facts and shape them into great creative meanings. So he could meditate on the profound elements of Christian faith,

as in his epoch-making *On the Holy Trinity*. So also he could
be the most authoritative voice of the church against what he
believed to be false movements in act and in thought, as in his
controversy with the fanatically violent sect of the Donatists
in North Africa, and with the monk Pelagius who seemed to
Augustine to treat too lightly man's desperate need of God.
What he wanted to say he could express in terms of no heavy
pedantry, but with a vital reality which all men could understand.

Probably the one of his writings which has come closest home
to innumerable human souls is his *Confessions*. Next to the Bible,
it stands with Thomas à Kempis' *Imitation of Christ* and Bunyan's
Pilgrim's Progress as more widely read than anything else in
Christendom. The *Confessions* was a new creation. Never before
had there been the self-analysis of a personality so unsparing, so
penetrating, and so profound as this; and in these last fifteen
centuries innumerable men and women have been helped by it to
confess to God, as Augustine did, "Thou madest us for Thyself,
and our heart is restless until it rests in Thee."[8]

The two other imperishable written works of Augustine may
best be considered in relation to the third aspect of his greatness:
namely, his effect upon the long history of the church and upon
the beliefs that would struggle for dominance within it.

One of these two books was *The City of God*. It was written
when Rome had already been captured by the barbarian tribes
which had broken through the frontiers that the legions could
no longer defend; and when North Africa was being ravaged
by the vandals, and Hippo itself was besieged. The end of all
earthly stability seemed at hand. Then in that moment of what
must have been the world's despair, Augustine proclaimed the
rise of the City of God. That City was the Christian fellowship
of the redeemed. *This*, and not any earthly power, should endure. By that immense affirmation Augustine laid the basis for
what he could not foresee; the rise of the medieval church, and
the papal claims to a spiritual dominion centering, like the empire of the Caesars, again in Rome.

But at the same time, and by what would have seemed incredible contrast, Augustine's *The City of God* helped to inspire the Reformation. For in his imagination the City of God which was to be a hierarchical organization was also something deeper and more primal; it was first of all the *congregatio sanctorum*, known best, therefore, not by its outward form but by its spirit, and thus leading directly to Martin Luther's great proclamation of the priesthood of all believers in a living church of God.

So also Augustine's other greatest work, his treatises against Pelagius, had a double result. From his own religious experience and from his reading of Paul, he had known man's sinfulness and the inability of the human soul to save itself. He maintained, against Pelagius, the utter dependence of man upon God for anything that could be good in his own life. Especially through the Dark Ages and in the medieval period, the sense of human helplessness was immensely deepened, and the power of the Catholic Church which claimed to be the one instrument of super-natural salvation was correspondingly increased. Only divine grace could redeem, and the church controlled that grace.

But in the Reformation the great authority of Augustine was turned another way. As Martin Luther read the facts, the Roman Church no longer represented the gospel of a saving grace that comes from God alone. It was in effect preaching salvation by works—men making themselves acceptable in God's sight by going to Mass, venerating relics, repeating prescribed prayers, giving money to the priest and sending "Peter's pence" to Rome. To Luther, that could become a blasphemous denial of the truth. No ecclesiastical control could take over the grace of God and appropriate it to serve the church's own profit and power. Grace could come direct to every soul whom God chose to make his own. In this conviction Luther had caught again the living fire that had burned in the soul of Augustine; for Augustine—as the article concerning him in *The Encyclopaedia of Religion and Ethics* truly says—"first among Church teachers gave adequate expression to that type of religion which has since attached to itself the name of 'evangelical'; the religion, that is to say, of faith, and distinct from the religion of works; the religion which, despairing of itself, casts all its hope on God."

Thus out of Augustine's theology has come a mixed inheritance; and Roman Catholicism and evangelical Christianity have interpreted his teaching in different ways. Not even so great a mind and soul as his could conceive and express the Christian gospel so perfectly that what he said would be free from misrepresentation or, indeed, infallible and completely satisfying even when rightly understood. As we have seen, his doctrine of the authority of the church as the destined City of God and his doctrine of salvation by grace were like two children struggling in the womb of his mind, and the balance between them is not always clear. Also, his emphasis on the sovereignty of God led him in his controversy with Pelagius to such a complete denial of any freedom of the human will that out of it there grew the kind of predestinarianism which John Calvin preached with appalling sternness. Even Augustine could sometimes forget that the mysteries of God cannot have an assured path driven through them by relentless logic, and that the greatest intellect must often stand hushed before that which is not yet fully revealed.

So it is not with Augustine as the thinker—pre-eminent though he was in that respect—that the final word belongs. His glory was and is in the religious passion which illuminated all that he tried to learn and then sought to convey. When all is said and done, his supreme gift to Christendom is the example in himself of the Truth he expressed in the *Confessions* concerning the relationship of the soul to God: the truth that shines through the never-to-be-forgotten words already quoted: "Thou hast made us for Thyself, and our heart is restless until it rests in Thee."

⊸§ X §⊸

Monks and Missionaries

In the second century, Irenaeus, looking out upon the facts of the general life, said of the order and stability which had been created by the rule of Rome: "The world is at peace, and we walk on the highways without fear, and sail where we will."[1]

Two hundred years later the kind of world that Irenaeus knew was disappearing. The barbarian tribes from north of the Rhine and the Danube had broken the defenses of the empire and disrupted the civilization which for so long had been safeguarded by what men thought of as "the eternal city." Rome itself had fallen; and with its central power broken, life throughout the empire lost its cohesion and dissolved like sand in a flooding river. The invading tribes had no concern for the culture which the patient, creative centuries had evolved. Conquest and plunder were all that they cared about at first. The great Roman roads disintegrated, the flow of commerce and communication was cut off, the aqueducts were broken, and paralysis fell upon the life of what had been the cities. In the open country, weeds grew in the fields no longer cultivated, and around the half-abandoned villages could be heard the howling of wolves when the sun went down. People huddling together to keep alive had little chance to preserve what they might have cherished: schools, works of art, the rich resources for mind and spirit which had been familiar in the long years of the Roman peace. Over all Western Europe there fell the shadow of the Dark Ages.

One great influence beyond all others saved the future. That was the life which centered in the monasteries. Before the Roman empire fell, the monastic movement had begun. Religious commitment led many men to devote themselves—some of them fanatically—to complete withdrawal from the secular world. In the chaos which followed the barbarian invasion the numbers of those who thus withdrew increased. It was in part a despairing flight from conditions that seemed hopeless; but it carried also the indestructible spark of the will to live, from which would come a flame of hope for the years to follow. When most of civilization fell into deepening shadow, the monasteries were like little islands where even in the worst times the flickering lights of promise burned. And that light would grow stronger, and men from the monasteries would carry it out into the surrounding darkness. The activities of the mind would be revived for a world which had descended into ignorance, and the Christian evangel for men's souls carried to the invading pagan tribes.

The later history of monasticism would reveal the fact that there are weaknesses in human nature by which even the most religiously conceived institutions can be infected. The time came when in many monasteries there was no actual holiness, but a fat and sheltered life fed by greed and special privilege, and at its worst morally corrupt. But monasticism could not have come into existence without the spark of an ideal which was possible only because there is a part of human nature which is noble. Montalembert, in *The Monks of the West*, wrote with a fervid piety which set monasticism in a glamorous light, but he expressed what monasticism at its best was supposed to be. A monk, he said, "is a man who withdraws from other men, not in hatred or contempt of them, but for the love of God and his neighbor, and to serve them so much the better, as he shall have more and more purified and regulated his soul."[2] As to the effect which monasticism had upon the future of Europe in the period when the break-up of the Roman empire brought an eclipse from which it seemed that civilization might not emerge again, Montalembert was stating substantial truth—even if rhetorically— when he wrote: "God brought forth a host of blackrobed men, more intrepid and patient, more indefatigable and less indulgent to themselves, than Romans or Barbarians ever were. They spread themselves noiselessly over all the empire and when the hour of its ruin had come they are to be found everywhere, in the West as well as in the East. . . . The Roman empire, without the Barbarians, was an abyss of servitude and corruption. The Barbarians, without the monks, were chaos. The Barbarians and the monks united re-created a world which was to be called Christendom."³

Who, then, were some of the men who, with a devotion that reflected in part at least the influence of the monasteries, were witness-bearers of the gospel between the fourth and the seventh centuries?

Over almost the same span of years through which Jerome was preaching and living in ascetic devotion in the East, another figure rose into greatness in the West. This was Martin, the patron saint of France, who was born about A.D. 316 in the province of Pannonia, the child of heathen parents. His father was a tribune in a Roman legion; and Martin, who as a boy had become a Christian catechumen, was himself drafted into the army. Sent into what was then the province of Gaul, and later separated from the army, he came into contact with Hilary, bishop of Poitiers. Having been baptized, Martin chose to go to a desert island off the coast near Genoa, where he subjected himself to rigorous self-discipline and mortification of the flesh. Returning to Gaul, he was made bishop of Tours; and until his death, about the year 400, he was so powerful an influence in combating the paganism of the invading tribes and in establishing Christianity that he was afterward canonized. Not long after his death, the chronicle of his life was written by his disciple Sulpicius Severus; and though that chronicle contains naïve accounts of reputed miracles and what may be credulous exaggerations, there emerges from it the picture of a man of great spiritual devotion who deserved the honor in which he has ever since been held. It may have been from some element of fact and not from legend only that there has come the story most lastingly associated with him: the story of Martin, when he was still in the Roman army, taking his sword and cutting his cloak in two to give half of it to a shivering beggar.

While he was bishop of Tours, Martin founded the monastery of Marmoutier; and after his death there rose in what is now France another monastery, which was to be still more renowned, that of Lerins. It was here that the monk Vincent of Lerins lived in the fifth century—he who gave the definition of orthodox faith which has been quoted in theological discussions from that time to this: "*Quod semper, quod ubique, quod ab omnibus creditum est;* that which always, everywhere, and by all, has been believed."

But a still more important figure had some connection with Marmoutier and Lerins. About the year 389 there was born somewhere near the western coast of Britain the boy Patrick. Christianity had come to Britain long before that, although no one now can know who the first bringers of the gospel message were: perhaps some soldiers in the occupying Roman armies who had been won to Christianity at home, perhaps some other official of the empire, or perhaps some humble traveler on business whose name is long since forgotten but whose witness has outlasted time. So there was Christianity in Britain, perhaps as early as the first century; but in the regions near the Channel such Christian beginnings as once existed had largely been scattered and almost extinguished by the pagan invaders who came in their dark ships down from the North Sea. Yet, driven back into the fastnesses of the West, Christianity survived; and it was a presbyter of the church and a deacon who were the grandfather and the father of Patrick. It was not to be in the shelter of any Christian community, however, that Patrick was to grow up. When he was about sixteen years old, there was a sudden raid by marauders from across the Irish Sea. They captured Patrick, and carried him to Ireland as a slave, where for six years he tended the herds of an Irish tribal chief.

At length Patrick escaped by means of a ship that carried him around the south of Britain to the coast of Gaul. Landing there, he made his way to the monasteries of Marmoutier and Lerins, where he stayed for several years. While returning to Britain he had a dream concerning Ireland, the land of his onetime enslavement. "I imagined," he said, "that I heard in my mind the voice of those who were near the wood of Fochlut, which is near the western sea, and thus they cried: 'We pray thee, holy youth, to come and walk again amongst us as before.' "

From that point on, the story of Patrick becomes a saga embroidered with miracles and wonders—including the tradition that there are no snakes in Ireland because Patrick drove them out. Through the mist of the far-off time it is impossible to sift out the objective realities from the rainbow of pious marveling. But among the facts are these. After his dream, Patrick went again to Gaul, to prepare himself for what he believed now to be his mission. There he was ordained and ultimately made a bishop. Then he did go back to Ireland, launch upon a long struggle with the Druids and other pagan influences among the Irish tribes, overawe by his spiritual forcefulness some of the Irish chiefs, found churches and the monastery at Armagh. Before he died in 461, he had made Christianity—Latin Christianity—part of the warp and woof of Irish character. And if Patrick, because of what he helped to produce in the Irish tradition and the Irish temperament, has been identified as a saint with Irish Romanism, nevertheless as a man he bore witness for all Christians to a devoted courage which could say, as in the opening words of the so-called St. Patrick's hymn,

> I bind unto myself today
> The power of God to hold and lead,
> His eye to watch, His might to stay,
> His ear to hearken to my need.

As Patrick went *to* Ireland, so another great missionary came *from* Ireland. In county Donegal, in 521, was born Columba, the son of an illustrious family. He became a monk, and he himself afterward established the monasteries that were to become famous, Daire Calgaich (or Derry), and Dair-magh (or Durrow). But his most significant work was beyond the borders of his own land. In 563, with twelve companions, Columba embarked from Ireland for the coast of Scotland; and landed on the little island of Iona, of the Inner Hebrides. There, separated by a narrow strip of ocean from the Scottish mainland, he built a church and a monastery, and from it he and his followers launched their bold attempt to bring Christianity to all the unconverted peoples of Scotland and northern England. Columba himself was a man of such purity of spirit and such fearless dedication that he won a response which only a great and rare soul could achieve. He converted Brude, king of the Picts, and his evangelizing influence reached out over wide areas of Scotland. Other monasteries were established on the mainland by his companions who went out from Iona, but Iona itself had a special meaning as the mother-house. There Columba lived until 597, thirty-four years after he had come from Ireland. Then on an evening in June, he was in his cell transcribing one of the psalms. When he heard the bell that sounded midnight, he made his way to the chapel; and it was there, kneeling to pray, that he sank down and died.

Already, while Columba lived, many worshipers had begun to come to Iona as to a shrine that was blessed because Columba was there. After his death, it became increasingly a place of pilgrimage; and now that the church held his body, the whole island came to be regarded as holy ground. For centuries, all the kings of Scotland were buried at Iona, and so, apparently, were eight kings or princes of Norway and four kings of Ireland. In the vicissitudes of the centuries, the buildings of Columba long ago disappeared, a medieval church built to replace them fell into ruin, and even of the great sculptured crosses that marked the graves, most have disappeared. But in this century, under the leadership of Dr. George MacLeod, the broken church has been restored, and Iona made again, not a monastery, but a holy place where men who want to learn to serve God better in their own communities come to study and work and pray.

A generation earlier than Columba, European Christianity, and especially the development of monasticism, had been profoundly affected by another great career. In the Sabine town of Nursia, not far from Rome, in 480 there had been born of noble parents a boy who was baptized Benedict. When he was only fourteen, Benedict left behind him the wealth and privilege which were his inheritance, went out into the rocky hills near Subiaco, and hid himself in a cave. There for three years he lived alone, praying, wrestling with the fleshly imaginations and desires that assailed him, and mortifying his body with extreme austerity. The report of him and of what was regarded as his sanctity spread through the neighboring region, and a group of monks from that area persuaded him to become their abbot; but Benedict had not been long in the monastery when the monks, angered at his correction of irregular and dissolute habits of their own, tried to poison him. Back to his solitary cave he went, yet not again to be left alone. Disciples resorted to him, and some of the Roman patricians brought him their sons for his instruction and his discipline. Soon he had organized twelve small monastic communities; but the jealous hostility of a nearby priest so undermined his influence that he resolved to leave. With a few followers he went south to Cassino, halfway on the road from Rome to Naples.

Now, however, after the first years of what had seemed a checkered and partly frustrated life, his career blossomed into immense significance. On the great hill of Cassino he founded the monastery which was to become the most famous and the most powerful monastic institution that the Western world would know. What constituted its influence was not only the personality of Benedict while he lived; it was the influence of the specific regulations for the monastic life which he wrote and put into effect at Cassino, and which spread through Europe as the Benedictine Rule.

The beginnings of the monastic movement had been in the impulsive acts of individuals—individuals like Anthony who in the third century had been moved by disillusionment with the world to go off alone into the Egyptian deserts, in a complete asceticism which broke every contact with the general human life. Later, some of these solitaries of the desert came together into communities, but the nature of their communal life was loose and vague, with no clear pattern. Basil, bishop of Caesarea in the fourth century, had issued directions which for the first time gave some clear guidance as to how the monks should live. But it was Benedict who had the genius to conceive and implement a plan of monastic organization so complete that it would prevail in all the countries of the West. His rule, set forth in seventy-three chapters, went into elaborate detail concerning the government of a monastery and the behavior of its monks; but the power of the rule lay in the fact that Benedict understood both the capacity of the human soul for heroic dedication, on the one hand, and the down-to-earth needs of the human body, on the other. So he made drastic requirements for spiritual commitment and religious discipline, and at the same time he rooted monastic life in the wholesome labor which is the elemental ground for the existence of human beings. He understood "that man was a creature of flesh and spirit, but that the spirit could not function except in and through the flesh. Man was a thinking reed, but the reed must be anchored firmly in the black earth, watered at the roots, warmed by the sun."[4]

In Benedict's conception, there was to be no idleness, either in worship or in work. Seven times a day the monks were to recite their offices of devotion, beginning with vigils before dawn, and then at three-hour intervals prime, terce, sext, nones, vespers, and compline before they went to sleep. Every monastery was to be a self-sustaining unit, with its fields and garden where food was grown, its mill, and its bakery; and every monk was to do the work assigned to him, regardless of who he was or what his rank had been in the world.

The threefold vow of poverty, chastity, and obedience was taken for granted. From the moment one entered the Benedictine Order, he possessed and would possess nothing of his own. As he was bound to chastity, so was he also bound to obedience, and the Benedictine Rule made unmistakable what that obedience would mean. The abbot of a monastery was elected by the monks themselves; but once elected—except for some grave charge of immorality or gross unfitness—he held authority for life. In important matters, he must consult the community, but when all had been heard, the final word was his. As it was his business to help the weak, so it was equally his business to make those who were tempted to pride and self-assertion realize instead that they had come into "a school of divine servitude," and to make them know that "our life in this world is like the ladder which Jacob saw in his dream: in order to reach heaven, it must be planted by the Lord in a humbled heart. We can only mount it by distinct steps of humility and discipline."[5]

Thus the rule of Benedict was strict, but it was also understanding; austere, but not demanding the fanatical excesses of asceticism which some of the solitaries like Anthony, and Simeon Stylites who lived forty years on top of a pillar, had exhibited. Basil of Caesarea, in the previous century, checking pious exhibitionism with common sense, had said, "If fasting hinders you from labor, it is better to eat like the workmen of Christ that you are."[6] And Benedict likewise, although his requirements both for work and for discipline were rigorous, drew the line against a degree of mortification which he thought had no reasonable meaning. Hearing once of a solitary in a neighboring mountain who had not only shut himself up in a cave but had fastened himself to its rock walls by a chain so that he could not move beyond the chain's length, Benedict sent him word to have no more of it. "If thou art truly a servant of God, confine thyself not with a chain of iron, but with the chain of Christ."[7]

Thus the Benedictine monks, as long as they exemplified the spirit of the great man whose name they bore, could be moral salt and spiritual leaven in a world that needed both. And that is what sometimes the best of them were: men who had sought the cloister in a genuine desire for closer communion with God, and who in their prayers and in their studies kept the candles of religion and of learning lighted in centuries when most of what had been civilization had gone into eclipse. Eventually—the weaknesses of human nature being what they are—the world and the flesh crept back within the monastery walls. Individual monks were sworn to poverty, but there was no similar inhibition upon the monasteries as such. From many sources—including bequests from frightened sinners near death who thought they might win merit for their souls—the monasteries acquired great properties; and what had once been disciplined life and labor was corrupted by luxury and sloth and the sleek arrogance of protected privilege. Nevertheless, the fact remains that in critical times the spread of the gospel in Western Europe was accomplished by individuals whom the monasteries had nurtured and inspired.

The man who proved to be the greatest bishop of Rome in the first one thousand years of Christianity, Pope Gregory I, had been a Benedictine monk, and it was another Benedictine monk who carried out a mission which Gregory had conceived. In ancient chronicles dating as far back as the first history of England, written in the early eighth century by the Northumbrian monk called the Venerable Bede, there is the story, which seems to be authentic: One day in Rome, Gregory saw a sale of slaves who had been brought from Britain, where in the continual collision between earlier and later invaders,—Angles, Saxons, Jutes and Danes—captives taken in the tribal battles were marketed as men had been marketed ever since the days of imperial Rome. Struck by the appearance of these particular men and boys, Gregory asked who they were, and he was told that they were Angles. "They are well named," he said, "for they must become brethren of the angels in heaven." So when he had become pope he commissioned Augustine—not, of course, the great Augustine of Hippo, but a man of the same name—to set out with a group of companions to preach the gospel in what now is England.

Making their slow way on foot from Italy through Gaul and finally to the coast, Augustine and his companions crossed the Channel and landed in the southeastern part of England which was then the kingdom of Kent. Ethelbert, the king, was a pagan; but his queen, who had come from Gaul, was already a Christian. After a time Ethelbert himself was converted and baptized; and Augustine found a place to live and work, at the little church of St. Martin, near Canterbury, where Bertha the queen was accustomed to worship. There had been Christians in Kent in earlier centuries, but most of Christianity in the east of England had been overrun and nearly obliterated by the pagan invaders from across the sea. Now the Christian church would be reestablished, and Canterbury would become the shrine and center of continuous Christian witness, down to and through the Reformation, by which the whole history of England would be molded, and the heritage of which would be carried from England to the New World.

So to those who are accounted as the church fathers must be added the later names of Martin of Tours, Patrick, Columba, Benedict, Gregory, and Augustine of Canterbury as torchbearers of the gospel fire.

✦ XI ✦

Francis of Assisi

Some who carried the message of the gospel were torchbearers of fiery demands, controversialists such as Tertullian and Jerome; but the gospel could come also as the gentler flame of a candle on the altar of a soul's devotion. Thus it was in the thirteenth century when there appeared the astonishing figure of "the little poor man" of Assisi, Francesco Bernadone. Born in 1182, the son of a prosperous merchant named Pietro, Francesco was to adopt the life of complete devotion and detachment from this world's advantages which has made him remembered through all the succeeding centuries as St. Francis. His career would have been extraordinary in any time. In his own time, it was the more so because it represented so complete a contrast to the facts with which his world was most familiar.

Europe was only beginning to emerge from the long night that had followed the breakup of the Roman empire. After the old imperial civilization had been torn to pieces by the invasion of the barbarian tribes, the struggle back to some relative world order and stability was slow and painful. For masses of the people contemporary with Francesco Bernadone, there was little to kindle any generous emotion. Feudal nobles in their fortified castles looked down upon the hovels of peasants who grubbed their living from fields they did not own. All the towns were walled, not only for defense against brigands but because there was frequent, organized fighting of town against town. Small communities were caught also in wider conflicts; war between

97

the emperor of Germany and the Lombard League of North Italy, war radiating out from Rome against German and Norman-French invaders who had established their local kingdoms on Italian soil. The crusades, which had been launched a hundred years before in religious fervor for the redemption of the Holy Land, had sunk into a futility of empty violence which had its backwash in all Europe when disillusioned armies drifted back from the East. The common people were ignorant and superstitious, and their masters not much more enlightened. Not only in the peasants' huts but in the castles and in the towns, crude conditions of existence bred disease; epidemics, including the Black Death, broke out with terrifying frequency. Life was apt to be cruel, brutish, and short. Yet although the age seemed to have all the vices, there was one vice it did not have—the vice of triviality. "Life was rude enough to kill feeble organisms; and thus characters had an energy not known today."[1]

Meanwhile, what of the church?

It included contrasts more dramatic than any century before or since has witnessed. In the first place, it had become morally corrupt. The lower clergy were uneducated and undisciplined, many of them as remote from the people's actual needs as the Latin they mumbled in the Mass was remote from the people's understanding. The bishops and other clergy of the higher ranks competed for the rich benefices by unashamed intrigue and bribery. The great monastic orders which had proliferated in the eleventh and twelfth centuries had so lost their first ideals that to the popular mind they could be characterized by such crooked and greedy pretenders as the monk and the pardoner whom Chaucer later portrayed in *Canterbury Tales*.

Thus, with regard to its inner life, the church had sunk far down. Yet the extraordinary accompanying fact was that its outward power had never seemed so immense. In 1198, the cardinals in Rome had elected as pope thirty-eight-year-old Lothario di Segni, young and vigorous, and distinguished already by noble birth, by natural intellect and wide education. He took the name of Innocent III, and in his pontificate of eighteen years he became one of the greatest in all the long line of those who have sat upon the papal throne. He carried to its ultimate expression the claim which some of his predecessors had begun to make: that the popes had inherited a primacy given first to Peter, that thus they were the "vicars of Christ," clothed with a divine authority to which all earthly potentates must bow. To the patriarch of Constantinople, Innocent wrote: "The Lord left to Peter the governance not of the church only but of the whole world"; and against John, the king of England, he asserted a supremacy which had been given to him, he said, by "the King of kings."

Nor were these empty words. He backed them with a double power: the physical power of astute armed alliances, and the more awful power of excommunication and the interdict. In that age when the mass of men implicitly believed that the church held the keys of heaven and hell, and when their pictures of the Last Judgment had a dreadful vividness, the threat of being shut out from all the instruments of salvation could become an appalling terror. Before the imperious will of Innocent, resistance crumbled. He forced the king of France to take back his queen whom he had tried to divorce; he compelled obedience of the kings of Aragon and of Portugal; and as for John of England, he reduced him to such abject surrender that John declared his kingdom subject to the pope's authority and he himself a vassal to his overlord. If a spiritual dominion could have been established by fear, Innocent thus would have established it. But the ultimate victory of the spirit of Christ cannot be won by the weapons of the world. Coming as it seemed from nowhere and with empty hands, Francis of Assisi would let loose a power more redeeming than anything possessed by the great pope in Rome.

Yet, at the beginning, there was no sign that this son of Pietro Bernadone would ever be significant. He seemed only a part of his world's pattern, no creator of anything new. He shared in his father's business, and he shared even more in the careless pleasures of the young crowd he went with. If it was laughter and gay excitement, he was for that; if it was fighting, he could be for that. When he was eighteen he went out from Assisi to one of the endless little local wars among the Italian towns, this time against Perugia; he was captured and spent a year in a Perugian prison. Not long after that, he started off to fight under Walter De Brienne, a knight who was championing the authority of Innocent against enemies of his power south of Rome. But this venture came to a quick and frustrating finish. When Francis and his companions had ridden only as far as Spoleto, thirty miles south of Assisi, a sudden sense of the futility of what he was about came to him as imperatively as a voice out of the sky that told him to go home again. So back he went, to the bewilderment of his parents and his friends. But then immediately he took up the old associations; and no one would yet have known that there was any essential difference between Francis and the young blades of his generation.

But under the surface there *was* something different—the restlessness of a disturbing spark which came from beyond the things of earth. That hidden spark was to break suddenly into a flame which would illumine and inspire all subsequent life for Francis. It was as sudden and as dramatic as the conversion of Saul of Tarsus on the Damascus road.

One evening Francis was going through the streets of Assisi as "master of the revels." There came a moment when his friends went noisily on, and then looked about in astonishment—for where was Francis? They turned back, and saw him standing in the middle of the street like a man transfixed. What was the matter with him, they wanted to know. Had he fallen in love, and gone into a trance about it? Whatever answer he made was beyond their understanding at the moment, but from that day on they saw the shattering fact of what had happened.

All the fabric of what Francis had thought was satisfaction had suddenly crumbled into dust. Wealth, privilege, irresponsible gaiety—what right did he have to these in a world where he could see around him the stark facts of poverty and wretchedness? He began deliberately to go among the poor, and to give away what his father had given him. One day he met a leper. Overcoming his instinctive horror of leprosy and its contagion, he not only gave money to the leper but kissed his hand; and he

went to the nearby leper colony to give what help he could.
Near Assisi was the obscure little church of St. Damian. Francis
began to go there to kneel and pray. At one of these times as he
gazed at the crucifix it seemed to him that the figure on the cross
became alive, and that it drew him with the awful love of the
One who had taken upon himself the sufferings of mankind.
What should Francis do? One obvious thing occurred to him.
He would help restore the neglected and half-ruinous little
church itself. He took all the money he himself had, and he sold
goods of his father's and brought the proceeds to the priest, who
was prudent enough to refuse to accept it; but Francis left it in
the building anyway. Meanwhile the poor priest gave him shelter.

Pietro Bernadone, Francis' father, was outraged. He came in
violent anger to drag Francis home. That day he did not find
him, but later, when Francis appeared in the streets in ragged
clothes, Pietro seized him and locked him up. Shortly afterward,
Pietro being away on a short journey, Francis' mother set him
free; and Francis went back again to St. Damian's, and to begging
in the streets for material with which to repair it.

For Pietro matters had gone beyond the limit of his endurance.
He tried to take Francis before the magistrate to accuse him of
giving away his (Pietro's) goods; and failing to take Francis
there, he did take him to the bishop. There he made his angry
denunciation of his son. But Francis' reply was more startling
than his father's anger. His father wanted him to pay back what
he had taken, and to renounce his right to an inheritance? Very
well; he would do more than that. Going aside from the bishop's
audience hall to another room, he reappeared presently, naked,
holding in his hands a bundle in which he had rolled his clothes,
and a little money which he laid down before the bishop. "Listen,
all of you," he said, "and understand it well; until this time I have
called Pietro Bernadone my father, but now I desire to serve
God. This is why I return to him this money, for which he has
given himself so much trouble, as well as my clothing, and all that
I have had from him, for from henceforth I desire to say nothing
else than 'Our Father, who art in heaven.' "

The bishop sent out hastily for a castoff piece of clothing that had belonged to one of his laborers and put it around Francis; and Francis went out from the bishop's palace in an exaltation of release and joy. As one of his biographers has written, Francis' gesture had been dramatic, but it was also symbolic. "It marked a complete break with the past. . . . If he had come naked into the world, he would go out of it naked, into a new world, a world where 'worldly' standards would mean nothing, a world where love alone reigned. By this sudden action he had irrevocably declared his purpose. There could be no going back."[2]

Exactly what he did next is uncertain; some of the early accounts of his life say that he knocked at the doors of a monastery, where he was churlishly admitted and put to work in the kitchen. In any case, before long he was back in Assisi, trying again to obtain stones to rebuild the church of St. Damian's, and begging his own food from door to door.

There was another neglected little church which Francis tried to rebuild, Santa Maria Degli Angeli, to be famous afterward as the Portiuncula. There one day in the winter of 1209, he listened as a Benedictine priest read Mass; and this is what he read as the Gospel for that day: "Wherever ye go, preach, saying 'The Kingdom of heaven is at hand. Heal the sick, cleanse the lepers, cast out devils. Freely ye have received, freely give. Provide neither silver nor gold nor brass in your purses, neither scrip nor two coats, nor shoes nor staff, for the laborer is worthy of his meat.' "

To Francis, the words came as with the blazing authority of heaven. Here was his commission! He would obey it to the letter. He threw away his scrip, his purse, his shoes. Henceforth, in mystical completeness, he would walk with the only companion who he said had been faithful to the Lord Christ and gone with him all the way to the cross—Lady Poverty. He would be stripped of every utmost thing which the world reckoned as its resources. Empty-handed, he would go out to preach the gospel of him who said, "He that seeketh his life shall lose it; and he that loseth his life for my sake and the gospel's, shall save it."

At first in Assisi the crowds mocked him and reviled him, but there was a passion in his preaching which none could ignore.

Presently his own example was "like a flaming sword penetrating to the very depths of conscience." As Paul Sabatier has written, he struck at men "with the holy boldness of love" for "he spoke only of that which he had himself experienced, proclaiming repentance, the shortness of life, a future retribution, the necessity of arriving at gospel perfection";[3] and this he did knowing that although the world may seem full of men who pass through life with souls asleep, there are always those who are waiting for some tremendous message to stab their spiritual energies wide awake.

It was not long before Francis won his first follower and companion, Bernard of Quintavalle, a man of wealth and of high standing in Assisi. He invited Francis to spend a night at his house, and the next morning he told Francis that he was wholly purposed in his heart to forsake the world that he had known and to go with Francis wherever he might go. He would give all his wealth away to the poor, and this he proceeded to do. The contagion of Francis' spirit spread. Pietro de Catonio, a priest and canon of the cathedral at Assisi, gave up his position to join himself with Francis and Bernard; and soon afterward came a man from a different class, apparently a poor laborer, Egidio. They had no formal organization nor any regular place of their own at which to gather, except a makeshift shelter in which they might sleep near Santa Maria Degli Angeli. They had accepted, each one, the same commitment to which Francis had given himself—the commitment to follow with absolute completeness the charge which the Gospels said that Jesus had given to some of his disciples when he sent them out; to go preach in his name, with no money and no possessions, and with no provision even for food or lodging except what might be offered to them on their way.

So out into the Italian countryside they went, wearing the coarse, brown robes of the peasants, girded with a piece of rope, sleeping sometimes in haylofts or under the porch of a church or even in some leper hospital. Their religious life was to be among the people, not apart from them as was the life of the monastic orders behind their convent walls. They were to labor at any skills they had, or in any humble service in farm or village, taking whatever bare living they could earn; and if they found no work, then they were to beg from door to door for bread. Humility, simplicity, poverty, and prayer: those were "the four foundation-stones of what we may call 'the Franciscan way.' "[4] In Francis and those around him there was a joyousness of spirit that might have seemed incredible: incredible except that they had found the mystic secret in the words of Jesus, "Unless you become as little children, you cannot enter into the kingdom of heaven." In their deliberately accepted poverty and in the simplicity of life from which all anxiety and apprehension were stripped away, they were like souls reborn.

It was from Francis himself that they caught this spirit. One bitter winter day Francis was walking from Perugia toward Assisi with one of his followers, Brother Leo, and he began to talk to Brother Leo on what would be "perfect joy." Would it be to win world-wide fame for "holiness and edification"? No, not that. Would it be to have all knowledge, to work miracles, to preach with such eloquence that infidels would be converted? No, not that. But if the Brothers could be so humble and so devoted that when they were most maltreated and abused they could feel most near to God, then *that* would be perfect joy. "Above all the graces and all the gifts which the Holy Spirit gives to his friends," said Francis, "is the grace to conquer oneself, and willingly to suffer pain, outrages, disgrace and evil treatment, for the love of Christ."

The name of Brother Leo indicates that others were being added to the Brothers Minor, as Francis chose to have their fellowship called. And that was true. Men were enlisting who would play their unforgettable parts in Franciscan history: Rufino, Leo, Masseo, and the incomparable simplehearted Brother Juniper, who, being left in charge of a chapel by a foolish sacristan, handed over to a beggar some silver bells from the altar, and who could never be restrained from giving away the clothes he wore even when he had nothing else to put on.

Now that the Brothers Minor were growing more numerous, it seemed necessary to Francis that he should have the approval

of the church. So he and some of the Brothers set out for Rome
—to Rome where the pope was the great Innocent III, whose
awesome authority had humbled the pride and power of kings.

Exactly what happened first is uncertain. One account says
that Francis made his unauthorized way into the gardens of the
Lateran Palace, where Innocent was walking alone upon a
terrace; and that when the pope found himself confronted by
this man from nowhere in his rough peasant's robe, he dismissed
him imperiously and told him to go roll in the dirt with the
pigs. Whether that was true or is only legend, the subsequent
fact was that Francis did have an audience with the pope through
the mediation of Cardinal Giovanni di San Paolo. Francis presented to the pope the rule which he desired for his companions:
to live in obedience, in chastity, and without property, and to
follow the teaching and footsteps of Christ. As he described
further the implications of the rule, with its complete sacrifice of
all worldly goods, its unqualified humility and poverty, and its
obligation upon the Brothers "in whatever place they may be
staying with other peoples, to serve them and cook for them,"
the pope replied: "Your life appears to me too severe; I see indeed
that your fervor is too great for any doubt of you to be possible,
but I ought to consider those who shall come after you, lest your
mode of life should be beyond their strength." Why could not
Francis and his companions be satisfied to enter one of the more
conventional monastic orders which already existed?

But Francis persisted, with the holy stubbornness of a conviction anchored in something higher than the authority of the pope.
He could not be satisfied with a kind of monasticism that was
more than half-conformed to the values of this world. He wanted
his Brothers Minor to be so free from self-concern that there
would be no possible barrier between them and uncalculating
service to the poor, the suffering, and the sinful. So, finally, the
pope gave his qualified approval. The Brothers Minor should
elect a responsible superior; they should have the tonsure as a
mark of ecclesiastical regularity; they could continue their
preaching and their way of life—and the pope would watch and
see what happened.

That qualified approval was enough. Francis and those who had gone to Rome with him went back to Assisi jubilant. It was Francis, of course, whom the Brothers Minor chose as their superior, and under his inspiration they went out everywhere to preach. The order grew by leaps and bounds, not only in Italy but in France and in Spain and later in Germany and in England. A seventeen-year-old girl named Clare, of the noble family of Scifi, heard Francis preach in the cathedral at Assisi, and she determined to break with all that seemed to her to be the trivialities of her luxurious life, and to become—like Francis—a servant of the poor. She came to the Portiuncula, where Francis was, and took the vows of a nun; and she, and afterward her younger sister, were established by Francis in a building at St. Damian's which was given to him by the Benedictine monks. From that beginning grew the sister Franciscan Order of the Poor Clares. Not long afterward there developed "the Third Order" of people still in the ordinary environment of the world who would try as best they could to reflect the Franciscan spirit, in moral behavior, abridgment of their luxuries, self-discipline, and prayer. So the influence of Francis was carried far and wide, like the fertilizing pollen of a flower.

Meanwhile, Francis was revealing in himself those qualities which would be described devotedly by his biographers, and some of which would be expanded into legend. In his eyes and in his bearing there was a spiritual serenity which made living creatures of every kind come toward him without fear. It is recounted that birds alighted on his shoulders and the little animals of field and wood ate out of his hand; and it was told also that once he tamed a wolf that had terrified the village of Gubbio. He had a delight in all things beautiful, and an adoration for the wonder of the works of God that broke into poetry and song, as in his *Canticle of the Sun*. People were amazed at his gaiety and gladness, as though for him God's whole created world was filled with light and joy. And so it has come to pass that the most instinctive pictures of St. Francis in Christian art are those which portray him against an idyllic background where the more tragic aspects of existence do not appear.

But that would represent only a fragment of the truth concerning him. The same Francis who could be so debonair among the little things was forever sensitive to those realities of human life which touch its depths of suffering and tears. His boundless compassion for all who were distressed gave him a spiritual power which made men think of the power of Christ. In the adoration which his closest followers had for him, the descriptions of what he did were doubtless magnified, and it is not possible to separate the exact original facts from the growing legends; but only something very wonderful about him could have inspired the lovely stories recorded in the writings which date from the years almost immediately after his death in 1226: the first *Life* by Thomas of Celano in 1228, and the recollections of Brother Leo, Brother Angelo, and Brother Rufino not many years thereafter. The Francis whom they remember, as one of his modern biographers has truly written, "was dedicated to the service of God and the winning of souls to greater love and obedience. Other interests were but a background to that work, a source of joy and satisfaction in their way but not to be compared in importance with the ministry of reconciliation. If Francis could choose the sort of stained glass window which he would like to be erected in his memory he would certainly choose one which depicted him surrounded not by birds and butterflies, but by the sick and the leprous, by cripples and tramps, by all the dregs of society whose life he so bravely shared and whose souls he so dearly loved."[5]

It is told that one day Francis approached a leper who had shouted at Francis' companions with insult and blasphemy. He asked the leper what he would have him do. "I wish you to wash me from head to foot, for I smell so bad that I disgust myself," the leper replied. So Francis heated water; and putting into it some sweet-smelling herbs, and taking off the leper's rags, he did wash the man from head to foot. Whereupon, the tradition says, the leper's flesh became like the flesh of a little child, "and in proportion as the flesh was healed, the soul of the wretched man was also healed and he began to feel a lively sorrow for his sins, and to weep bitterly." So runs the account, which could seem beyond belief. "But before one casts away the story as incredible," writes another modern commentator, "let him remember that few things are impossible to the completely unselfish, to those whose greatest happiness lies in service. Let him remember that there is no limit to the power of the man who lives wholly in the life of Christ. . . . Francis had broken through the ordinary limits of human energy. He, through his utter self-forgetfulness, his love, had entered into the energies that are Christ's and God's, and yet, none the less, his own."[6]

To preach in many areas of Europe was not enough for Francis. He wanted to follow the crusaders, and to preach also to "the infidel." After two unsuccessful efforts, he did get to the East. Touching first at Acre, he went on to Damietta, which was then being besieged by the Christian armies. Here Francis was shocked and disillusioned by the coarseness and loose-living of the troops who were supposed to represent the banner of the cross. At peril of his life he went through the lines until he came among the Arab armies, and demanded to be taken before the Sultan, the commander of the Muslims against whom the crusades had been launched. He offered to go through the ordeal by fire if—he being delivered—the Sultan would embrace the Christian faith. The Sultan seems to have been deeply impressed by this strange saint who had dared to come to him, but naturally he would make no promise. Conscious of what seemed to him his failure, and bitterly disappointed, Francis was sent back to the crusaders' base, there to be met with grievous news. During his absence, disintegrating influences had spread in the Franciscan Order. There was crucial need that Francis should come home.

He returned as quickly as he could, and he found that the troubling report which had been brought to him was true. The powerful Cardinal Ugolini (afterward Pope Gregory IX) who in his intention was a friend of Francis but who instinctively had the point of view of the conventional ecclesiastic, wanted to regiment the Franciscans under more practicable rules. Also among the greatly increased numbers of the Brothers themselves were those who wanted to relax the completeness of Francis' commitment to what he believed to be for him and for them the way of Christ: with its renunciation of all possessions, its following of him who had no place to lay his head, its unlimited identification with the lot of the poor. Elias, an able and, in his way, a devoted man, had been made vicar-general of the Order during Francis' absence. But Elias was also ambitious for the Order in a way not according to Francis' conception, willing to compromise its spirit if necessary in order to make it a force more shrewdly adjusted to what he thought were the realities of the world.

Slowly Francis realized that his vision for the Brothers Minor was being lost. The official pressure of the church, and a creeping worldliness within the Order, were turning it into something different from his soul's desire. It was becoming less a brotherhood in saintliness and more an organization covetous of supposed prestige and success. Francis could be an inspirer of men seeking to follow the example of Christ; he could not be the administrator of a machine. So, with deep distress of soul, but with complete humility, he resigned his headship of the Order, and left its direction in Elias' hands.

From that time on, Francis gave himself increasingly to solitude and prayer. His mind was filled with contemplation of the passion of Christ. With three of the Brothers, Angelo, Masseo and Leo, he had followed the lonely footpath that led from the valley of the Arno to the high plateau of Monte Averno where there had been built for him a rude shelter surrounded by woods. There he could pray alone. When one whole night he had agonized in prayer, there came to him, as the morning broke, a vision: the vision of a six-winged seraph nailed upon a cross. From that time there appeared upon his body what those who loved him told of with hushed and reverent awe—the stigmata: on his hands and feet black welts like the heads of the nails that fastened Christ to the cross, and in his side an open wound, such as that which Christ received from the Roman spear in the death-thrust at the crucifixion.

Two years after that, in 1226, Francis, who had been slowly weakening, was brought back to Assisi. He was only forty-four, but his bodily strength was burned away. With some of the Brothers gathered about him, he had them sing his *Canticle of the Sun*, which begins with praise to the Lord God for all his creatures, "and specially our brother the sun, who brings us the day and the light," and goes on to its climax in "Praised be my Lord for our sister, the death of the body, from which no man escapeth. Woe to him who dieth in mortal sin! Blessed are they who are found walking by thy most holy will, for the second death shall have no power to do them harm." Then at last at his own insistence he was stripped of his robes and laid on the ground at Santa Maria Degli Angeli, where he first had made his great renunciation; and there at the humble little church which his soul loved best, on October 3, 1226, at nightfall, death came. "I have done my duty," he said to the Brothers. "May Christ now teach you yours."

With Francis gone, the rule and life of the Franciscan Order began to slip into gradually increased conformity to the natural world which Francis' incredible saintliness had transcended. Innocent III perhaps was right when he had said to Francis, "I ought to consider those who shall come after you, lest your mode of life should be beyond their strength." Human nature cannot move enduringly on the level of St. Francis.

Yet there is forever in the human soul something that answers to the provocation of his ideal. It has been truly written of Francis:

There is probably no one figure in Christian history who exercises anything like such influence or holds such a compelling fascination over the mind and heart of the modern world. No milder phrase will do than to say that he "haunts" us. He has become for us the personal symbol in which we objectify our recognition that a secret has faded out of life which it would be worth all progress to recapture. . . . He had no interest whatever in most of the things which for us give life its value [secular learning, bodily well-being, material enrichment]. But . . . he achieved a certain tone in his response to the claims of life which sounds on unforgettably. What makes him a moral and spiritual leader whose fire still burns in the most unlikely hearts, for great numbers of modern men and women the one "real Christian" they have heard of, is not the *width* of his response to life so much as its quality and intensity.[7]

And even yet the beautiful and terrible spark of St. Francis' dedication may kindle again in actual human lives. Geoffrey Studdert-Kennedy, that flaming prophet of early twentieth-century England, was moved always by what he called "a passion of pity for the poor." And in this immediate time there has appeared from Madonna House, in Cambermere, Canada, a woman's description of "Launching a Lay Apostolate."

I was just a woman [she writes] in love with God, wishing to make the slums her cloister, hoping to witness to Christ "by being" on the badly re-paved pavements of slum streets and in the crooked and dilapidated houses. . . . He who gives that particular vocation, brought to my doorstep two young women and three young men. . . . They came to offer themselves in the same manner, and in the same way to God!

What did we do? The usual. We fed the hungry, clothed the naked, wept with those who mourned, gave drink to those who thirsted, and buried the dead. But above all we realized from the beginning, that *being* before the Lord mattered more than *doing*, and that the corporal and spiritual works of mercy had to be done with a flaming charity. We had to be part and parcel of those we served. We ate the same food that we gave them, humble as it was. We dressed ourselves in the same sort of second-hand garments we gave them. We lived in the same uncomfortable, cold, or over-heated homes they lived in. We were equally poor. . . . Whatever the call, whatever the vocation, whatever the Apostolate, it is always a call to *caritas*—to love.[8]

❧ XII ❧

Martin Luther

At the beginning of the thirteenth century when Francis of Assisi lived and Innocent III sat on what was called the throne of Peter, the power of the Roman papacy was at its awesome peak. In the centuries immediately following, the central element in that power still stood unbroken, even though crises in the history of Europe eclipsed the immense political influence which Innocent III had wielded; for the hold that the papacy had on the imagination of men went so deep that no change in outward circumstances could suddenly disturb it. Ever since Augustine in the fifth century, when the empire of the Caesars was breaking up, had written *The City of God*, there had been implanted in the mind of Europe the conception of the church as the refuge for the souls of men and the only ark of ultimate salvation. Little by little, what Augustine had thought of as a communion of the Spirit in contrast to the powers of this earth had become embodied in an institution. The process which led from Augustine's *The City of God* to the dominating actuality of the vast ecclesiastical structure that centered in Rome was shaped by the strangely mixed influences which so often mark human history. On the one hand, there was a deep religious yearning that there *should* be some voice to speak unfailingly for God and his righteousness in the midst of the voices of this earth—some infallible chief shepherd to be the vicar of Christ. But the desire that there might be such, which with our imperfect human nature there could never be, turned into devices out of which the desire might be realized. So there was developed the claim not only that Peter had founded the church in Rome, but also that he had transmitted a divinely commissioned primacy to all who might follow him as bishops there.

Nor was that all. As strong and masterful popes asserted this authority declared to have come from Peter, ecclesiastical jurists translated the claims into terms of the old imperial law. "Precedents, needed by the legal mind to unite the past with the present, had been found in a series of imaginary papal judgments extending over past centuries. The forged decretals of the pseudo-Isador (used by Pope Nicholas I in his letter of 866 A.D. to the bishops of Gaul), of the group of canonists who supported the pretensions of Pope Gregory VII (1073-1085) . . . gave to the papal claims the semblance of the sanction of antiquity." And in the thirteenth century "Thomas Aquinas set himself to prove that submission to the Roman Pontiff was necessary for every human being."[1] Thus, long indoctrination had made the mass of men in Europe believe implicitly that in the hands of the pope were the keys of heaven and hell, for he controlled the vast machinery of the church, from the dread shadow of which men's consciousness could never fully escape. Eternal destiny was reckoned to depend upon the mediation of the priest and the supernatural power of the sacraments. These the pope could grant or could withhold; and therefore, for fear of what might happen after death, the men of medieval Europe had little impulse to challenge the awful authority of the church.

But in the early years of the sixteenth century there arose a man who did challenge it—though at the outset nothing so formidable as that was involved in what he thought to do. The man was Martin Luther, born in the little German town of Eisleben, on November 10, 1483, the son of Hans Luther, a miner, and Margarethe, his wife. In Eisleben and later in Mansfeld to which his hard-working father moved because the Counts of Mansfeld would hire out small smelting furnaces to miners who had some skill, the boy Martin seemed certainly marked to be none other than an obedient and docile child of the church. He learned the Creed, the Ten Commandments, and the Lord's

Prayer; he learned that the church was the "pope's house," and that forever to be remembered were hell and purgatory and the Judgment to come. He told in after years of how he used to look at a stained-glass window in the parish church and shrink from the sight of the frowning Jesus in it, who came girded with a sword against the wicked. In Eisenach, where he was sent to school when he was in his teens, there were nine monasteries and nunneries; and pilgrimages and the veneration of relics and all the Catholic cultus were part of his matter-of-course picture of religious life. To question the divine appointment of the pope to rule would have seemed to him nearly as blasphemous as to question God. Yet two influences would converge to make him do exactly that. One was what happened in his own inner life; the other was the drift of events in Europe which made the times ripe for a revolt against the papacy, once a growing disillusionment concerning it should be touched by some spark of protest that would make resentment leap to flame.

Consider the second fact first.

In the century and a half before the birth of Martin Luther, the power of the papacy in the temporal affairs of Europe had gone up and down with changes as violent as the shock lines of an earthquake. From 1309 to 1376, later to be called the period of "the Babylonish captivity," the so-called popes—some of them with rival claimants—were not in Rome but at Avignon, in France; and after the return of the papal court to Rome, there followed an even worse time of chaos, "the Great Schism," when repeatedly there was pope and antipope, and at one moment *three* men, each of whom claimed to be the rightful occupant of "the throne of Peter."

From that low point of ignominy, the papacy made its way upward again, at least so far as concerned its prestige in a world which had few moral standards left. The last half of the fifteenth century was the period of the Renaissance, with a great flowering of art and culture and an immense increase of wealth in Europe due to the dramatic opening up of new avenues of commerce both by land and sea. Riches flowed into Rome, and the papal court had never been so magnificent nor ever before so powerful with the kind of power that money can give. Julius II brought the great architect Bramante to Rome to build St. Peter's, and Michelangelo and Raphael to adorn the Vatican; another part of his increasing revenues he used in armed warfare to enlarge the papal states. His predecessor, Pope Alexander VI (Rodrigo Borgia), a man of gross and unblushing immorality, so far re-asserted the papal claim to a sovereignty superior to that of all earthly kings that he issued in 1493 a papal bull which declared how the newly discovered continents and islands of the Western world should be divided. But back of this splendid front was a perversion of the church's spiritual reality to which even the humble and patient multitudes who had always believed in the popes as the vicars of Christ could no longer be blind. "The un-reformed papacy of the closing decades of the fifteenth and of the first quarter of the sixteenth century was the open sore of Europe, and the object of execrations by almost all contem-porary writers."[2] If anything should bring the great institution of the papacy under general scrutiny, men might see that the golden image had clay feet.

But for Martin Luther, in his little corner of Germany, this was at first outside the circle of his thought. He had no troubled feeling concerning the church at large. He took it for granted that everything was as it should be, and that what the pope said in Rome was the truth, which every devout soul should listen to and trust. But what did trouble him was unrest in his own soul. The church with its sacraments was the ark of sure salvation, but what if he were not fit to be sheltered in it? This was the haunt-ing question which conscience and imagination could not escape.

In the Germany of the last years of the fifteenth century there were massive influences out of which religious anxiety could dismayingly come. Old paganisms still permeated the thinking of the common people, making them believe in witches and demons that lurked in hidden corners of their world. The Devil himself and his malignant power were no vague notions, but realities forever threatening the soul. The sanctions of the church were built on inculcated fears: fear of death, of hell, and of eternal punishment. Life on earth was made to seem only a

prelude and a probation for the awful final verdict of a God
before whose wrath the wicked and the careless must tremble.
All mortal existence lay under the long shadow of the coming
fact; and the question of the soul's ultimate destiny made every
other consideration seem insignificant. In 1493, one Hartmann
Schedel wrote and published in Nürnberg a history of the world,
recounting the story of mankind from Adam on, and ending
with a woodcut of the Dance of Death. This was in the year
after Columbus had found his way across the Atlantic and landed
on the shores of the newly discovered Western world. All subsequent human history was to be gigantically affected by that
event, but Hartmann Schedel wrote no word of it. How astonishing it would appear that the news had not reverberated
enough through Europe to have reached him—for Columbus
had come back from his voyage three months before the book
was finished; or how much more astonishing must it seem that, if
he had heard it, he ignored it as of small concern. Yet he may
have considered the mere finding of a new continent on which
mortal existence might expand to have been only a trivial matter.
He could not have failed to know of the discovery of the Cape
of Good Hope in 1488, yet he never mentioned that. As Roland
Bainton has written: "The reason is that he did not think of
history as the record of humanity expanding upon earth and
craving as the highest good more earth in which to expand. He
thought of history as the sum of countless pilgrimages through
a vale of tears to the heavenly Jerusalem. Every one of those now
dead would some day rise and stand with the innumerable host
of the departed before the judgment seat to hear the words,
'Well done', or, 'Depart from me into everlasting fire.' "[3]

That somber sense of present life as chiefly "a vale of tears"
could have come to anyone in medieval Europe, and most of all
to a child and growing boy who was sensitive and emotional, as
Martin Luther was. Moreover, the facts in his own family and
in his environment tended to make his whole world of experience
seem grim and formidable. "His parents were hard, thrifty, and
superstitious, and beat their boy; and school was monotonous
and cruel. Martin gleaned from the combined harshness of home,

school and what he considered the Church's exclusive preoccupation with the last judgment, a world-mood of guilt and sadness."[4]

Of course the color of life for Martin Luther was not always one of guilt and sadness. The underlying anxiety was like a hidden river which only now and then broke through to cover his spirit with its dark flood: of those crises we shall speak later as well as of the final crisis when the river of his anxiety suddenly made its junction with a great, clear stream of redeeming energy which gave to his whole life a transfigured power. But through most of the years when he was growing up, his life on the surface did not seem too different from the life of his companions. Hans Luther, his father, was determined that this son of his should make his mark in the world—the new world of opportunity opening up in a Europe that was passing from the Middle Ages into a quickened era of fresh ideas, ambitious ventures, and expanding wealth. He sent Martin to school at Eisenach when the boy was fifteen; and two years after that to the University of Erfurt, which had an academic prestige not outranked by any other institution.

Hans Luther was confident that the hard-earned money he had invested with fierce determination would bring the honors he coveted in the person of his son. Erfurt, a walled city of some twenty thousand people (a large population for that century), was an important center of international trade, and its university had the most numerous student body in Germany. Martin seemed to adapt himself auspiciously to its life. He had a love for music which opened special companionships. He studied hard and mastered what the university offered in the classics, in logic, philosophy, astronomy, and physics. In a year and a half he took his bachelor's degree, and in two more years his master's. Now he was ready to enter the most distinguished department of the university, the school of law. His father presented him with the expensive books which the school required, sure that the proud ambitions he had cherished for Martin were about to be fulfilled.

But with shocking suddenness there came an event which for the tough old miner turned his expectation into outrage, as it reversed and confounded what he had thought would be the clear current of his son's career. Martin had gone home for a visit before the new term at the university began. What turmoil there may have been in his mind, what possible doubt about his father's driving purpose, what clash of loyalties, cannot now be known. But somehow and somewhere within him there was division which made him vulnerable to outer shock.

On the road back to Erfurt there came a crashing thunderstorm, with bolts of lightning that struck near Luther. Terrified, he cried out to St. Anne, the patron saint of miners and, therefore, the saint associated with his father. "Help me, Saint Anne! I will become a monk." At the brink of death as it seemed, he turned instinctively to the commitment which he thought would save his soul.

When he got back to the university, some of his companions tried to argue him out of his purpose. But he had been too deeply stricken for that. He knocked at the gates of the Augustinian priory in Erfurt and begged to be let in.

Admitted, he was brought presently before the prior. Prostrated at the foot of the steps leading to the altar, he was asked "What seekest thou?" "God's grace and thy mercy," he replied. Then the prior, raising him up, examined him as to whether he was ready for the renunciation of self-will, the reproach of poverty, the mortification of the flesh, and all the rigors of the monastic life. "Yes, by God's help," he answered, "insofar as human frailty allows." Then he was clothed with the habit of a novice. For one year he would be on probation, and in his ears were the admonishing words of the prior, "Not he that hath begun but he that endureth to the end shall be saved."

From home there came no encouragement, but only echoes of his father's indignant repudiation of what the son had done. To Martin Luther, the knowledge of that anger must have been like another thundercloud hanging always on the rim of his consciousness. But to all seeming he adjusted himself with relieved acceptance to the quieting regimen of monastic life; with its unvarying ordering of existence, its prayers and fastings, its seven hours of devotions beginning with the cloister bell that called the monks for matins between one and two o'clock in the morning, and continued at their appointed intervals until the day ended with compline, after which the monks went to bed on their cots of straw in the barren cells. It appeared that Luther's soul had found its peace. At the end of his novitiate, he took his final vows. Later he was made a priest. Then came the day when he celebrated his first Mass.

This was made the great festal moment in a new priest's life. All his family and friends were supposed to come. But what about Hans Luther? Would *he* come? Actually he did, with a whole retinue from Mansfeld. But his coming was to have a tempestuous sequel. When Martin and his father met at the monastery table after the celebration of the Mass, Martin said: "Dear father, why did you resist so hard and become so angry because you did not want to let me be a monk, and maybe even now you do not like too much to see me here, although it is a sweet and godly life, full of peace?" Whereupon Hans Luther burst out in anger, before all the company. Had no one ever heard of the commandment that a child should honor his father and mother? And as to the call of God to be a monk which Martin had claimed to have heard in the thunderstorm, "God give it that it wasn't a devil's spook!"

Martin Luther was caught again in a devastating spiritual conflict. A psychoanalyst, Erik H. Erikson, wrote in 1958 an exciting study and attempted explanation, *Young Man Luther*. His conviction is that the root of the religious doubt and near-despair which made Luther's next years in the monastery a torment to his soul was due to the conflict of his feelings about his father. He was drawn toward him in a bond he could not break, and yet he rebelled against him. The same conflict was transferred to his relationship to God. God became established "in the role of the dreaded and untrustworthy father . . . the God who *turns his back*, who looks away into the eternal darkness—the terrible, the hidden God."[5]

Whatever may have been the full reason, Luther went through a time of agonized distress. He knew himself to be under condemnation of his father. How could he be sure that he was not also under the condemnation of God? He set himself with desperation to try to achieve somehow a righteousness that might save him from the certainty of hell. In the monastery he multiplied his fastings and his penances; he starved and mortified his body almost to the point of physical collapse; he poured into the ears of his confessor such a recital of imagined sins that the confessor grew weary of his obsession. But Luther got no nearer to inward peace. The more he tried to accumulate righteousness, the more hopeless seemed the distance between his sinfulness and the implacable judgment of the holy God.

Luther's deliverance came at length in a great discovery—a discovery which became not only a personal experience for him but the opening of a new world of illumination for innumerable souls. His deliverance was made possible by the common sense of the vicar of the Augustinian Order, Johann Staupitz, who took Luther away from his morbid introspection in the Erfurt convent, and sent him out to work. He appointed him as a teacher in the new university which the Elector Frederick the Wise was trying to build up in Wittenberg. He announced to Luther that he was to lecture on theology and on the Bible. Luther was dismayed, but he had to obey. He began to study anew, particularly the Psalms, and then Paul's epistles to the Romans and to the Galatians.

One day he was reading the epistle to the Romans and shrinking, as he had so often done, before the thought of the awful justice of God whose wrath must be "revealed from heaven against all ungodliness and unrighteousness of men." Then he turned to read what Paul had written as to how men who had sinned "shall live by faith." Suddenly there flooded upon him, with a light as dramatic in its consequence as that which came to Paul on the Damascus road, the recognition that God does not wait for men to make themselves fit for his forgiveness. By the love that was revealed in Christ he calls them home, and all that is first required is trust in the outreaching hand. "Night and day I pondered," wrote Martin Luther afterward, "then I grasped that the justice of God is that righteousness by which through grace and sheer mercy God justifies us through faith. . . . To

me, an unworthy, condemned and contemptible creature, altogether without merit, God of his pure and free mercy has
given us in Christ all the riches of righteousness and salvation,
so that I am no longer in want of anything except faith to believe
that this is so. . . . Thereupon I felt myself to be reborn and to
have gone through open doors into paradise."[6]

Actually he did become like one reborn. He was a man now
with a new message and a new power. In place of doubt and
inner division he had wholeness, and the impact of his personality would shake the whole life of Germany.

It was in 1508, when Luther was twenty-five years old, that
Staupitz had sent him first to Wittenberg. Recalled to Erfurt, he
was sent on a mission to Rome in 1510, where the grossness of
the Italian priests disturbed him but where, as he visited the
churches and gazed at relics, he was awed anew by what he
thought was the sanctity of the Roman Church. In 1512, he was
sent back to Wittenberg permanently. He taught in the university and preached in the Castle church. With his new theological convictions, he had a message which students and general
congregations crowded to hear. But all that he said and did
moved within the regularity of the Augustinian Order and the
faith and discipline of the Church of Rome.

Now, however, events moved toward making him what in his
monastic obedience he would once have thought incredible—the
prophet of a Reformation. The reigning pope was Leo X,
worldly and unprincipled, and incapable of any spiritual concern. The corrupt papal court always seemed to need more
money, and Leo needed it now. So he hit upon the plan which
he thought most likely to secure it. There had grown up the
practice of indulgences, based upon the theory that Christ and
the saints by the measure of their goodness above all expectation
had created an overplus of merit which the church could dis-
pense to ordinary sinful souls. Leo made a bargain with Albert,
bishop of Brandenburg, who wanted to be also archbishop of
Mainz. For a large sum, Leo assigned him the right to have indulgences proclaimed in his ecclesiastical jurisdiction, and the
money that came from the sale of them would go to Albert, after

the proper share had come to Rome. A monk named Tetzel appeared not far from Wittenberg, setting up the papal banner, a platform from which he preached, and a box for the money the people would be called upon to pay. Here was the supreme chance, he said, for sinners to obtain forgiveness. Here was the chance, too, for all decent and dutiful men and women to help their dead fathers and mothers and friends escape from purgatory. The letters of indulgence he was selling, straight from his holiness the pope, were like the keys of heaven and hell. Who could be so hardened, who could care so little for their souls, as to turn their backs on this bargain for salvation?

Both as a theologian and as a man of moral conscience, Luther was revolted at the grossness of Tetzel's preaching. What should he do? Well, he could bring the whole matter to public notice, so that people could stop and think and see the truth for themselves. Therefore, on October 31, 1517, he posted on the bulletin board of the Castle church in Wittenberg a long list of theses which he was ready to maintain in discussion or debate against any who might question them. He denounced the promises which Tetzel was making in the name of the pope. The pope had authority over the church on earth; but it was false, he said, for Tetzel to declare that even the pope himself had any authority over purgatory. If any man was truly sorry for his sin, and trusted in God's mercy through Christ, he would be forgiven; without that godly sorrow and repentance, no written indulgence could save a man's soul. Believing that he spoke only what all right-thinking persons in the church would echo, Luther had no idea when he nailed his theses among the notices at the Wittenberg church door that he was setting in motion events that would be catastrophic.

But in Europe and particularly in Germany there were smoldering questions to which some positive word could come like a spark to light a spreading flame. Too many men were aware of what Luther himself had not yet fully recognized: venality and corruption at the papal court that made a mockery of its spiritual pretensions. People were growing tired of the ecclesiastical exactions which drained German money off to Rome. A new national-ism also was arising that would look twice at assertions of life-and-death authority hawked about in indulgences signed by an Italian pope. Luther's theses proclaimed what many persons had been waiting to have said. Copies of the theses, made possible by the newly invented printing press, were spread everywhere in Germany. The sale of indulgences dropped.

When Leo X first heard report of Martin Luther, he dismissed the matter with contempt. "Some drunken monk," he said. "When he is sober, he will talk differently."

But before long the tune changed. Albert of Brandenburg wrote to the pope that people were not buying the indulgences. He was not getting the revenue he had expected, and the pope would not get his either. Something needed to be done.

Accordingly the pope ordered the head of the Augustinian Order to see that Luther stopped talking; but it was not only Luther who was talking now. What he had said already was echoing throughout Germany. Some of the German princes and multitudes of the people were saying that Luther was right. There were abuses in the church that had to be ended.

Still Luther thought of himself as a conscientious spokesman of the gospel and of the Catholic faith to which he was yet obedient. If there were abuses, like Tetzel's preaching, he believed almost naïvely that the pope would want to correct them.

But Dr. John Eck, a learned scholar and able controversialist, challenged Luther to a debate. When they met in Leipzig, Eck set out to show who it was that Luther had actually been attacking. Luther had denounced Tetzel. Everybody knew that Tetzel spoke by the pope's authority; therefore, Luther had attacked the authority of the pope. He was preaching notions he claimed to have got from the gospel; but interpretation of the gospel was the province of the pope, not of an unruly monk. For preaching notions contrary to what the church in Rome proclaimed, John Hus had been burned as a heretic a century before. Luther was a heretic now.

That accusation was a shock to Luther. "God forbid!" he cried.

But as the debate proceeded, Luther was driven to positions

which laid him open increasingly to this charge of heresy. He had already said that the pope had no power over purgatory. He was saying now that popes had been in error and could be in error again; and that he, Martin Luther, could appeal to an authority of the Bible greater than the authority of the pope. By the direct mercy of Christ, and not through the machinery of the Mass or through indulgences, the sinner could be redeemed. To say that was to challenge the totalitarian claims of the Roman Church to hold the keys of heaven and hell.

The die was cast now. Infallibility could not permit that sort of defiance. Accordingly, the pope put Luther under the ban, which meant that he was forbidden to preach or to teach. If he disobeyed, the next penalty would be excommunication. Now Luther must either surrender completely or precipitate a struggle from which there could be no retreat. And what he did was this. When the ban was brought to him at Wittenberg, he put up a public notice inviting all the city to assemble at the Chapel of the Holy Cross outside the gates. He held up the papal document which ordered his submission. Then he burned it. Popes had sent alleged heretics to the stake and to the flames. Very well. He would put what he declared now to be the pope's false claims into the fire.

When the news of that spread along the roads of Germany, the country was electrified. Men caught their breath to wonder what would happen next.

What did happen is now remembered as one of the supremely dramatic scenes of history. Charles V, sovereign of the ancient and still awesome authority called the Holy Roman Empire, summoned the princes and nobles, the bishops and archbishops, of Germany to meet in imperial Diet in the city of Worms. Luther was ordered to appear for judgment. He was under condemnation by the pope, and the emperor was hostile. If he went to Worms, it might be at peril of his life.

He wrote to Duke Frederick of Saxony: "You ask me what I shall do. . . . I will go even if I am too sick to stand on my feet. If violence is used, as well it may be, I commend my cause to God. . . . This is no time to think of safety. I must take care that the gospel is not brought into contempt by our fear to confess and seal our teaching with our blood."[7]

On April 2, 1521, Luther set out from Wittenberg to answer the summons to appear at Worms. Traveling in a rough Saxon cart, he was two weeks on the road. On April 16, the word spread in the streets of Worms that Luther was approaching, and a great crowd of people swarmed out to meet him; for Worms, as one of the most ancient towns in Germany, had a fierce pride of independence and had little use for emperor or pope. The common people saw in Luther a champion, but he knew well enough that the heavy odds were on the other side. The next day when he was on his way to the palace where the Diet was assembled, an illustrious old soldier, General Frundsberg, clapped him on the shoulder, and said to him, "My poor monk! my little monk! thou art on thy way to make a stand such as I and many of my knights have never done in our toughest battles!"

As he entered the crammed audience hall, Aleander, the papal legate, looked closely at him, and said afterward, "The fool entered smiling; he looked slowly round, and his face sobered." There was reason to be sobered; for in that glittering assembly, with its background of banners, were gathered the might and majesty of medieval church and state.

On a table were Luther's books. Would he admit that they were his? Yes, he would admit it. Then came the question, "Do you wish to retract and recall them and their contents; or do you mean to adhere to them and to reassert them?"

Luther asked for time to deliberate, "that I may answer the question without injury of the Word of God and without peril to my own soul."

Grudgingly, the emperor allowed the Diet to adjourn until the next day; then it reassembled. Now Luther would have the chance he had coveted to make his full defense. He reviewed the books that lay before him and the truths of the gospel which he believed them to contain. To the gospel he appealed, and to the free soul's reception of it. As to what he had written, "It is impossible for me to recant," he said, "unless I am proved to be in the wrong by the testimony of scripture or by evident reasoning; I cannot trust either the decisions of Councils or of Popes, for it is plain that they have not only erred but have contradicted each other. My conscience is bound to the word of God, and it is neither safe nor honest to act against one's conscience. God help me! Amen!"[8]

Thus he stood then, in his monk's robe and cowl, alone and seemingly unfriended. Yet he was not altogether without friends, even in that august assembly which stared at him in what seemed its ominous, grim silence. Charles V, as well as the papal legate, was outraged. Here was this presumptuous monk exalting his individual conscience above the divinely given authority of emperor and pope. But there were others who were ready to see that authority challenged, and they were on Luther's side because he dared to challenge it. Princes of Germany had read Luther's summons *To the Christian Nobility of the German Nation*, his *Liberty of a Christian Man*, and his scathing arraignment of the papacy, *On the Babylonian Captivity of the Church*. So while Spaniards in the Diet shouted that Luther should be condemned as a heretic, German knights ringed him round and escorted him from the hall.

The next day the Diet met again, and the emperor proposed that Luther be condemned. German nobles resisted that, wanting to work out some compromise. This came to nothing. A week later Luther was ordered to return to Wittenberg, without preaching. On April 26, his safe conduct would expire, and after that he was liable to be seized and put to death as a pestilent heretic.

But Luther was not seized on April 26 or thereafter. He had vanished. In Worms and elsewhere, the word spread that he had been assassinated. As a matter of fact, a group of armed knights had suddenly laid hold of him on the road—knights who were not his enemies but sent in secret by some powerful friend. They carried him to the castle of Wartburg, to stay there hidden and protected.

Germany was too divided for the emperor to venture to such length as hunting Luther down. For a year, he remained at Wartburg. Meanwhile, his writings were spread everywhere, and so was his influence. Great numbers of monks and parish priests, and even bishops, espoused the evangelical doctrine which he had preached. The papal excommunication of Luther and all who might support him was still in effect, but in a fierce wave of independence a large part of Germany began to treat the papacy as though it had ceased to exist.

The church was in revolution—a revolution that might go too far. There was danger that unbalanced and violent men might throw all religion into chaos, repudiating everything that was orderly and traditional in revolt against what had formerly been. Luther's friends at Wittenberg were dismayed. They sent him a message desperately urging him to come back. And back he came, regardless of the threat of arrest and execution which still hung over him.

Luther checked the excesses of those who were leading the new movement to extremes. He was resolute to retain the essential elements of the church as they had come down through all the centuries: the orders of the ministry, the sacraments, and the creeds, while at the same time cutting away what he believed to be parasitic growths—the rule of the papacy, the superstitions and corruptions associated with the Mass, and the exploitation of the fear of purgatory and of hell. What he sought was not repudiation of the central Catholic heritage; what he sought was reformation.

For a time it seemed that the Lutheran movement would sweep all Germany, but then for more than twenty years the country was torn with increasing conflict. One party wanted to restore the power of emperor and pope. The other party espoused the new conception of the faith and the new liberties which Luther represented. Neither party was strong enough to prevail. Enough of the princes stood by Luther to prevent his enemies from seizing him as a heretic. But the terrifying Peasants' Revolt in 1525 against intolerable poverty and oppression frightened many in the ruling class and provoked reaction in every line. At Speyer in 1529, the princes who took the side of Luther were first called Protestants, and in many of the principalities Protestantism was established. But other territories fell back under the dominance of Rome.

In 1525, to the whole of Germany's astonishment, Luther was married. He had left the Augustinian Order and ceased to be a monk when he had broken finally with the pope. His studies had convinced him that there was no warrant in the Gospels for required celibacy; and that, instead of monasticism, religious dedication ought to be identified more closely with the general life. As the influence of his preaching spread, monks and nuns listened, and many left their cloisters. Among the nuns was Katherine von Bora, daughter of a nobleman, born in 1499, who had been in a Cistercian convent since she was nine years old. She, and a number of her sister nuns, abandoned the convent at Easter, 1523. It was this Katherine whom Luther married two years afterward, and his life with her was happy and serene. Six children were born to them; and the same Luther of storm and struggle who wrote the great Reformation hymn "A mighty fortress is our God" revealed himself in his family life the man of tenderness to children who could write also the lovely Christmas carol:

> Ah, dearest Jesus, Holy Child,
> Make thee a bed, soft, undefiled,
> Within my heart, that it may be
> A quiet chamber fit for thee.

Driving himself with the same intensity he had always had in preaching and in the spread of the evangelical allegiance, Luther lived until 1546; and his death came as the result of a long journey in bitter cold January weather when he had gone on an errand to Mansfeld to try to reconcile two friends. Becoming ill at night, he died the next morning. "Reverend Father," said Justus Jonas who was with him, "wilt thou stand by Christ and the doctrine thou hast preached?" Luther raised himself for a single word, "Yes."

One of the supreme forces in history, he seems the more real because he was so human: passionate, explosive, sometimes uncontrolled in sudden temper and in speech that could be violent and coarse. But he gave the almost incredible example of the moral power which one man of lonely courage can exert. He woke the conscience of Germany and created the Reformation. And as one transformed by his own experience of the redeeming gospel, he gave afresh to Christendom the great conviction that it is not by their self-righteous works but by faith in the undeserved love of God in Christ that men are born anew.

XIII

John Wycliffe and William Tyndale

John Wycliffe

Martin Luther is rightly accounted the creator of the Reformation, if by the Reformation is meant the establishment of organized Protestantism set free from the domination of the Church of Rome. But Martin Luther, and men like Calvin and Knox and others yet to be named who were the spearheads for a new religious freedom in the sixteenth century, could not have succeeded except for the fact that in various countries discontent had long been gathering. Corruptions in the medieval church had been so flagrant that many people everywhere were ready to hear them challenged. And in the years when the privilege and power of the ecclesiastical system was still too deeply entrenched to be broken, even then courageous voices spoke their protests and men of intrepid spirit blazed the roads of thought and action which led to decisive ends.

In the famous debate at Leipzig, when John Eck in the name of the Pope arraigned Martin Luther for Luther's attack upon indulgences, Eck accused Luther of being a follower of John Hus. Luther recoiled from that charge with horror, because in his own thought he was still a loyal son of the church, and Hus had been condemned by the Council of Constance a hundred years before and burned at the stake as a pernicious heretic. Later he came to recognize that what Hus had preached did in fact foreshadow what he, Luther, was maintaining. The Bohemian martyr was his forerunner. Back of Hus was another great figure, whose writings Hus had read and whose opinions Hus had dared to espouse, namely, John Wycliffe, of fourteenth-century England.

Wycliffe was born in or near the year 1320. Educated at Balliol College, Oxford, he became a brilliant and influential lecturer on theology. In his earlier years, his thought and teaching dealt with scholastic matters which might provoke disagreement but were not of a kind to give any serious ecclesiastical offense. But then he moved to more dangerous ground. In the popular mind there was a growing disillusionment with the church and with those who represented it. Wycliffe's contemporary, Geoffrey Chaucer, in his *Canterbury Tales*, had satirized the easygoing worldliness of clerics, the fat laziness of monks, the rascality of lecherous friars. The man of letters, amusing and delightful, could get away with his goodhumored mockery. But Wycliffe was a priest; and assault by a priest was a different matter. When Wycliffe saw the hypocrisy and corruption which had become all too familiar, and began to denounce it, he spoke not with any amusement but in straight words that blazed with indignation. What outraged him most was the fact that many priests were so ignorant or so indifferent that the real message of the gospel never got to the common people. What could the people make of church services mumbled in Latin, and what could they learn from perfunctory sermons—or from no sermons at all? Meanwhile, there was no Bible they could read. Consequently, Wycliffe set out to do two things. He translated the Latin Vulgate into English, and he enlisted a company of priests who shared his own concern to go out and preach in villages and countryside.

Ecclesiastical authorities and the reactionaries in general looked upon these preachers with contempt. They called the preachers and their listeners "Lollards", a nickname of scorn which probably meant "idle babblers." But the response of the people to the preachers, and the spreading influence not only of Wycliffe's translation of the Bible but of the English tracts which he wrote and circulated, soon woke official alarm and anger. As John Richard Green expressed it in his *Short History of the English*

People, "The rough, clear, homely English . . . the terse, vehement sentences, the stinging sarcasm . . . roused the dullest
mind like a whip. . . . Pardons, indulgences, absolutions, pilgrimages to the shrines of the saints, worship of their images,
worship of the saints themselves, were successively denied. A
formal appeal to the Bible as the one ground of faith, coupled
with an assertion of the right of every instructed man to exam-
ine the Bible for himself, threatened the very groundwork of the
older dogmatism with ruin."[1] What might happen if the ordinary folk took it into their heads to form their own ideas about
religion instead of listening to what the priests and prelates had
to say? A contemporary chronicler wrote of Wycliffe's translation of the Gospel "from the Latin into the Anglican language"
that thus he "made it the property of the masses and common to
all and more open to the laity and even to women who were
able to read than formerly it had been even to the scholarly and
most learned of the clergy. And so the Gospel pearl is thrown
before swine and trodden underfoot."

Powerful figures in the church, particularly Archbishop Sud-
bury and the bishop of London, outraged now by what they
regarded as Wycliffe's false teaching and sedition, repeatedly
ordered him to trial. But he had vigorous defenders in Oxford
University, which was near the parish of Lutterworth of which
he was rector, and in John of Gaunt, the most powerful nobleman in England. The result was that his enemies were never able
to carry through their desire to condemn him as a heretic and to
burn him at the stake as they were grimly ready to do—the more
so because in his last years he denied the doctrine of transubstan-
tiation and the miracle of the Mass on which the supernatural
authority of the priesthood rests. Instead, the end came for Wycliffe in his own parish of Lutterworth, where he was stricken
with paralysis during a service in the church; and there in
Lutterworth he was buried.

But his body was not to stay there. Archbishop Arundel, writing to the pope in 1412, called Wycliffe "that wretched and
pestilent fellow of damnable memory, son of the old serpent,
and the very herald and child of anti-christ . . . who crowned

his wickedness by translating the scriptures into the mother tongue."[2] And four years earlier the provincial council of Oxford decreed that "no one shall in future translate on his own authority any text of holy scripture into the English tongue or into any other tongue, by way of book, booklet, or treatise. Nor shall any man read this kind of book, booklet or treatise, now recently composed in the time of the said John Wycliffe, or later, or any that shall be composed in future, in whole or part, publicly or secretly, under penalty of the greater excommunication, until that translation shall be recognized and approved by the diocesan of the place, or if the matter demand it, by a provincial council."[3] In 1415, the same Council of Constance which condemned John Hus, ordered that Wycliffe's body be dug up and burned and the ashes thrown into the river—which was done.

Thus Wycliffe's body could be disposed of; not so readily could the world have done with his spirit. It was reflected in the heroic witness of John Hus. It continued as a light kept burning among the Lollards in England, especially "in villages along the Chiltern hills, in the Thames Valley and in Essex. Theirs seems to have been a simple, pious, anti-clerical religion, and the evidence from the bishops' courts suggests that they had only a few tattered, precious copies of single gospels and epistles which went the rounds from one congregation to another."[4] So, the influence of Wycliffe may have seemed to be not much more than a flickering candle, in danger of being blown out by the winds of reaction; but it was not extinguished, and when the times should be more propitious, it could kindle a greater flame.

The more propitious time did not come quickly. For more than a century after the death of Wycliffe the church in England was back in the rut from which Wycliffe had tried to lift it. The greed of prelates and the immorality of priests continued to be notorious. "Priests, monks and nuns swarmed, large numbers living idle and useless lives. The ecclesiastical orders had amassed to themselves, in the name of God, enormous riches and a great proportion of the land, and on this they claimed to be exempt from taxation. . . . An open scandal also was the unchastity of the clergy and of the monastic bodies. While claiming to be too pure for holy matrimony, they were at liberty to keep concubines, and in many parts of Europe could square the episcopal authorities by paying an annual tax."[5] Except in the case of a few, there was abysmal ignorance. In 1222, a visitation at Salisbury had revealed the fact that five out of seventeen priests in charge of churches could not translate the Latin words of consecration in the Mass; and more than three hundred years later, Archbishop Warham was to complain of the monks at Canterbury that, when conducting divine service, they were "wholly ignorant of what they read."

But in 1453, the capture of Constantinople by the Turks brought about the influx of Greek scholars into Western Europe. The era of the Renaissance and of the New Learning began. At almost exactly that same time, Gutenberg, in Mainz, had invented the printing press; so that henceforth what men thought and wrote could be spread not only by manuscripts laboriously copied one by one, but through printed books and tracts which could come off the presses in unlimited numbers. At the end of the fifteenth century and the beginning of the sixteenth, John Colet began to lecture at Oxford on the epistles of St. Paul, with a freshness of interpretation which aroused the suspicious hostility of reactionaries in the church, but which woke excited interest among the many who came to hear him; he continued these lectures in London when he became dean of St. Paul's. To Oxford while Colet was there came Erasmus of Rotterdam, destined to be the most famous scholar of the age, and later Erasmus taught in Cambridge University from 1511 to 1514.

Returning to the Continent, Erasmus brought out in 1516 his Greek New Testament, by which the Gospels and the epistles in their original language were first made available in Europe, and in comparison with which men first became aware of the many inaccuracies in the Latin Vulgate, which had been the only Bible of the medieval church. Devoted to the classics and to the humanities in general, Erasmus was only casually concerned with theological questions. He was disgusted with the corruption in the monasteries and other institutions of the church, and he assailed it with devastating sarcasm; but he accepted the church's doctrines with a routine conformity, and he steered clear of any quarrel with the pope. His scholarship was recognized as so authoritative that he had vast influence among all who had any education, and he stimulated everywhere a thirst for further knowledge. With the cool temperament of the intellectual, he never had the crusading zeal that might have made him a champion of the Reformation; but with the scholar's impatience with ignorance, he said things that could open roads along which the Reformation could advance. In the Preface to his Greek New Testament he wrote: "I vehemently dissent from those who are unwilling that the sacred scriptures, translated into the vulgar tongue, should be read by private persons. . . . I would wish even all women to read the gospel and the epistles of St. Paul, and I wish that they were translated into all languages of all Christian people. . . . I wish that the husbandman may sing parts of them at his plow, that the weaver may warble them at his shuttle, that the traveller may with their narratives beguile the weariness of the way."

Measured against the cruel repression which was the church's actual answer to any effort to make the Bible available in English, those might have seemed subversive words. But as coming from Erasmus, the ecclesiastical authorities did not take them too seriously. They might be the rhetoric with which the man of letters pleased himself; there was no likelihood that, with Erasmus, they would lead to disturbing action.

The man was about to appear, however, who would not shrink from action. What Erasmus had expressed as pleasant wishes, this man would put into bold and challenging fact. As one of the chroniclers of the time was presently to write: "Midnight being now past, some early risers were beginning to strike fire and enlighten themselves from the scriptures."

William Tyndale

In 1494 or thereabout, in Gloucestershire near the border of Wales, was born William Tyndale, of a family of relatively prosperous yeoman farmers. As a young boy he was sent to school at Magdalen Hall in Oxford, from which he entered Magdalen College. Whatever other learning he got there, he did not acquire easily any of that which later would be his passionate concern. "In the universities," as he afterward wrote in *The Practice of Prelates*, "they have ordained that no man shall look on the scripture, until he be noselled in heathen learning eight or nine years, and armed with false principles, with which he is clean shut out of the understanding of the scripture; . . . and when he taketh his first degree, he is sworn that he shall hold none opinion condemned by the church." For some twelve years Tyndale remained at Oxford; and then he went to Cambridge, where the ecclesiastical atmosphere was less repressive and the New Learning more advanced. In the two universities he became a proficient scholar in Greek and probably in Hebrew also, and at Cambridge —in the words of John Foxe—he "further ripened in the knowledge of God's word."

After three years in Cambridge, Tyndale left the university in 1519, to go back to Gloucestershire as a tutor to the children of Sir John Walsh, at Little Sodbury Manor. He had been ordained, probably when he was at Oxford. The diocese of Worcester, to which the Cotswold country belonged, exemplified as glaringly as any part of England the contrast between the gross worldliness and complacency of the existing church and the spirit of the Gospels by which Tyndale had been stirred. Three successive bishops of the diocese were Italians who took their ease in Rome and drew their revenues without so much as setting foot in England. In Gloucestershire were six great priories whose mitred abbots had seats in the House of Lords, and at the abbey of Hailes there was a shrine which claimed to possess drops of the blood of Christ and to which the credulous came in pilgrimage because it was promised that to worship before that blood was to win salvation. Many of the clergy, great and small, were as ignorant as the people; and, as is usually the case with ignorance, quick to resent any influence by which the empty routine of religious forms might be disturbed.

But Tyndale was on fire with a new purpose. He preached in the manor chapel which was the parish church for Little Sodbury village, and he preached also in the city of Bristol, where little groups of Lollards had kept the message of Wycliffe alive. At Sir John Walsh's table he spoke his mind to the ecclesiastics whom the master of the manor had there as his guests: "divers great beneficed men, as abbots, deans, archdeacons, and other divers doctors and learned men." There is graphic record of what happened; for when John Foxe in this same sixteenth century wrote his *Book of Martyrs* he got some of his material first-hand from men who had seen or heard what they described; among them was a Gloucestershire man, probably Richard Webb, who knew Tyndale and to whom Tyndale talked. So it is related that "the said Master Tyndall, being learned . . . did many times therein show his mind and learning; wherein as those men and Tyndall did vary in opinions and judgments, then Master Tyndall would show them on the book the places, by open and manifest scripture: the which continued for a certain season . . . until . . . those great beneficed doctors waxed weary, and bore a secret grudge against Master Tyndall." Their grudge became the more embittered when they saw that Tyndale's superior knowledge had made them lose face with Sir John Walsh at Little Sodbury Manor, so that "those great prelates were no more so often called to the house, nor when they came had the cheer nor countenance as they were wont to have."[6]

Before long they lodged complaint against Tyndale with John Bell, the archdeacon and chancellor of the diocese, alleging that he was "an heretic in sophistry, an heretic in logic, and heretic in his divinity." And when Tyndale was called before him, the chancellor "threatened him grievously and rated him like a dog."

Instead of being intimidated, Tyndale now made up his mind that the one thing he would set himself to do would be to provide a translation of the New Testament which could be read by the people of England, and by which they could see for themselves the contradiction between what went on in the church and the neglected message of the gospel. "I had perceived by experience," he wrote afterward in the Preface to his translation of the Pentateuch (1530), "how that it was impossible to stablish the lay people in any truth except the scripture were plainly laid before their eyes in their mother tongue, that they might see the process, order and meaning of the text."

But in England, with the decrees of the Council of Oxford still in effect, no translation could be put forth unless some high dignitary were persuaded to sanction it. The new bishop of London, Cuthbert Tunstall, was an accomplished scholar, and supposed to be of a liberal spirit. Tyndale would go and make appeal to him. "Sir," he said to Sir John Walsh, "I perceive that I shall not be suffered to tarry long here in this country, nor shall you be able to keep me out of their hands; and what displeasure you might have thereby, it is hard to know, for the which I should be right sorry."[7] Might he have, therefore, Sir John's consent to leave his engagement at Little Sodbury and go to London?

The consent was given, together with a letter of introduction to Sir Henry Guildford in London, who might have influence with the bishop. To London, therefore, Tyndale went, and after some delay he was given audience by Tunstall. But Tyndale's plea that the bishop lend his sanction to what he, Tyndale, wanted to do was heard with chilling dislike. The prelate had no mind to be associated with an enterprise so questionable. Nor did he have any place in his household for this unimportant priest from Gloucestershire. He had chaplains enough already. Let Tyndale look somewhere else for a place in London.

In the city there was a wealthy cloth merchant, Humphrey Monmouth. While Tyndale had been waiting for his appointment with the bishop, he had been invited to preach in St. Dunstan's Church, Fleet Street. There Monmouth had heard him; and with a generous kindness he invited Tyndale to come and stay at his house—an act which later was to bring to Monmouth heavy cost and punishment when Tyndale's name had become anathema in the church.

After the rebuff by Tunstall, it was evident to Tyndale that any translation he might make could not be printed in England; and that even the knowledge that he was attempting it could bring his own immediate arrest. But there might be a better chance in one of the countries of the Continent where Lutheranism was already spreading and where repression was not consistent. So in 1524 he sailed for Hamburg, leaving the homeland, which he would never see again.

From Hamburg, according to the consensus of imperfect records, he went to Wittenberg; and there in Martin Luther's town and university he made his translation of the New Testament, using as his sources the Vulgate, but more decisively his own fresh study of the Greek text, and, for comparison, the German version which Martin Luther himself had completed. After some nine months, having his manuscript nearly completed, Tyndale and a companion, William Roye, made their way to Cologne, where Tyndale hoped to have his translation published because Cologne was "nearer to England, more frequented by commerce, and more convenient for transport by boat."

He did find a printer who would undertake the work. But it had progressed only a little way when a Romanist got wind of it, made report to the authorities in Cologne—who prohibited the printers from any further dealing with the "two English apostates"—and wrote to the bishops in England "to keep the strictest watch in all the parts lest that most pernicious merchandise should be imported into the country."

Tyndale and Roye—a man who became more trouble than help to Tyndale and from whom Tyndale presently parted—escaped to Worms, where the protecting influence of Lutheranism was strong. And in Worms, in 1526, were printed some five or six thousand copies of one of the epoch-making books of history, Tyndale's translation of the New Testament, which for the first time made the Gospels and the history of the early church and the epistles available in printed form in the English language to all who could read in England.

Now began the dangerous process of trying to get the books into England. There were booksellers ready to run the risk of receiving them if that could be done secretly. So the books were shipped to England hidden in bales of merchandise: some on ships that went down the Rhine, some from Antwerp, some through the book market at Frankfurt where merchants of many countries came and went. Soon the New Testaments were cropping up in England: in London, in towns where the Lollard groups were still existent; and in the universities. Agencies of state and church were alerted now to find the books and any persons who were guilty of their circulation. A royal pronouncement by Henry VIII declared, "We, . . . with the deliberate advice of the most reverend fathers of the spirituality, have determined the said and untrue translations to be burned, with sharp correction and punishment against the keepers and readers of the same." Tunstall, bishop of London, summoned the booksellers of the city, and warned them that "certain children of iniquity . . . declining from the way of truth and the orthodox faith, have with crafty trickery translated the holy gospel of God into our vulgar English tongue, intermingling certain articles of heretical depravity and pernicious erroneous opinions, pestilent, scandalous, and seductive of simple minds." He threatened with excommunication and indictment for heresy all who should have any part in circulating this "pestilent and pernicious poison in the vulgar tongue." Wadham, archbishop of Canterbury, and Wolsey, cardinal and papal legate, issued similar denunciations; men in Christ Church College, which Wolsey had established at Oxford, who were suspected of having bought the prohibited books, were arrested and jailed, and three of them died in prison.

Meanwhile, Tyndale remained for a year in Worms, where the strong Lutheran influence gave him at least a temporary refuge. After that, apparently he was at Marburg, and at Frankfurt, and then in Antwerp. In 1528, there was printed at Antwerp the first of Tyndale's writings which openly bore his name—for the title page of his New Testament translation had named neither author nor printer. The new book was *The Parable of the Wicked Mammon* and in it Tyndale launched his indignant protest against those in England who were trying to keep the gospel from the people. "They love you so well," he wrote, as though he were speaking directly to the English people, "that they had rather burn you than that you should have fellowship with Christ. . . . They would divide you from Christ and his holy testament, and join you to the pope to believe in his testament and promises. . . . Nevertheless in translating the New Testament I did my duty, and so do I now, and will do as much more as God hath ordained me to do."

The powers in England redoubled their efforts to find and destroy every book of Tyndale's and to hunt down Tyndale himself. The bishop of London confiscated all the copies of the New Testament he could find in London, and burned them publicly at St. Paul's Cross. Furthermore—unwisely—he sent his agents to buy up copies on the Continent, where his authority for seizure did not reach, and in that process there came into the whole grim conflict a glint of ironic humor. For it is recounted that one of those whom Tunstall sent as an agent, Augustine Packington, was actually a friend of Tyndale's; and having delivered copies of the New Testament to the bishop at a high price to be burned at St. Paul's, Packington sent the receipts to Tyndale to pay for the printing of many more copies than had been burned. "And so," as was written in Halle's *Chronicle,* "forward went the bargain: the bishop had the books, Packington had the thanks, and Tyndale had the money."

Money was the last thing Tyndale cared about except as a means to pursue his one devoted purpose—the purpose which had begun to form in him when he was at Little Sodbury. There one day when a pompous cleric was revealing his own complacent ignorance, Tyndale had burst out: "If God spare my life, ere many years I will cause a boy that driveth the plough shall know more of the scripture than thou dost." With unflagging energy Tyndale drove himself toward the accomplishment of nothing less than that. He would pour into England such a flood of new knowledge of the Bible that thousands among the common people could begin to read and understand. Besides the translation of the New Testament which afterward he twice revised, he wrote an introduction to the Epistle of Paul to the Romans, expositions of Matthew and of I John, *The Obedience of a Christian Man, The Practice of Prelates,* a prologue to the Gospels called *Pathway into the Holy Scripture,* and a little tract on *The Supper of the Lord.* Having translated the New Testament, Tyndale turned to the Old; by midsummer of 1530, his translation of the Pentateuch, printed probably in Antwerp, had begun to appear in England.

With its coming there was roused among the English prelates

a hatred of Tyndale which became implacable, and which put his life in constant peril. For with the translated text of the Pentateuch, Tyndale printed marginal notes—notes which reflected his sense of outrage at the way his New Testament had been treated and the gospel itself denied. In Numbers 18:24, it is set forth that the Levites should have certain specified tithes from the Temple sacrifices, but beyond that no inheritance; alongside which Tyndale wrote, "Ours will have tithe, and lands, and rents, and kingdoms, and empire and all." In Deuteronomy 23:18, it is commanded that "thou shalt not bring the hire of a whore . . . into the house of the Lord thy God"; and Tyndale commented thus: "The pope will take tribute of them yet, and bishops and abbots desire no better tenants."

Blistering words were those, out of place beside the text of Scripture; yet there was truth in their indictment, and the vindictiveness that was let loose against Tyndale came from ecclesiastics who still were protecting some of the evils which he had dared denounce. By fair means or foul, the powers in England tried to apprehend him. At first it was not known where Tyndale was. Then when he was discovered to be in the Netherlands, unsuccessful efforts were made to get the authorities there to arrest him as a heretic. In 1531, Henry VIII sent an agent, Stephen Vaughan, to promise Tyndale safe conduct for return to England. Vaughan wrote to the king that at first he hoped Tyndale would respond, "but the bruit and fame of such things as hath chanced within your realm has led him not only to refuse, but to suspect a trap to bring him into peril." The "such things" included the recent burning at the stake of three men and a woman, one of them a friend of Tyndale's accused of heresy. Still the pursuit of Tyndale continued; and at length, in 1536, he was trapped in Antwerp by another emissary from England, imprisoned at the castle of Vilvorde near Brussels, tried and condemned by the Inquisition, and there, early in October, 1536, strangled by the public executioner, and his body burned.

So William Tyndale was put to death, but the supreme achievement of his life's devotion could not be destroyed. He had brought the New Testament and much of the Old Testament into the hands of the people of England. The eagerness to possess the scriptures, which he had inspired, grew so strong that within one year after his martyrdom, at the urging of Thomas Cranmer who had succeeded Warham as archbishop of Canterbury, royal assent was given to a Bible printed under the fictitious name of Thomas Mathew, but made up almost entirely of Tyndale's translation text.

From that time on, a succession of Bibles repeated or directly reflected Tyndale's words, and determined the character of all English editions. "In phrasing, rendering, vocabulary, rhythm, and often in music as well," this continuing power of Tyndale's translation was due, as Professor Isaac of the University of London has described it, to Tyndale's "honesty, sincerity and scrupulous integrity, his . . . directness, [and] his magical simplicity of phrase." Once that had been heard, the echo of it could never be absent from the thought and the instinctive speech of subsequent translators. In the King James Bible of 1611, known for centuries as the Authorized Version, one-third of the New Testament is a direct repetition of what Tyndale wrote, and in the remaining two-thirds the sentences follow his general pattern. Before his enemies apprehended him, Tyndale had not had time enough to translate the whole of the Old Testament, but even so all subsequent translations were affected by the "magical simplicity" of his style. Tyndale never got so far as to the book of Psalms, and so there is no version of these that has his immediate accents. But here, as elsewhere, the King James Bible is in the pattern of language which he set, and the rare beauty of it can be recognized by a comparison with another translation, the Rheims-Douay version, completed in 1582 by Roman Catholic scholars trying to bring back Catholicism into England. Here, with its stilted Latinisms, is its version of the opening and closing verses of the twenty-third psalm:

"Our Lord ruleth me, and no thing shall be wanting to me. In place of pasture there he hath placed me; upon the waters of refection he hath brought me up. . . . Thou hast fatted my head with oil, and my chalice inebriating, how goodly it is. And thy mercy shall follow me all the days of my life, and that I may dwell in the house of our Lord in longitude of days."

As against that, read "The Lord is my shepherd. I shall not want"; and the words that follow to the end of the psalm as it stands in the beautiful, familiar language of the Authorized Version. For more than three centuries, that Bible has exerted its immeasurable influence upon the thought and life of English-speaking peoples everywhere; and first and noblest among all the men who laid the foundations for it was William Tyndale, who gave his life that the Word of God might be set free.

XIV

John Calvin

Towering among the great figures of the Reformation in the sixteenth century was John Calvin in Geneva.

John Calvin, as he is generally known (though the family name was originally Cauvin and his baptismal name in France was Jean), was born at Noyon, Picardy, France, in 1509, the son of loyal Catholic parents. His father, a lawyer, was a secretary of the bishop, and attorney for the cathedral chapter at Noyon. At the time of John Calvin's birth, Martin Luther was in his first provisional assignment as a teacher at the new University of Wittenberg, so far as any general recognition was concerned an unimportant and almost unknown monk. Nothing then indicated that his words would presently light a fire that would spread through Europe. But already there were influences that made for religious change. The New Learning which had come with the Renaissance had stirred men's minds to question old ideas. The great scholar Erasmus of Rotterdam, and others of the humanists, had exposed superstitions of the church and corruptions among all ranks of the clergy, including the papal court at Rome, which began to arouse a moral conscience that had too long been dormant. Here and there were lay people, and also some ecclesiastics, who wanted correction of manifest abuses. "They looked to reform without 'tumult,' to a reformation of the Church by the Church and within the Church, brought about by a study of the Scriptures, and especially of the Epistles of St. Paul, by individual Christians weaning themselves from the world while they remained in society, and by slowly leavening the people with the enlightenment which the New Learning was sure to bring."[1] Most distinguished among these was Marguerite D'Angoulême, queen of Navarre, and sister of Francis I, king of France. A woman of deep personal piety, she was the center of a little circle which included the bishop of Meaux, and Jacques Lefèvre who translated the Bible into French. Among them, and wherever their influence reached, there was genuine desire for a living religious experience different from what was often the dead ceremonialism of the Catholic Church.

In his early years, John Calvin was altogether the child of the old order. When he was twelve, his father secured for him a benefice in the church at Noyon, and a more lucrative one in a church nearby—a practice which no one then considered to be extraordinary, although the duties of the benefices had to be carried out by hired substitutes of adequate age. Most of the revenues accrued to the boy, and his father sent him at fourteen years of age to study theology at the University of Paris. John Calvin was there until he was nineteen, and then the father, having quarreled with the ecclesiastical authorities at Noyon, decided that there was "a surer road to riches and honors," and sent his son to Orleans and later to Bourges to study law.

Meanwhile, Martin Luther had nailed his ninety-five theses on the door of the castle church of Wittenburg, and began his increasing challenge of the papacy which came to its climax four years later in his epoch-making defiance at the Diet of Worms. The excitement of this spread to France, and galvanized there all the gathering unrest. Just how directly and at what point decisively the message of Luther began to affect John Calvin cannot now be known, but about 1532 he was converted to the full evangelical gospel of the Reformation. In 1533, his friend, Nicholas Cop, was to be inaugurated as rector of the University of Paris. Calvin, already a brilliant and accomplished scholar both in theology and in law, was believed to have largely written the revolutionary inaugural address which Cop delivered, to the outrage of the Sorbonne and of all reactionary Catholics. Forced to flee from Paris, Calvin was briefly imprisoned at Noyon, and then banished from France.

After a time he found a haven in Switzerland. There, in 1535, he wrote, and in the next year published, the book which would take its place among the few that have had immeasurable influence on religious thinking: *The Institutes of the Christian Religion.* His purpose was to show that the Reformation gospel was the true and uncorrupted gospel of the church at its beginning, and so he based the *Institutes* on an exposition of the three great affirmations of the Apostles' Creed: belief in God the Father, God the Son, and God the Holy Ghost, with a final section on the nature, the meaning, and the authentic marks of what should be "the holy Catholic Church." He dedicated it "To His Most Christian Majesty, Francis, King of the French" to whom he, John Calvin, wished "peace and salvation in Christ." As to those, and particularly the priests, who resisted the Reformation and entrenched themselves in what he denounced as the superstitions and falsehoods of Rome, he wrote:

> They think it unimportant what anyone holds or denies concerning God and Christ, provided he submits his mind with an implicit faith (as they call it) to the judgment of the Church. Nor are they much affected, if the glory of God happens to be violated with open blasphemies, provided no one lift a finger against the primacy of the Apostolic See, and the authority of their Holy Mother Church. Why, therefore, do they contend with such extreme bitterness and cruelty for the mass, purgatory, pilgrimages, and similar trifles, and deny that any piety can be maintained without a most explicit faith, so to speak, in these things; whereas they prove none of them from the word of God? Why, but because their belly is their God, their kitchen is their religion.

And as to the two conceptions of the church which were in collision between the papists and the Reformers, he wrote:

> Our controversy turns on the two following points: —first, they contend that the form of the Church is

always apparent and visible; secondly, they place that form in the see of the Roman Church and her order of prelates. We assert, on the contrary, first, that the Church may exist without any visible form; secondly, that its form is not contained in that external splendour which they foolishly admire, but is distinguished by a very different criterion: the pure preaching of God's word, and the legitimate administration of the sacrament.

Instinctively a scholar and a thinker, Calvin wanted—or thought he wanted—a quiet life. But forces were converging which would lay hold upon him unpredictably and involve him in a relentless conflict that would last almost until he died.

The awakening message of the Reformation had come early to Switzerland. Its appeal to the thought and conscience of the individual found ready echo among a people who in their alpine strongholds had been fighting for independence from the House of Hapsburg and from feudal overlords since the thirteenth century. One of the first voices to stir, in Switzerland, a challenge to the Church of Rome parallel to what Luther had begun in Germany was that of Ulrich Zwingli. As a student in Swiss universities, he became a humanist after the pattern of Erasmus. In age almost an exact contemporary of Martin Luther, what he did in Switzerland was closely parallel to what Luther first did in Germany—and yet with a profound difference. Luther's gospel of redemption from sin by the free mercy of God in Christ had come to him in a transforming spiritual experience, and therefore when he challenged Tetzel's preaching of the pope's indulgences he did so with a flaming religious earnestness because he saw the saving truth perverted, to the peril of men's souls. Zwingli, who had been a parish priest at Glarus and then became the preacher at the Great Minster in Zurich, also denounced the selling of indulgences; and he went on to challenge other medieval doctrines of purgatory and intercession of the saints. There was not in him the moral passion that was in Luther, but he had the devastating power of intellectual scorn for what he held to be the superstitions and abuses which had grown up in the church. Under his influence, the Great Council that governed Zurich as a free city called a Public Disputation, for which Zwingli drafted sixty-seven theses for debate. As a result, the Mass in its medieval form was abolished in Zurich, monasteries were secularized, pictures and images taken from the churches. The first Evangelical communion service was held in the Great Minster in 1525. In Zurich, as in Germany, the new order was built upon appeal to what the Reformers believed to be the recovered truth of the Gospels rather than upon what they regarded as the distortions made by the Church of Rome.

Elsewhere in Switzerland the Reformation spread. Of greatest importance was its establishment in the powerful canton of Bern. By 1528, this canton had become decisively Protestant, and its ruling Council had a militant purpose to plant the new faith wherever the influence of Bern could reach. The authority and protection of the Council was promised to preachers of the gospel. Among these was William Farel, like Calvin born in France, and one of the little group who had been inspired at Meaux by the piety and devotion of Jacques Lefèvre and Marguerite, queen of Navarre. Driven here and there by the Romanist authorities in France, Farel came to Switzerland, first to Basel and later to a little town near Bern. After a time he became the leader of an organized group of missioners, young men for the most part well educated, of unbounded courage, daunted by no threat or peril, ready to risk death in their complete devotion. In the towns to which they went they could be sure of the implacable resistance of bishops and most parish priests, and often of the violence of incited mobs. To use a twentieth-century word, they were the commandos of the Evangelical crusade, the assault wave of the Reformation advance.

In eastern Switzerland, near the borders of France, was the strategic city of Geneva. Farel sent there his most trusted assistant, Antoine Froment, who opened a school, which the Romanists presently tried to close; and once he was hunted by a mob from house to house until he escaped by hiding in a barn. Now the Council took action. It sent Farel himself to Geneva, and with him a demand that Geneva, with which Bern was in alliance, hold a Public Disputation, with the right for Farel to confront any who might appear against him. There were murderous riots and an attempt to poison Froment and Farel. This last outrage finally turned the tide against the Catholic group. The Council of Geneva, stirred by rising demands from among the people, announced the Public Disputation which Bern had called for. The Romanist spokesmen proved to be no match for the flaming eloquence of Farel, and on May 21, 1536, the citizens of Geneva confirmed a vote of the Council to abolish the Mass and saint worship, and proclaimed their action "by sound of bell and by trumpet."

The Reformation had taken possession of Geneva, by formal action at least. But to vote a change in religious ritual and to reform the life of a city were not the same thing, as Farel soon found out. He was a pioneer evangelist, reckless in courage, eager, generous and warmhearted, but not naturally suited for the relentless purpose and the steady plan which would be needed for building the structure of a Reformed Church out of the diverse elements in Geneva.

The stage was set for Calvin, although he did not know it; a will more sovereign than his own was calling him to the center of that stage. After he had finished the *Institutes*, he was on his way to Strassburg, where he intended to devote himself to quiet study. But difficulties on the road compelled him to detour by way of Geneva, where he meant to spend no more than a single night. Farel heard that he was there. To Calvin's lodging he came, filled with his own passionate devotion to the Reformation cause. Should Calvin immerse himself somewhere in study? No! Let him come and be the Lord's instrument in Geneva. Finding that his first persuasion did not avail, Farel, as Calvin himself told afterward, "proceeded to utter an imprecation, that God would curse my retirement and the tranquility of the studies which I sought, if I should withdraw and refuse assistance when the necessity was so urgent." At that moment the power of Farel's conviction seemed as awful as the thunder of Sinai. "I was so stricken with terror," said Calvin, "that I desisted from the journey which I had undertaken." He stayed with Farel in Geneva, to remain there, except for one brief interlude, until his life's end.

The crucial influence which Calvin was destined to exert in Geneva had no preliminary sign. "Professor in sacred learning to the Church in Geneva" was his title; and the Council, in assenting to what it said was Farel's statement of need for a teacher, referred to Calvin merely as "this Frenchman in St. Peter's."

It was not long, however, before the impact upon the city of Calvin's mind and purpose became evident. Growing numbers of people came to St. Peter's Church to listen to his daily lectures on the epistles of Paul. More important were the plans he began to formulate for the organization of the Genevan Church. Farel would present these to the ruling Council of the city, but back of Farel's voice was the incisive thought of Calvin. At work in him now was not only the learning of the theologian but the systematic precision of the lawyer. He wanted to create a church so definite in faith and structure that it would be stronger than the resistance it would have to deal with in Geneva: the double resistance which came, on the one hand, from the resentful group that still clung to the Church of Rome as against the Reformation, and, on the other hand, from the large number of the so-called Libertines—the people of easy morals and loose living who did not want any new religious control from any quarter.

The cornerstone on which it seemed to Calvin that an effective church must be built was a right conception of the Holy Communion. This Communion, or Lord's Supper, was the sacrament of union with the redemptive life of Christ, and therefore Calvin wanted it to be the center of the congregation's worship every Sunday, stripped of what he believed to be the perversions of the Roman Mass. At the same time it could be the instrument of the church's discipline, if the church should have authority to exclude from the Communion those adjudged to be heretical or blasphemous or of evil life, and to subject them thus to the punishments not only ecclesiastical but civil which every sixteenth-century community would visit upon the excommunicate.

Accordingly, Calvin recommended that the church rule upon the fitness of any person to come to the Lord's Table. He also drew up a statement of faith which every citizen of Geneva should be required to sign, and a catechism in which all children should be instructed.

The Council of Geneva did actually adopt Calvin's confession of faith, and it had the people of the city brought in batches to the cathedral church and made to raise their hands and take the oath. But the Council balked at giving the ministers of the church the power of excommunication. It wanted possible domination by ministers no more than it wanted the now repudiated domination of priests. So in January, 1538, it voted "that the Supper be refused to no one."

Thus began an increasing conflict. Farel and Calvin had against them from the beginning not only the unconverted Romanists but all that part of the population which had no use for the moral strictness of the Reformers. And now they had to deal with the Council's insistence on the ultimate authority of the state. The issue came to a head when the Council presumed to order that the Communion be administered with unleavened bread, instead of with the ordinary bread which the ministers meant to use. In April, 1538, on the day set for a Communion service, Calvin announced that in the mood prevailing in the city, the carrying forward of the service would be a desecration, and that there would be none.

The next day the Council met and ordered Calvin and Farel to get out of Geneva within three days.

Calvin went to Strassburg, where he was made preacher and professor of theology. There he developed the form of liturgy which later was adopted wherever Calvinistic influence spread; he set the psalms to music for congregational singing, and above all he magnified the preaching of the Word of God, as against the former Roman emphasis on the ritual. For six months in Strassburg the meager salary promised him was not paid at all, and he was desperately poor; nevertheless, he was happier than he had been in Geneva.

Meanwhile at Geneva there was trouble: quarreling in the

Council, breakdown of leadership in the church, flaunting immorality and loose living in the city. In two years and a half, the Council had had enough of the worsening conditions. There seemed nothing to do but, by any means, to bring Calvin back again. So in September, 1540, they voted to call him. Calvin dreaded to return to what he said had been a hell of torment. But his overmastering sense of duty compelled him to do so, lest, he said, he be reckoned among "those who have more care for their own ease or profit than for the edification of the Church."

Farel, when he and Calvin were expelled from Geneva, had gone to Neufchatel, and he remained there. Calvin therefore would be the one outstanding spokesman of the church in the city which had called him back. He knew at once what he wanted to do. He submitted to the Council new Ordinances for the Genevan Church. There should be four ranks of church officials: pastors, teachers, elders, and deacons. The pastors would preach, administer the sacrament, advise and admonish members of the congregation, and furthermore they were to meet each week to discuss the scriptures and to point out shortcomings among themselves. But the most original element in the Ordinances was the provision for the elders, twelve laymen to be known as the Consistory. They were "to watch over the life of each individual, to admonish affectionately those who are seen to err and to lead a disorderly life, and where there shall be need, to make report to the body which shall be appointed to make fraternal corrections." They would have power to debar offenders from the Communion, and to recommend to the Council drastic civil punishment.

At first, the Council voted to give the Consistory this power of excommunication. Then, two years later, it withdrew that power. Calvin had to face again the crucial controversy between the authority of the church and of the state. It took him twelve years to prevail. At length, in 1555, the Council surrendered to the Consistory the power of excommunication. To Calvin, this meant the accomplishment of his supreme ideal: the life of a whole city subject to theocratic rule.

What would a theocracy be? For Calvin exactly that which

is the definition of the word: "government of a state by the immediate direction or administration of God." His unqualified belief was in the sovereignty of God over all life. The Bible revealed the will of God; and as God's minister, it was John Calvin's commission—so John Calvin held—to interpret that will as the Bible declared it and to make it prevail. From the moral law of the Ten Commandments every human law must be derived; and gross offenders against morality and religion must be punished in the name of God. Regulation of personal life and conduct in the most particular matters was nothing new in medieval towns. There were laws against cursing and swearing, against gambling and some kinds of dancing, against extravagance in dress and dinners that were too ostentatious. The police strictness which many resented and which Calvin's enemies charged to him would have been the same in most matters if Calvin had not been in Geneva at all. But the difference was that under his preaching and his influence all offences that had to do directly with the church were magnified. Any man absent from worship might have his home entered and searched; three men were jailed for laughing during a sermon, and others for criticizing what the preacher said.

What Calvin was trying unbendingly to do was to lift the life of a whole community to what he believed to be demanded by the Word of God. With him, therefore, the one unforgivable offence was anything that challenged what he regarded as the pure Word. No instinct of human pity should mitigate the punishment of a heretic; for heresy was worse than murder; it could destroy not the body only, but the soul. From this implacable conviction came some of the actions of Calvin which are not pleasant to remember. Sebastien Castellio, a teacher in Geneva who wanted to be ordained a minister, was rejected by Calvin because he questioned the inspiration of the Old Testament book, the Song of Solomon, and had irregular ideas about the creedal phrase, "He descended into hell." Jacques Gruet, who had put up in St. Peter's Church a placard reading, "We no longer wish to have so many masters," was arrested and jailed, and his house searched. There were found notes of his saying that the laws of

Moses were no better than so many empty words, and that what Calvin had written in one of his books about immortality was "all nonsense." He was tortured, found guilty of blasphemy and treason, and beheaded. But most unforgettable was Michael Servetus, a Spanish scholar, settled in Vienne, France, who, in a book called *The Restitution of Christianity*, questioned the orthodox doctrine of the Trinity. Arrested by the Inquisition, he escaped and rashly tried to pass through Geneva. Recognized and seized by the Genevan police, he was put on trial as a pernicious heretic, and it was Calvin who furnished evidence against him. Largely because of Calvin's evidence, he was condemned to death, although the method of his death—being burned alive —did not have Calvin's approval.

In the dedication of her book, *John Calvin: The Man and His Ethics*, Georgia Harkness calls Calvin "a man of great faults and great virtues." Great virtues he did have: utter devotion to what he believed to be the truth of God, courage, fortitude, and magnificent steadfastness of aim. Great achievements were his also: the formulation—by his preaching, his confession of faith, and the written pages of his *Institutes*—of the Calvinistic doctrines on which numberless churches in Europe and the New World would be built; his conception of presbyterian government by an educated clergy and by the ruling elders from the congregation; his development of the University of Geneva; and the power of his moral and religious influence in making Geneva a citadel to which the persecuted of other lands could come and from which they could go out again as bolder and more enlightened preachers of the Reformation.

"Great faults"? Yes, as that may be true of any intense and positive human being. But "great *limitations*" might be a juster phrase. John Calvin had the limitations of his age: its fierce commitments, its literal assumptions, and therefore sometimes its terrible intolerance. Calvin was more at home in the Old Testament than in the New, an interpreter more of law than of grace. Therefore, in the name of the Lord he could preach a religion that was relentless in its demands, and sometimes narrow to the point of cruelty. But he bore his unswerving witness to the truth that human souls must forever choose and fight for what is right as against what is wrong; and the magnificent integrity of conscience appearing in subsequent history as the Puritan spirit owes much of its essential strength to Calvin.

⊷ XV ⊶

John Knox

To speak the name "Scotland" is to call to mind the country which more instantly than any other land will be thought of as Protestant and Presbyterian. It contradicts one's sense of familiar fact to be reminded that there was a time when Scotland was completely under the dominance of the Church of Rome. But that was true: no longer ago than at the beginning of the sixteenth century, when John Knox was born. And this one man, John Knox, became the decisive force to shape the religious character and change the religious loyalty of a whole people.

Scotland had its king and a powerful nobility. Knox came from among the common folk. His father was a small farmer, of what might earlier have been called the peasant class, but he was thrifty and he wanted his son to get ahead. Young John went to grammar school, where he learned Latin, and then he was able to enter St. Andrews University. After that, the only obvious avenue of advancement was the church, and so John Knox became a priest—not because of any religious crisis such as took Luther into the monastery at Erfurt, and not at first to be either a pastor or a preacher, but only as a kind of ordained clerk in the ecclesiastical machine. In the years that immediately followed, he himself seemed as insignificant as his work was unimportant.

Yet under the surface something was happening. Knox was only four years old in 1517 when Luther began his assault on the indulgences, but by the time he went to the university, the questions Luther had asked and his attacks upon corruption in the church were finding their echo in the minds of men in Scotland. Gradually Knox began asking more searching questions of his own. What was the nature of the true church, and what was its authority? He studied the early church fathers, such as Jerome and Augustine. He read his New Testament, especially the Gospels. Presently he began to believe that the true church was not the huge and heavy institution ruled by pope and priests, under the relentless weight of which new movements of the Spirit could be crushed and stifled. The church was the invisible company of those who were genuinely trying to be disciples of Christ, known only to God, and owing obedience to God alone. In sixteenth-century Scotland, anyone who had such ideas did best to keep them secret. They were Protestant heresy, and the answer that the Church of Rome in Scotland—as on the Continent—had ready for heretics was the stake and fire.

In 1528, when Knox was fifteen, one Patrick Hamilton, high born, scholarly and gentle, had been accused of Lutheranism. Denounced by one of the Dominicans, he was brought before the archbishop of St. Andrews, tried with indecent haste, and put to death with ghastly tortures following his refusal to recant. When he went to the stake he took off his coat, gave it to his servant, and said to him: "This stuff will not help in the fire, yet will do thee some good. I have no more to leave thee but the example of my death, which I pray thee keep in mind! For albeit it be bitter to the flesh, and fearful before men, yet it is the entrance unto eternal life, which none shall possess that deny Christ Jesus before this wicked generation."

The years went by, and Knox, moving in the round of petty ecclesiastical duties, remained obscure. But when he was about thirty-two, there appeared in Scotland a man as devoted as Patrick Hamilton and more arousing as a preacher—George Wishart. Knox was drawn to him, heart and soul, as Wishart preached the new spiritual freedom of the Reformation gospel to the common people, and he made himself Wishart's bodyguard. But the entrenched priestcraft of the ruling church was angered by this new disturbing influence, as it had been angered before by Patrick Hamilton. Knox and some others who rallied round Wishart

were not sufficient to protect him. Seized by the cardinal archbishop of St. Andrews, nephew and successor to the archbishop
who had done away with Hamilton, Wishart—like Hamilton—
was condemned for seditious and heretical doctrine, and forth-
with executed.

By this time a considerable number of the Scottish nobility
had espoused the Protestant movement, partly because of its religious message but also because any movement toward greater
freedom suited their political antagonism to the rapacious power
of the Church of Rome in Scotland. A group of them made their
way by surprise into the archbishop's castle. Entering the keep,
they hunted the archbishop down. Then and there James Mel-
ville denounced the primate's sins, told him he had better make
his quick confession—and ran him through with a sword.

The rebels fortified themselves in the slain archbishop's castle,
and others rallied to them. Knox had been a tutor of some of
their children; and he was ordered to bring them and come himself into the fortifications. There he became preacher to the
garrison, although an increasingly unwelcome one, for he assailed the sins of the men shut up there as vehemently as though
they were the enemies outside. Meanwhile, the nobles who held
to the old order and resented the killing of the archbishop laid
siege to the castle, and with the aid of a French fleet they captured it and all who had been among its defenders, including
John Knox.

What happened to him then is a startling reminder of how
much nearer in many ways the world of the early sixteenth century was to the world of the first century than to the twentieth.
In the navies of that time some of the fighting ships were little
different from the ships of Greece and Carthage and Rome.
They included galleys, rowed as in the time of the Roman empire by galley slaves chained to the benches alongside the banks
of oars. Knox was sentenced to a galley in the French fleet, and
for nearly two years he served there, under the eye of the *horta-
tor*—a title given by the Romans—who beat time for the rowing
and brought his whip down mercilessly on the back of any man
whose oar was dragging. Many men might not have survived

that long, but Knox did survive; and having endured the galleys, there was little likelihood that any threats of violence to be used against him could intimidate him thereafter.

In 1549, when he was about thirty-six years old, Knox was released. Scotland was still controlled by the Romish faction; but in England under Henry VIII, both church and state had broken free once for all from papal domination. To England, therefore, John Knox went. Committed now completely to the Reformation, he was welcomed by Archbishop Cranmer and others who in the brief reign of Edward VI were changing the medieval Roman rituals into the new and more Protestant worship of the Book of Common Prayer. Scotsman though he was and not to the English manner born, it appears that Knox nevertheless was strongly influential in the shaping of the second Prayer Book of 1552, which made more explicit the transformation of the priest-manipulated Roman Mass into the Communion that should belong to all the people.

But Knox's stay in England was cut short by the early death of Edward VI, and the accession to the throne of the fanatically devoted Roman Catholic, Mary. He stayed long enough to denounce the crowd that welcomed her in London, and then he escaped to the Continent. For more than four years—except for a brief visit to Scotland during which he married Margaret Bowes, whom he had known when he was in England—he preached and ministered in Switzerland and in Germany: in Geneva, which under Calvin seemed to Knox "a school of Christ," in Zurich, and in Frankfort.

Meanwhile in Scotland the Protestant spirit was spreading. To John Knox in Geneva there came a letter signed by four of the Scottish nobles. They wrote that they had "a godly thirst and desire" for his presence, and that if he would come back again to preach in Scotland they would "be ready to jeopard lives and goods for the forward setting of the glory of God."

Advised by Calvin in Geneva that "he could not refuse that vocation, unless he would declare himself rebellious unto his God, and unmerciful unto his country," John Knox went to the seaport of Dieppe, ready to embark for Scotland. There he received and read new messages which suggested that the resolution of the nobles who had first written to him was weakening. He sent an indignant answer. Declaring that "if any persuade you, for fear or dangers that may follow, to faint in your former purpose, let him be judged of you both foolish and your mortal enemy. . . . I am not ignorant that fearful troubles shall ensue your enterprise, as in my former letters I did signify unto you; but joyful and comfortable are those troubles and adversities which man sustaineth for accomplishment of God's will, revealed by his word!"

Two months later the Scottish nobles sent a message in accord with John Knox's own fiery spirit. They had had a new consultation, and had committed themselves to God's hands for whatever action was necessary in order that the people of the Scottish realm should no longer "be defrauded, as they had been, of the only food of their souls, the true preaching of Christ's evangel"; and so far as the Church of Rome was concerned, they bound themselves to "renounce and forsake the congregation of Satan, with all the superstitions, abominations and idolatry thereof."

Therefore in May, 1559, Knox appeared again in Scotland. The most powerful figure in the government of the kingdom at that moment was the regent, Mary of Guise. She was the widow of James V of Scotland, and the mother of Mary Stuart who, already proclaimed the sovereign of Scotland, but betrothed when she was ten years old to the Dauphin of France, had been sent to the French court for her royal training. As a Roman Catholic and sister of the Cardinal of Lorraine, Mary of Guise, the regent, was determined to maintain the old order in the church if craft and power could do it. Concerning that, she was under no illusion about John Knox. When Knox had been in Edinburgh during his previous return to Scotland, he had dared to preach that there could be no real Reformation in Scotland until the Mass was abolished, and the whole ecclesiastical system of the Church of Rome—which he called the Babylon of Antichrist—overthrown. Moreover, Knox had written and published in 1558 a pamphlet entitled, *The First Blast of the Trumpet against the Monstrous Regiment* [by which he meant the rule] *of Women*. To his mind the reign of Mary Tudor in England, and the regency of Mary of Guise in Scotland, were an offense to man and God. Now that John Knox had returned, there was bound to be collision.

The Queen Regent had been wise enough to recognize that the Reformation spirit had grown so strong in parts of Scotland that concession had to be made to it, at least where it was espoused by some of the nobles and other men of power. So the activity of evangelical preachers was tolerated as long as it was inconspicuous. But nothing that had to do with John Knox could remain inconspicuous. Everything he thought and did was passionate. In his nature there was a terrible intensity, like the molten fires at the center of the earth which can break out in volcanic explosions, awesome and overwhelming. In his thinking nothing could be neutral; a principle was white or it was black, with no room for shading or for compromise. It was not enough for him that Protestantism be permitted to exist; he wanted it to prevail to the point at which it could smash completely the power of the Church of Rome in Scotland, together with all its archbishops and bishops, its monks and friars; and in his estimation the Queen Regent was "a woman crafty, dissimulate, and false." When he began to preach in Edinburgh, he was branded an outlaw. Escaping to Dundee, he preached there and in other towns of central Scotland. In Perth he denounced the "idolatry" and "abomination" of the Mass; and the next day when a priest in one of the churches opened the tabernacle on the high altar and was proceeding with the service, there was a shout, "This is intolerable, that when God by his word hath plainly damned idolatry, we shall stand and see it used in despite." The disturbance increased, and grew quickly into riot. The tabernacle above the altar and the statues in the church were knocked to pieces; and then a mob stormed the two priories of the Franciscans and the Dominicans, broke into them and left these buildings, of "wondrous cost and greatness, so destroyed that walls only did remain of all these great edifications."

The Queen Regent was enraged. She ordered the arrest of those who had committed the breach of the peace, and of all the preachers whom she accused of having provoked it. But many of the Scottish lords rallied to their defense, and John Knox was like a firebrand in their midst. He determined to preach in St. Andrews where he said that he had been first called "to the dignity of a preacher," before he had been taken as a galley slave to France. Warned that St. Andrews was then in possession of his enemies, he answered—as is recorded in the long and vivid *History of the Reformation* which he himself afterward wrote —"As for the fear of danger that may come to me, let no man be solicitous, for my life is in the custody of Him whose glory I seek; and, therefore, I cannot so fear their boast nor tyranny, that I shall cease from doing my duty, when God of his mercy offereth the occasion." He did preach there on "the ejection of the buyers and sellers forth of the temple of Jerusalem," and "applied the corruption that was then to the corruption that is in the papistry." The result was armed collision between the forces of the Queen Regent and the defenders of John Knox who "appeared as men . . . rained from the clouds." Civil war had broken out in Scotland.

Troops came from France to support the Queen Regent. Attacking from the seaport of Leith, they drove the defenders of the Reformation cause back into Edinburgh and then out of it, in what John Knox called "our dolorous departure," which seemed to bring his fortune and that of his friends "to the depth of the dungeon."

Now the Scottish lords who stood with Knox appealed for help to Elizabeth of England. She personally had no use for Knox, but her counselors persuaded her that it was not politic to permit French troops to have a foothold in Scotland. Consequently, English forces were sent north, and the balance shifted in the Scottish struggle. When matters had been at their lowest ebb, John Knox had never lost his flaming courage. As one of the English emissaries recognized and declared, he was "able in one hour to put more life in us than five hundred trumpets blustering in our ears." The Queen Regent was obliged to make a truce. Scottish nobles began to abjure their allegiance to her. Soon thereafter she fell ill; and in the coarse language which in that century of bitter controversy was not unusual even on the lips of the religious, John Knox's *History* records that then "began her belly and loathsome legs to swell, and so continued, till that God did execute his judgments upon her."

With the Queen Regent dead in June, 1560, the effective power in Scotland passed for the time being to the Parliament, made up mostly of the nobility. The acknowledged sovereign was the young Mary Stuart, but she was absent from the realm, being still in France. The Dauphin of France to whom she had been married in April, 1558, had become king at the death of his father in July, 1559. Mary Stuart was thus queen of France, and also by inheritance queen of Scotland; but since she was not *in* Scotland, the Scottish lords were in control. In July, 1560, the month after the Queen Regent's death, the Parliament met, and adopted "The Confession of Faith" of which John Knox was the chief author, "professed and believed by the protestants within the realm of Scotland; as wholesome and sound doctrine, grounded upon the infallible truth of God's word."

The Confession embodied and expressed the stern Calvinism which from that time forward was to shape the thought and character of Scotland. It affirmed the doctrines of original sin and of the salvation only of the elect, set forth the signs "by which the true kirk is discerned from the false," denounced "the blind papists," and as contrasted with the resurrection into blessedness promised to "the society of the elect," declared that "such as now delight in vanity, cruelty, filthiness, superstition, or idolatry, shall be adjudged to the fire inextinguishable, in which they shall be tormented forever, as well in their own bodies, as in their souls."

The same Parliament adopted statutes putting an end to all authority in Scotland of the bishop of Rome, and forbidding any and all persons, under criminal penalties, to say Mass, hear Mass, or "be present thereat." And a copy of these statutes was sent to Mary Stuart and her husband, the king of France, "rather to show our dutiful obedience"—as the ironical words of John Knox expressed it—"than to beg of them any strength to our religion, which from God has full power, and needeth not the suffrage of man."

In December, 1560, Mary's husband suddenly died; and in August, 1561, Mary returned to her realm of Scotland. Most of the nobles and the people in general, wanting order and quiet again, were ready to welcome her, even though she always had been and still was a Roman Catholic. The Mass had been outlawed in Scotland. Nevertheless, for the sake of peace, let the queen have Mass, if she wanted it, in her own chapel. So said the majority; but not John Knox.

It was not long before Mary Stuart became aware of this troublesome disturber haranguing against what he called "footsteps of antichrist and dregs of papistry." Young, imperious, and charming in her femininity, the queen could win most men to her side, but John Knox looked upon her as "of proud mind, crafty wit, and indurate heart against God and His truth." She had brought her priest from France to celebrate Mass in her palace of Holyrood. John Knox looked upon this as Joshua might have looked upon strongholds still in the possession of the Canaanites that threatened the people of the Covenant; and in the face of any sovereign he could be as formidable as Elijah denouncing Ahab and Jezebel. Nevertheless, the queen determined to try her arts of conciliation. Within two weeks of her arrival, she summoned Knox to Holyrood. He had written a book against the authority of queens; but was it not in the word of God, she asked him, that subjects should obey their princes?

"If princes exceed their bounds, madam," Knox answered, "and do against that wherefore they should be obeyed, it is no doubt but that they may be resisted. My travail is that both princes and subjects obey God. . . . And this subjection, madam, unto God, and unto his troubled kirk, is the greatest dignity that flesh can get upon the face of the earth, for it shall carry them to everlasting glory."

"Yes," said she, "but ye are not the kirk that I will nurse. I will defend the kirk of Rome, for it is, I think, the true kirk of God."

"Your will," said he, "is no reason; neither doth your thought make that Roman harlot to be the true and immaculate spouse of Jesus Christ. And wonder not, madam, that I call Rome harlot;

for that kirk is altogether polluted with all kind of spiritual forni-
cation, as well in doctrine as in manners."

"My conscience," said she, "is not so."

To which the implacable Knox replied, "Conscience, madam,
requires knowledge, and I fear that right knowledge ye have
none."

Infuriating though that interview must have been to one accustomed only to respectful deference, Mary Queen of Scots
(and through her descent from Margaret, eldest daughter of
Henry VII, claimant also to the throne of England) was to
listen to John Knox frequently. She could not ignore or escape
the power of his spirit over the people—and therefore in some
crises over her. He challenged her right to have the Mass at
Holyrood. He denounced what he said were her frivolities. And
when it was rumored that she might marry a prince of Roman
Catholic Spain, he preached against such a marriage as no less
than treason to the Scottish Reformation.

Now Mary Stuart was almost beside herself with anger. When
she had summoned Knox, she burst into passionate weeping. "I
cannot be quit of you," she sobbed. "But I avow to God, I shall
be once revenged."

"What have you to do with my marriage?" she demanded; "or
what are you within this commonwealth?"

To that Knox made his simple but tremendous answer: "A subject born within the same, madam," he said. "And albeit I neither
be earl, lord, nor baron within it, yet has God made me a profit-
able member within the same. Yea, madam, to me it appertains
no less to forewarn of such things as may hurt it, if I foresee
them, than it doth to any of the nobility."

And when some of the court wondered that Knox was not dismayed at the queen's inordinate passion, he answered: "Why
should the pleasing face of a gentlewoman fear me? I have looked
in the faces of many angry men, and yet have not been afraid
above measure."

The queen did not make the marriage which had been supposed, but she was to make one that would prove not less calamitous. In 1565, she became infatuated with her cousin Henry

Stuart, Lord Darnley, and took him for her husband, and she proclaimed also that he should be considered joint sovereign with herself. As Darnley gathered power to himself, some of the Protestant nobles were driven into exile. In Darnley, Knox had a new enemy—and scant wonder; for he had preached a sermon in which he had compared Darnley to King Ahab and the queen to Jezebel. Therefore he stood in increasing danger.

But it was the royal pair and not Knox who were moving most surely toward disaster. Mary had an Italian secretary, Rizzio, who had great influence over her. One day at Holyrood armed men dragged him out of her presence and stabbed him to death; and many at the court believed that Darnley was an accomplice to his killing. A son was born to Mary, but nevertheless her feeling for her husband had turned sour. Not long afterward he was found strangled in a garden, and within a few months Mary was married to James Hepburn, Earl of Bothwell, who may have been the murderer.

The nobility of Scotland rose in arms and forced Mary's abdication; and although she escaped from a castle where they held her, she dared not stay in Scotland, and fled to England. But England was to prove no happy refuge. Refused an audience by Elizabeth, she was kept as a virtual prisoner in Sheffield Castle and finally at Fotheringay; and in 1587, she was executed under a warrant for treasonable conspiracy, which Elizabeth's counselors at long last had persuaded her to sign.

After Mary's abdication, the influence of John Knox became great again in Scotland. He preached at the coronation of Mary's infant son, who was to become James VI of Scotland, and, early in the next century, also James I of England. Knox had already been the driving power in the adoption of the Scottish Confession of Faith. At that time, in 1560, he had drawn up also the Book of Discipline, according to which all Scotland would be organized into congregations each electing its own minister of God's Word and sacraments; establishing in every parish a school for universal education; and providing for the support of church and school from the revenues that had belonged to monasteries and to the prelates of the Church of Rome. Powerful men in Scotland who had already got hold of some of the plundered riches of the Catholic Church were in no mood to see this new discipline fully established; they pushed it aside as "devout imagination." But ultimately this Book of Discipline was adopted, and the Church of Scotland, Protestant and Calvinist, established as the embodiment of the convictions which John Knox had championed as the essentials of "the true kirk." It represented in some respects the fierce intolerance which was the inevitable accompaniment of the life-and-death religious struggles through which that generation had passed. In the "contrary doctrine to be utterly abolished . . . we understand," the Book of Discipline declared, "whatsoever men by laws, councils, or constitutions, have imposed upon the consciences of men, without the express commandment of God's word, such as . . . the superstitious observance of fast days . . . keeping of holy days of certain saints . . . christmas . . . and epiphany." Moreover, in order for "Christ Jesus to be truly preached, and his holy sacraments rightly ministered," it was declared that "idolatry," which included "all monuments and places of the same," such as "chapels, chanteries and cathedral churches," should be "utterly suppressed."

But over and above these extremes of puritanism stands the great fact that the Book of Discipline fashioned a church which —in its zeal and its integrity, its provision for instruction in the Bible and devotion to it on the part of both ministers and people, and in the dignity which it gave to every Christian individual— has been the heart of the moral greatness of Scotland, and is the supreme monument to John Knox.

When John Knox died in 1572 and was buried in the churchyard of St. Giles's in Edinburgh, the Scottish lord who then was regent said over his grave, "Here lies one who neither flattered nor feared any flesh"; and the reason why those words were true was because the only fear John Knox knew was the fear lest he should ever be found unfaithful to what he believed to be the will of God.[1]

❦ XVI ❧

Roger Williams, William Carey, and Adoniram Judson

The long roll of those who have been the bearers of the gospel message, and witnesses to the power of it, includes men of various origins and of diverse names: Lutherans, Church of England men, Calvinist Presbyterians, Baptists, Methodists, Independents, and Congregationalists. They have represented the truth spoken by John Robinson, the pastor of the Pilgrims as they set out from their exile in Holland for New England: "The Lord has yet more truth to break forth from his holy Word."

Roger Williams

Among the creative figures in the colonial history of America was Roger Williams. Born in London about 1603, and educated at Charterhouse School and Pembroke College, Cambridge, he was ordained in the Church of England; but he shared to an extreme degree the aversion of the Puritans from the fixed forms and regulations of the established Church, from the rule of bishops, and from the control of religion by the state. For a time he was chaplain to a nobleman in Essex, but he refused other appointments because of his nonconformity, and late in 1630 he left England with his wife for the freedom of conscience and of worship which he thought he would find in the New World.

He landed in New England shortly after the arrival there of John Winthrop and the others who had come to found the colony of Massachusetts Bay. Welcomed by the Governor as "Mr. Williams, a godly minister," he was appointed teacher for the congregation in the town which had just been given the name of Boston. But the independence of ideas and convictions which he had exhibited in England was no less determined in the new surroundings. He refused to be associated with the Boston church because it continued to use the ritual of the Book of Common Prayer, which he pronounced "as glorious an idol . . . as any invention now extant." This was too much for the ruling Council of the colony, who from their own angle of theological and political convictions were as dictatorial as the authorities in England had been, so that Roger Williams was about to learn that he had left the rule of the "lords bishops" only to fall under the rule of the "lords brethren." Thus, shortly after Williams' arrival, when he was elected by the congregation at Salem to be their minister, the General Court at Boston wrote to the Salem church "that whereas Mr. Williams had refused to join the congregation at Boston, because they would not make a public declaration of their repentance for having communion with the churches of England while they lived there; and besides had declared his opinion that the magistrate might not punish the breach of the Sabbath nor any other offence that was a breach of the first table [the first four commandments of the Decalogue of Moses]; therefore the Court marvelled that Salem would choose him without advising with the council; and withal desired that they would forbear to proceed till they had conferred about it."[1]

On account of this objection, Roger Williams did not go to Salem. Instead, he went to Plymouth, not holding any office of pastor or teacher in the Plymouth church, but he "spoke on the Lord's Days and week days . . . exercising by way of prophesy." Wherever he was, he was certain to be doing that, and at Plymouth, as in Boston, not always to the satisfaction of the authorities. "He began," as Governor Bradford later wrote, "to fall into some strange opinions and from opinion to practice; which caused some controversy between the church and him. . . . He is to be pitied and prayed for, and so I shall leave the matter, and desire the Lord to show him his errors and reduce him into the way of truth and give him a settled judgment and constancy in the same."[2]

However much the people in the church at Plymouth might wish that Roger Williams had the same "settled judgment" which they had in theological ideas, they had reason to be grateful to him then and afterwards for his contacts with the Indians. In the first, bitter winter after the landing at Plymouth, it had seemed to the colonists, in Bradford's words, that what they faced was "a hideous and desolate wilderness, full of wild beasts and wild men . . . The savage barbarians were readier to fill their sides with arrows than otherwise."[3] In the succeeding years, there had been established more friendly relations with the surrounding Narragansett Indian tribe, but always on an uncertain balance. The average colonist was slow to have dealings with Indians unless he had his musket close at hand. But Roger Williams deliberately set out to win their confidence and friendship. He learned their way of life, their customs and their character; and this he did because God gave him "a painful patient spirit to lodge with them in their filthy, smoky holes to gain their tongue. . . . My soul's desire," he said, "was to do the natives good."[4]

The people in Salem still wanted Williams, and in 1633 he went there, and the next year was elected to be their minister. But soon he was embroiled again with the authorities in Boston. He was preaching that magistrates had no right to regulate any man's religious practices, which was a challenge to the whole theocratic constitution of the colony; and that neither the king of England nor anyone else could grant land in Massachusetts unless it were sold by the Indians, who were the possessors of it. Whereupon, in 1635, the General Court voted that "Whereas Mr. Roger Williams . . . hath broached and divulged divers new and dangerous opinions . . . and maintaineth the same without any retraction, it is therefore ordered that the said Mr. Williams shall depart out of this jurisdiction within six weeks next ensuing."[5] And when it was discovered presently that Williams had not only failed to "depart," but that "the infection" of his teaching might spread among the churches of Massachusetts

Bay Colony, the Council sent men to arrest him and deport him back to England by a ship then about to sail.

Before the arrest could be made, Williams had left Salem. Early in 1636, with a few young men as companions, he escaped in a small boat headed westward along the New England coast. "Unmercifully driven," as he afterward wrote, "to a winter's flight, exposed to the miseries, poverties, necessities, wants, debts, hardships of sea and land, in a banished condition. For fourteen weeks, in a bitter winter season, I was sorely tossed and knew not what bread or bed did mean."[6]

It might have seemed that his career in the colonies had ended in complete frustration. As a matter of fact, what became his great chapter of creative accomplishment had just begun. Landing at the head of Narragansett Bay, where two fresh rivers flowed into the salt water, Williams bought land of the Indians whose language he had already learned, and named the place Providence, "from the freedom and vacancy of the place and many other providences of the most holy and only wise."[7]

There were two great desires by which Roger Williams had continually been possessed. One was to be a missionary to the Indians; the other was to put into expression his passionate belief in religious freedom. In the long years that followed, he was to fulfill both. More than any other man in New England he reached out with a persuasive friendship to the Indians. He was the one person who could always negotiate with them, and he dared to take great risks in going out at critical moments into the Indian country when there had been murder or other violence and where there was danger of general war. He wrote once of how he had gone "all alone, in a poor canoe, to cut through a stormy wind, with great seas, every minute in hazard of life, to the Sachem's house. Three days and nights my business forced me to lodge and mix with the bloody Pequot ambassadors, whose hands and arms, methought, wreaked with the blood of my countrymen, murdered and massacred by them on Connecticut River, and from whom I could not but nightly look for their bloody knives at my own throat also."[8] Meanwhile, in the growing settlement of Providence, and for the whole new colony of which it was the center, he was creating something unprecedented in the seventeenth-century world: "a community where freedom of religious belief was assured to every person; where all were welcome whatever their belief; and where Church and State had full liberty to develop, without interference the one from the other."[9]

Williams' wife, whom he had had to leave in Salem when he was banished, joined him in Providence; and there with her and their children he was to spend the rest of his life except for two intervals in England, where he went to serve the cause that was closest to his heart. This was to secure, and later to have guaranteed against opposition, a charter of civil and religious liberties for the settlements at Providence, Newport, and Portsmouth, in the area that would ultimately be called Rhode Island. From June, 1643, until late summer of 1644 he was in London, and he came back bringing a charter for the towns to be known as "The Incorporation of Providence Plantations, in the Narragansett Bay, in New England," permitting "such a form of civil government as by voluntary consent of all, or the greater part of them, they should find most suitable to their estate and condition"; and the first General Assembly under that Charter, after adopting a code of laws for civil administration, provided at the same time that in religious matters "all men may walk as their consciences persuade them, every one in the name of his God."[10] From November, 1651, for more than two years, in wistful separation from his home and his wife, and at heavy personal expense, Williams was in London again, staying there until at last he succeeded in having the charter reviewed by the government of Oliver Cromwell, which had come to power after the beheading of Charles I. And in Providence until the end of his long life in 1683, Williams' influence made the Providence Plantation a haven for all who sought religious freedom, because he believed that there could be "no other prudent, Christian way of preserving peace in the world but by permission of differing consciences."[11]

In the Massachusetts Bay Colony, religious groups which were considered by the authorities to be disturbers of established beliefs were relentlessly punished by public whippings and in some cases by hanging. Among those who were accounted by the

Boston authorities as pernicious sectaries were Baptists and Quakers, numbers of whom found refuge in the Providence Plantations. Roger Williams himself was moved by a Baptist preacher, and was rebaptized. Later he was divided in his thought concerning this baptism. "I believe their practice comes nearer the first practice of our great Founder Christ Jesus than other practices of religion do," he wrote; "and yet I have not satisfaction neither in the authority by which it is done nor in the manner."[12] He did not again serve as a minister, nor would he call himself a Baptist or by any other denominational name. He reckoned himself only as "a Seeker."

Yet the Baptists have good right to consider him a witness to great convictions which Baptists have always championed, particularly the freedom of the individual from ecclesiastical control, and the separation of church and state. Their use of laymen in evangelism is in tune with the conviction which Roger Williams expressed for his own life: "I know no other true sender, but the most holy spirit. And when he sends, his messengers will go, his prophets will prophesy, though all the world forbid them."[13]

William Carey

Up to the time of Roger Williams, there had been little interest among Englishmen in carrying the gospel to others than their own race. At Jamestown in the early 1600's there had been efforts to teach and evangelize the Indians, but that concern was only fleeting. No one had followed the heroic examples of Francis de Sales and Vincent de Paul who had preached Christ in Asia. But, about eighty years after the death of Roger Williams, there was born in England the man who would inspire the modern movement for "foreign missions."

William Carey (1761-1834) was the son of a weaver in the little village of Paulerspury in Northamptonshire. His father and grandfather belonged, like most of the village folk, to the Church of England; and successively they were schoolmasters for the village and clerks of the ancient parish church. The boy William went as a matter of course to the Sunday services, probably got nothing much from the preaching, but knew the Prayer Book and listened to the clerk's "Amens" from beneath the pulpit, and at the proper time was duly confirmed. With a boy's prejudice in favor of familiar things, he disliked all dissenters; and he still did when at sixteen years of age his father apprenticed him to a shoemaker in the hamlet of Hackleton, nine miles away, where he found himself associated with another apprentice whom he looked upon "with contempt" because he was a dissenter.

But the religious convictions of Carey's fellow apprentice were so alive that Carey's Church of England beliefs began to seem to him only convention. In arguments about religion, Carey confessed that he "felt a growing uneasiness and stings of conscience."[14] He began to go to nonconformist prayer meetings, and then to hear Mr. Ryland, a Baptist minister, preach. Mr. Ryland, Carey said, "turned me over to his son"; and the son afterward reported: "October 5th, 1783, I baptised in the river Nen, a little beyond Dr. Doddridges' meeting-house at Northampton, a poor journeyman shoemaker, little thinking that before nine years had elapsed, he would prove the first instrument of forming a society for sending missionaries from England to preach the gospel to the heathen."[15]

The "journeyman shoemaker" was desperately poor so far as money went. He was married when he was twenty to a girl who was to become a victim of mental disease. What he earned by cobbling shoes was so little that often he did not have enough to eat. When he was commissioned as a Baptist preacher, for three years he walked sixteen miles to his chapel at Barton, and what the poor people of the congregation could give him was less than enough to pay for the wear and tear on his clothes. When he transferred to the village of Moulton, he still received from his ministry only thirty-six pounds a year.

But in a more important way he was not poor. He had had no education except in the village school at Paulerspury. There was no faintest chance for his father, the weaver, to send him to a college. Nor was there any library to which he could go. But he was one of those persons who now and then, with what would seem beyond all imaginable likelihood, develop like some miraculous flower growing up out of the common soil. From the time when he was a little boy, William Carey took delight in the beautiful English Midlands country and in all that he could see and learn as he walked about it; and his mind reached out for every kind of knowledge. He went without food to buy a few books, and others he borrowed. He would keep a book open before him on the work bench when he was mending shoes, and on the wall before him a map of the world which he had drawn, and notes on the map which he wanted to memorize. One who knew him and had seen him at work pointed one day to the crude little room that was the cobbler's shop and called it "Carey's college." In that college he taught himself Hebrew, Latin, and Greek, and also French and Dutch.

Meanwhile, there grew within him a burning concern for all the peoples of the earth outside Christendom. In 1786, he was present at a meeting of Baptist ministers in Northampton. The one who was presiding invited the younger brethren to propose a subject for discussion. At first there was silence, and then from Carey came these words: "whether the command given to the apostles, to teach all nations, was not obligatory on all succeeding ministers to the end of the world, seeing that the accompanying promise was of equal extent."[16] To an era of thought which Carey helped to create, that query would seem to carry its affirmative answer; but there in Northampton, the aged chairman of the group of ministers cried out, "You are a miserable enthusiast for asking such a question. Certainly nothing can be done before another Pentecost, when an effusion of miraculous gifts, including the gift of tongues, will give effect to the commission of Christ as at first."[17]

But Carey was not discouraged. He wrote a treatise which was afterward printed, through a gift from a man who had read it, entitled *An Enquiry into the Obligations of Christians to use Means for the Conversion of the Heathens*. The work of a cobbler who had no education except what he had given himself, it was nevertheless worthy of one who was born in the same part of England from which had come Shakespeare, John Wycliffe, and John Bunyan; clear and powerful in thought, and noble in expression. In it he took up the five objections which had been alleged against missions to heathen lands: their distance, their barbarism, the dangers that would be incurred, the difficulties of support, the unintelligible languages. One by one he answered these. The same objections, he said, had not prevented the adventures of world-wide trade, or been allowed to stand as barriers "to commercial men. It only requires that we should have as much love to the souls of our fellow-creatures, and fellow-sinners, as they have for the profits arising from a few otter skins, and all these difficulties could be easily surmounted." For those who would be missionaries there could be no "interested motives or great worldly expectations." But "the commission is a sufficient call . . . to venture all, and, like the primitive Christians, go everywhere preaching the gospel."[18]

Inspired by Carey, a society was formed among the Baptists, which urged that "every member of every congregation should take a part to the extent of fervent and united prayer, and of an average subscription of a penny a week." Andrew Fuller, a farmer's son who had been a laborer, stood at Carey's side. But six years went by, and most of those who called themselves Christians were still indifferent. Then, in 1792, the annual ministers' meeting was held in Nottingham, and Carey preached. He took as his text Isaiah 54:1, 2: "Enlarge the place of thy tent, and let them stretch forth the curtains of thine habitations: spare not, lengthen thy cords, and strengthen thy stakes." The time had come, Carey proclaimed, for the church to make a mighty venture, and to trust that power would be given to establish it. "Attempt great things for God! Expect great things from God."

For a moment there was dismaying silence. Then "what Andrew Fuller described as 'the much fear and trembling' of these inexperienced poor and ignorant village preachers gave way to the appeal of one who had gained both knowledge and courage, and who, as to funds and men, was ready to give himself."[19] They voted to have ready for their next meeting an actual plan for "propagating the Gospel among the heathen." Fuller was the secretary, and to some of those who were still timid and hesitant he said, "You excel me in wisdom, especially in foreseeing difficulties, I therefore want to advise with you, but to execute without you."[20]

In January, 1793, in the Harvey Lane Chapel at Leicester, Carey and John Thomas, a former surgeon of the merchant marine, were set apart—like Paul and Barnabas—to carry the gospel where it had not been heard before. They sailed for India, on a Dutch merchantman, and fortunately so, for what Carey called "the abominable monopoly" of the British East India Company had been empowered to keep out of India anyone whom the company did not want. After five months, they landed in Calcutta without the Company's knowledge. Trying in vain for some time to find a place where they could live and work, they found this impossible in the territory which the East India Company controlled; then a door of opportunity opened when an English indigo planter invited them to come to his plantation, at the edge of the jungle southeast of Calcutta. Two principles governed Carey from the beginning: "(1) a missionary must be one of the companions and equals of the people to whom he is sent; and (2) a missionary must as soon as possible become indigenous, self-supporting, self-propagating, alike by the labours of the mission and of the converts."[21] He made his livelihood by work on the plantation, and at the same time he devoted himself to learning the Bengali language so that he could reach the Indian people. Thomas set up a medical clinic, and, as Carey wrote, "his house is constantly surrounded with the afflicted." Carey procured a small boat on which he traveled up and down the rivers, and he walked from village to village, preaching and teaching. Also, he set up a school for some forty boys, at the same time grieving that in all India there was no school for girls. The subjection of women constantly appalled him; he had not been in India long when he saw—but was helpless to prevent—the burning alive of a child widow on the funeral pyre of her husband.

For seven years he stayed on the plantation. Then came a chance to establish missionary work at Serampore, a Dutch colony north of Calcutta, where the outreach of evangelistic work would not be subject to the suspicious hostility of the East India

Company. In Serampore, from 1800 until his death in 1834, Carey's life and work was to center, and from it his astonishing influence was to spread. Even the East India Company became a grudging instrument toward that end. When need developed to establish Fort William College to train the British civil service, the only man in North India who had mastered the dialects of Bengali, Mahratta and Tamil was William Carey, and he was appointed professor in the college. Carey learned Sanskrit also, and from the printing press which he set up in Serampore there issued a continual stream of Bibles and other books and tracts that could be read by some at least among the Indian millions. For seven years, with patient faith and undiscouraged devotion, Carey preached and ministered, and then at length the first convert from Hinduism was baptized. From that time on the response increased. By 1804 there were forty-eight, including Brahmans. A school for boys was established and now also one for girls. In 1810, there were one hundred and five new converts within that one year; and thereafter what Carey called the "fermentation raised in Bengal by the little leaven" was bringing to the life of northern India a redeeming hope and transforming power beyond all ordinary reckoning.

As a scholar, as a master of languages and translator, as an evangelist and as an organizer, William Carey, who began as a mender of shoes, became one of the makers of history for the great subcontinent to which a love for human souls made him dare to go. But it was not for the record of his own achievements that he would want most to be remembered. Late in his life, he was visited by the Scots missionary, Alexander Duff. As Duff was leaving, Carey called him back. "Mr. Duff," he said, "you have been speaking about Dr. Carey, Dr. Carey. When I am gone, say nothing about Dr. Carey—speak about Dr. Carey's *Saviour.*"[22]

Adoniram Judson

On the new paths of world evangelism which William Carey was the first to blaze, other men were to follow. In the *Encyclopaedia Britannica,* the eleventh edition, there is an article of less than five hundred words on Adoniram Judson. But the full story of this man's life and work fills more than five hundred pages in the absorbing biography written by his son.[23] From a reading of that biography there comes abundant confirmation of the words with which the sparse article in the *Britannica* concludes: In "his fervor, his devotion to duty, and his fortitude in the face of danger . . . Judson was perhaps the greatest as he was practically the first of the many missionaries sent from the United States into foreign fields."

The son of a Congregationalist minister, Adoniram Judson was born in Malden, Massachusetts, on August 9, 1788. At Providence College (now Brown University) which he entered in 1804, the religious loyalties which his home had planted in him were shaken by the skepticism which was part of the upheaval in all thought that followed the French Revolution; but various personal experiences turned young Judson's mind back to religion with an unqualified intensity. He entered Andover Theological Seminary, and he had not been there long when there came to Andover four young men from Williams College, who in prayer meetings which they held in a field by a haystack (where now the Haystack Monument stands) had formed a missionary society for work in foreign lands. Judson joined three of them in asking the Congregational Churches of Massachusetts to accept them as volunteers.

In response there was organized the American Board of Commissioners for Foreign Missions; and after some delay the Board resolved to send out Judson, Samuel Nott, Jr., Samuel Newell, and Gordon Hall. Meanwhile, Judson had been married to Ann Hasseltine, a beautiful girl of great vivacity of spirit. Because of her gaiety some of the somberly pious thought "she would have but a brief life, and be suddenly cut off."[24] That assumption was part of the pattern of Calvinistic theology then prevailing, and Adoniram reflected it in the language—as familiar then as it is astonishing now—of the letter he wrote to the father of the girl he wanted to marry. Would her father consent, he wanted to know, "to part with your daughter . . . to see her no more in this world . . . consent to her departure to a heathen land and her subjection to the hardships and suffering of a missionary life . . . to degradation, insult, persecution and perhaps a violent death? Can you consent to all this, in hope of soon meeting your daughter in the world of glory with a crown of righteousness brightened by the acclamations of praise which shall redound to her Saviour from heathens saved, through her means, from eternal woe and despair?"[25] And to Ann herself he wrote on New Year's Day, 1811, "May it be a year in which you will . . . be raised above sublunary things, and be willing to be disposed of in this world just as God shall please. As every moment of the year will bring you nearer the end of your pilgrimage, may it bring you nearer to God, and find you more prepared to hail the messenger of death as a deliverer and friend."[26]

Was a man who could write like that *real*, and ready to face the real world, not with rhetoric, but with stark courage and unflinching directness? To that question the years were to give unquestionable answer. Adoniram and Ann sailed for the Orient in February, 1812. During the long sea voyage, Judson, going out as a Congregationalist and looking forward to meeting the Baptist, William Carey, had a revolution in his thoughts. He came to the conviction that there ought to be only adult baptism, by immersion, and when they landed in Calcutta both he and Ann were rebaptized; and to the American Board in Massachusetts he sent the startling news that he was now a Baptist. The East India Company ordered the Judsons out of India. The only way they could escape the determination of the Company to send them home by way of England was to get on board a ship going somewhere else in Asia. They found passage on a Portuguese vessel out of Madras bound for Burma, and in July, 1813, they landed in Rangoon.

Probably no other country in the world could have been more formidable for missionary effort. Burma, one thousand miles long and six hundred miles wide, was governed by a king who ruled with absolute power, so awesome to the Burmese that to come into his presence was "to go up to the golden feet and lift up the eyes to the golden face." The kingdom had little commerce with the outside world, and no use for foreigners. A son of William Carey had managed to build a mission house outside Rangoon, but he himself had left. Rangoon was "a miserable dirty town, its houses being built with bamboo and teak planks, with thatched roofs—almost without drainage and intersected by muddy creeks, through which the tide flowed at high water."[27] "In all the affairs of this government," Judson wrote, "despotism and rapine are the order of the day. The present viceroy of this province is a savage man. Life and death depend on his nod." Nevertheless, he wrote also, "It was the evident dispensation of God that brought us to this country; and if the world was all before us, where to choose our place of rest, we should not desire to leave Burmah."[28]

As Carey had applied himself to learning Bengali, so Judson set himself to master the Burmese language, of which no grammar or dictionary had ever been compiled. The only writings in the language were on flattened palm leaves. As soon as he could make himself understood, Judson began to talk to individuals about Christ. When he had been in Rangoon a year and a half he was thankful that some seemed to listen, but he added, "I am not acquainted with a single instance in which any permanent impression has been produced."[29] Ann Judson was obliged to go to Madras for medical care in an illness, and for three months Adoniram was left completely alone. Their first child—whom they named Roger Williams—died seven months after his birth, and Adoniram himself was acutely ill, but neither he nor Ann ever lost their courage. The one plea they made was for volunteers from America to widen the mission work—"men . . . who live near to God, and are willing to suffer all things for Christ's sake, without being proud of it."[30]

Reinforcements did begin to come: George Hough and his family first, and later others, although few of them had the iron resolution to outlast every hardship which the Judsons had. Now also there was a printing press; and Judson could circulate among the Burmese the translations he was making of the Bible, and tracts in which he tried to make the gospel plain. Meanwhile, when he had to give so much time to study, to translation, to the creation of a Burmese grammar, and to what thus seemed mechanical work, he asked the people at home to pray that "I may not lose the life of religion in my soul."[31]

At length there came the fruits of all the patient sowing. Burmese who had come at first warily as inquirers, and for whom Judson never made Christian allegiance anything less than high and costly, began to be baptized. Knowing that they would be in immediate peril because of their change of faith, Judson determined to go by boat three hundred and fifty miles up the Irrawaddy River to the Burmese capital, Ava, and seek audience with the king, to win if possible permission for some of his subjects to turn, if they were so persuaded, from Buddhism to Christianity. He did get access to the king, in a setting of Oriental magnificence and splendor—a splendor which could not blunt awareness of the despotic cruelty of which the king was capable. The king listened indifferently to Judson's plea, and put aside with contempt the Bible which Judson had brought him as a present. The plea had come to nothing.

Back in Rangoon, Judson feared that the new converts would be frightened and would desert. But to his joy they answered, "This religion will spread of itself. The emperor cannot stop it."[32]

There came another occasion to go to Ava, and, as it seemed, a hopeful one. Jonathan Price, a medical missionary who had joined Judson in Rangoon, was summoned by the king, who had heard of his medical skill, and Judson went with him. But while they were in the capital, war broke out between Burma and the British on the Indian border. Immediately, all white men in Burma were arrested as suspected spies. On the 8th of June, 1824, Judson and Price were seized, and with others thrown into what was called the death prison in Ava, and then moved to a worse one in Oung-pen-la, ten miles away. In those prisons, Judson lay for seventeen months: at Oung-pen-la with nearly one hundred other prisoners chained night and day, stretched on the filthy floor, in a building forty by thirty feet with no means of ventilation except through chinks in the wooden walls, and with the tropical sun beating on the thin roof. On some afternoons, always at three o'clock, a heavy gong sounded outside.

The door opened, the jailer walked up to one of the prisoners and, with no advance warning, unchained him and took him out to execution.

With the approach of the British army and the defeat of the Burmese, Judson was released. He was found by his wife who had followed him to Ava and, in spite of the insults of the Burmese guards, had managed to get some food to him day by day.

With the British victory, part of the Burmese coast became British territory, and Judson, followed by some of his Rangoon converts, moved the mission center first to the new town of Amherst and then to Maulmain. "Life is short," he wrote. "Happiness consists not in outward circumstances. Millions of Burmans are perishing. . . . How great are my obligations to spend and be spent for Christ!"[33]

Most of the rest of Judson's life and ministry was in Maulmain. Great sorrows came to him, and also great fulfillments. While he was briefly away from home, his wife fell ill and died before his return. Twice after that he was remarried, each time to a woman who in courage and devotion was like the heroic Ann. Children were born to him; and his Burmese spiritual children were growing into a Christian church that would live long after he was gone.

In his fiftieth year, which was his twenty-fifth in Burma, he fell ill of what seemed to be consumption. That was in 1839, but his strength held out for eleven years more. Then, on a French ship for a voyage which it was hoped would bring him benefit, he died, April 3, 1850.

In the Baptist Meeting House at Malden, Massachusetts, a tablet in his memory, beginning with his name and the dates of his birth and death, continues:

Malden, His Birthplace
The Ocean, His Sepulchre
Converted Burmans, and
The Burman Bible
His Monument.
His Record is on high

❧ XVII ❧

John Wesley

England, like the whole of the west of Europe, was deeply affected by the Reformation, although the changes were less drastic and revolutionary than those which occurred in some of the other countries.

Through all the medieval period the church in England had been part of the widespread ecclesiastical system in which the papacy made its continual assertions of a right to rule. But since the struggle between Thomas à Becket and King Henry II in the twelfth century and the promulgation of Magna Charta in the thirteenth century, there had always been tension. Many in England resented the papal domination: the appointment by the pope of English bishops and archbishops, the claim of the papacy to be the final court of appeal in English controversies, the contributions and fees exacted and the great sums of money thus drained from the English realm. In the sixteenth century, the collision of purpose between an English king, Henry VIII, and successive popes concerning the king's marriages—an ugly matter which reflected credit on the motives of neither side—brought to an end the power of Rome in the politics of England. In 1534, the Convocation of the Church of England declared also that "the bishop of Rome hath not by Scripture any greater authority in England than any other foreign bishop."

For the next two decades, England was open to the quickening influences flowing into it from the Lutheran Reformation in Germany and from John Calvin in Geneva. Thomas Cranmer, who had succeeded Warham as archbishop of Canterbury, promoted new translations of the Bible, and in place of the Mass and the Latin service books, he created for England the Book of Common Prayer. In the brief reign of Mary, from 1553 to 1558, England reverted, so far as the queen could accomplish it, to Roman Catholic allegiance; but after Elizabeth came to the throne, the Protestant spirit was again dominant. In this, as in many other instances, there was that moderation so characteristic of the British temperament. The church in England was reformed, without having its continuity uprooted. The creeds, the central sacraments, the orders of the ministry, and many of the ancient ways of worship, were continued as before. Thus there were in England henceforth two forces that would be in shifting balance. There was the relative conservatism of the established church; but within the church, and breaking out among the people of England into independent religious movements, there was always the yeast of the Protestant freedom of conscience and the Protestant conviction of the right of the individual to reassert for himself what he believed to be the imperatives of the gospel. So there could be in England, on the one hand, the autocratic assertion of the divine right of kings and of bishops, and, on the other hand, the Puritan revolt which in the first half of the seventeenth century could execute Archbishop Laud and cut off the head of King Charles I.

In general result, the Church of England continued as the national organization of religion, reformed from the perversions of the pre-Reformation years, respectable, but in danger always of sinking into the stodginess and complacency to which every established institution may be liable. Such was the situation in the first half of the eighteenth century, which was presently to experience the religious awakening of Methodism, chiefly through the spiritual fervor and the organizing genius of one man, John Wesley.

Great creative personalities may come out of surroundings which seem to give no promise of anything extraordinary. John Wesley, who was to disturb profoundly the Church of England, first saw the light of day in a sleepy rural parish. His father,

Samuel Wesley, was rector of Epworth in Lincolnshire, and there in the rectory on the 17th of June, 1703, John Wesley was born, the fifteenth of nineteen children. Here and there in the Church of England were, doubtless, many other priests and pastors who, like Samuel Wesley, were of good character and respectable faithfulness; and there were lay people like Susanna, Samuel Wesley's wife, of evangelical fervor and devotion. But also in the church there was much complacent contentment with what the world and the flesh could offer. Bishops, with the large revenues then belonging to their sees, were the beneficiaries of what a historian of the period called "the scandalous practices of non-residence and pluralities." But to most of those who were part of the system there was nothing "scandalous" about it; instead, the order of things was a comfortable matter of course. Bishop Richard Watson of Llandaff, writing to the Archbishop of Canterbury, noted contentedly: "The provision of £2,000 a year, which I possess from the church, arises from the tithes of two churches in Shropshire, two in Leicestershire, two in my diocese, three in Huntingdonshire, on all of which I have resident curates." This bishop went occasionally to his diocese, but actually resided in the Lake district. There, he wrote, his time was "spent partly in supporting the religion and constitutions of my country, by seasonable publications, and principally in building farm-houses, blasting rocks, enclosing wastes, making bad lands good, planting larches etc. By such occupations I have recovered my health, preserved my independence, set an example of a spirited husbandry and honorably provided for my family."[1]

Many of the clergy occupied their livings in semi-idleness, carrying out their routine duties—although one could not always be too certain of that. Some were better than the average, and some were worse; but perhaps not untypical was an easygoing parson named James Woodforde who from 1758 to 1787 kept a *Diary of a Country Parson*, which has found its way into print.[2] He was a man, as the editor of the diary sums up what it reveals, who "loved good food and good drink; he loved sport, specially coursing hares and fishing; he loved a country life; he loved established institutions." Goodnatured, genial, and acceptable according to the standards of his times, the Rev. James Woodforde undoubtedly was. But no one could have expected of him, and no one received, any urgent message of the gospel. As one searches his diary, it is curious to note that, although there are occasional references to sermons, there is not a single reference to any sermon that seemed to arouse deep interest in him or any expectation that it would arouse a deep interest in anybody else. Kindly and essentially goodhearted, James Woodforde did what he was supposed to do, but the naïve admixture of religious responsibilities with the ordinary interests to which he turned back is shown in some of the spontaneous diary recordings. On an Easter Day, for instance, he wrote: "My Clarke Sam Hutchins sat up all last night drinking therefore he did not attend at the Holy Sacrament—for which I gave him a severe lecture. I had a piece of roast beef for dinner, and I had my Clarke Sam Hutchins, and his cousin Thomas Hutchins my gardener to dine." And in another entry: "Mr. and Mrs. Hodnes, Mrs. Davie and Mr. Hall dined and spent the afternoon with us. Mrs. Davie stayed and supped and slept here. I gave them for dinner a knuckle of veal and a tongue, a prodigious fine Cock Turkey and a Currant Pudding." And a few days later: "We did not go to bed till after 12 this night, the wind being still very high. We were as merry as we could be. I took of Mrs. Davie's Garter tonight and kept it. I gave her my Pair of Garters and I am to have her other tomorrow."[3]

So the Rev. James Woodforde went on his well-meaning way, fitting in pleasantly with the society of eighteenth-century England, but representing a church establishment which could hardly be said to be "not conformed to this world" but to be "transformed by the renewing of your mind."

Meanwhile, through the son of Samuel and Susanna Wesley there was to come a challenge to everything that was self-satisfied and stodgy in the church's life. Susanna was a woman of great strength of character, whose devotion to her children woke in them an answering love which made them want to be responsive to her expectations. Those expectations, born of her intense religious earnestness, would follow them wherever they went. When her son John had gone out from under her wing, first to Charterhouse School and then at thirteen years of age to Christ Church, Oxford, she wrote to him, "The way which leads to heaven is so narrow, the gate we must enter in so strait, that it will not permit a man to pass with one known unmortified sin about him."⁴

A friend of John Wesley's described him as "gay and sprightly, with a turn for wit and humor." Nothing harsh or narrow therefore had been bred in him in the Epworth rectory home. But he had strength and seriousness. The instinct for order which in the years still far in the future he would exhibit so conspicuously in the Methodist fellowships and the Methodist way of life appeared already in his student days at Oxford. At first not physically strong and needing to be careful of such energy as he had, he made for himself a scheme of study with a timetable for each day of the week, and he accomplished a wide amount of reading.

Meanwhile, John Wesley's religious interests were expressing themselves in ways that represented nothing startling, and may have been indeed not much more than the conventional routine by which many young men in the eighteenth-century English universities went on into a career. He was ordained a deacon in the established church in 1725, and in 1726 he became a fellow of Lincoln College, Oxford. For most of the next three years he was in Epworth to help his father as a curate; but in October, 1729, he returned to Oxford as a lecturer in Greek, and became associated with a special group of Oxford men who had begun to meet in the rooms of his brother Charles.

If Charles Wesley originally had been one of the number for whom religion was a decent family inheritance, it was also true that a day had come when he "awoke out of his lethargy." So did John. Together with some other students, they began to study the Greek New Testament, to review their lives in the light of it, to go to the Holy Communion each week, and to fast—as the Book of Common Prayer prescribed—on Wednesdays and Fridays. They began to visit, also, the prisoners in the jail, and the sick in parishes where the incumbent clergy would permit it. John Wesley had been much stirred also by reading

William Law's *Serious Call to a Devout and Holy Life.* He preached often, lived simply, and gave away most of his income to the poor. It would seem that he was already an exemplar of such "devout and holy life" as that of which William Law had written.

But later, as he looked back upon those years, Wesley said in his *Journal* that he had then no notion of inward holiness. "From the year 1725 to 1729," he wrote, "I preached much, but saw no fruit to my labor. Indeed, it could not be that I should; for I neither laid the foundation of repentance nor of preaching the Gospel, taking it for granted that all to whom I preached were believers, and that many of them needed no repentance. From the year 1729 to 1734, laying a deeper foundation of repentance, I saw a little fruit. But it was only a little; and no wonder: for I did not preach faith in the blood of the covenant."

In 1735, Samuel Wesley died, and John Wesley read the commendatory prayers of the Church of England by his father's bed. In the autumn of that year the brothers, John and Charles, sailed from England to the colony of Georgia, Charles to be the secretary of the governor, General Oglethorpe, and John commissioned by the Society for the Propagation of the Gospel to be a missionary among the Indians. Very little came of that particular effort, and John Wesley found himself ministering mostly to the colonists in Savannah. He gathered a little group who began to follow the same intensive religious regimen which the Wesleys and their friends had followed at Oxford—in the association which other students there had derisively called "The Holy Club." The Savannah society met on Wednesday evenings for "a free conversation, begun and ended with singing and prayer." Meanwhile, as still by training and instinct a High Churchman, Wesley followed strict interpretation of the rubrics of the Book of Common Prayer, and on one occasion refused the Holy Communion to a German whose baptism had not been at the hands of a priest episcopally ordained. He pursued his ministry with a devoted faithfulness, but there was something within him still unsatisfied.

In 1738, he returned to England. On the previous voyage, in the ship which carried John and Charles to Georgia, both of them had been greatly impressed by a group of Moravian fellow passengers, and especially by the calm courage and shining spirit of these Moravians in the midst of a violent ocean storm. In their faith there was a joyousness which seemed to the Wesleys above and beyond what they possessed. In England again, John Wesley met the Moravian, Peter Bohler; and in his presence Wesley began to feel that he lacked "that faith whereby alone we are saved." Then came what might have seemed an insignificant happening, but which for Wesley was spiritually transforming. He went one night—May 25, 1738—to a meeting of a society in Aldersgate Street, London; and there he listened to the reading of Luther's *Preface to the Epistle to the Romans*. In Wesley's own words is the account of what then swept over him—a sudden conviction so decisive that he could mark the instant at which his life seemed to begin anew. "About a quarter before nine," he wrote afterward in his journal, "while he (i.e. Luther, whose words were being read) was describing the change which God works in the heart through faith in Christ, I felt my heart strangely warmed. I felt I did trust in Christ alone, for salvation; and an assurance was given me that he had taken away *my* sins, even *mine*, and saved me from the law of sin and death."

As W. E. H. Lecky has written in *The History of England in the Eighteenth Century*, "It is scarcely an exaggeration to say that the scene which took place at that humble meeting in Aldersgate Street forms an epoch in English history." Because of it, John Wesley from that time on had a living gospel which he would carry out as fire to kindle what was too generally the dormant religious life of England.

Wesley went to visit Herrnhuth, the settlement in Germany which was the heart of the evangelical movement that had been begun there among the Moravians by Count Zinzendorf, and from which had come Peter Bohler and the other missionaries through whom Wesley had received his conversion. He hoped, he said, that "conversing with those holy men who were themselves living witnesses of the fine power of faith . . . would be a means, under God, of so establishing my soul that I might go on from faith to faith and from strength to strength."

The manner in which this hope was fulfilled is made clear in one of the most vivid and complete records of a man's life and work ever written: the *Journal* in which almost daily from 1735 to 1790, the year before his death, Wesley recounted where he went and what he preached and what happened, sometimes by way of welcome and more often in turbulent resistance, to his flaming message delivered to the eighteenth-century society which previously had known only "the drowsy, slippered armchair religion of the day."

From beginning to end, Wesley kept his loyal devotion to the Church of England in which he had been ordained deacon and priest. Commenting in his *Journal* on a communion service he attended in the Scottish Church, he wrote: "How much more simple, as well as more solemn, is the service of the Church of England!" Only four years before his death, he declared that some of his followers who wanted separation "had neither good sense nor even good manners left." "If you are resolved," he said, "you may have your service in church hours; but remember, from that time you will see my face no more. This struck deep, and from that hour I have heard no more of separating from the Church!" What Wesley wanted was to bring back into the church's life the moving of the Holy Spirit which it had forgotten; but in his ultimate decision it would be what he counted as the Holy Spirit and not the convention of the church to which he would be obedient. His own instinctive conservatism was progressively overcome by what, in the words of another, was "the lost ideal of the work of the Church—the universal compulsion of the souls of men."

In 1739, the year after his transforming experience in the Aldersgate meeting, Wesley was invited by George Whitfield to come to Bristol and join in the unfettered evangelistic work which Whitfield had begun. He wrote in his *Journal:* "I could scarce reconcile myself at first to this strange way of preaching in the fields . . . having been all my life (till very lately) so tenacious of every point relating to decency and order, that I should have thought the saving of souls almost a sin, if it had not been done in a church." But he went, because he felt a "bounden duty," stronger than his inhibitions, "to declare unto all that are willing to hear, the glad tidings of salvation." And twenty years later, when he had preached to untold tens of thousands in fields, streets, market places and village squares, he wrote: "What marvel the devil does not love field preaching? Neither do I; I love a commodious room, a soft cushion, an handsome pulpit. But where is my zeal, if I do not trample all these under foot, in order to save one more soul?"

When Wesley had once launched upon his work of carrying the gospel to the unchurched crowds, the energy and the indomitable determination with which he pursued his purpose reached an ultimate of achievement which might have seemed beyond the strength of any human being. In eighteenth-century Britain, railroads had not been dreamed of. Travel was by horseback or by stage over roads that might be morasses of mud when heavy rains fell, or dangerous in winter from ice and drifted snow. Many rivers had no bridges and could be crossed only by uncertain ferries. But Wesley went not once but again and again through and across England and Scotland, from Kent and the coasts of Cornwall to the Scottish highlands; through Wales and Ireland, to London, Birmingham, Bristol, Liverpool, Dublin, and other great cities and villages past counting; to the Isle of Wight, the Isle of Man, and the Scilly and Channel Isles. For fifty-two years, in fair weather or foul, he rode five thousand to eight thousand miles a year, which added up to more than a quarter of a million miles in his lifetime; and he tells that he discovered that his horse was never likely to stumble if he rode with a slack rein, which he always did, reading a book as he sat in his saddle. He preached fifteen times or more each week, and besides that, on the road or in the taverns where he stopped, he and any companion whom he took with him "were fully determined to lose no opportunity of awakening, instructing, or exhorting, any whom we might meet within our journey." It was hardly an exaggeration when Augustine Birrell called Wesley's *Journal*, in which he set down what he had done, "the most amazing record of human exertion ever penned by man."

Nor was Wesley's preaching any matter of smooth welcome and ready reception. In the cities and villages of eighteenth-century England, poverty and ignorance and general degradation had created a human element that could be quickly brutal.

Men half-drunk had no inclination to listen to a preacher, nor did townsmen in any village where there might be sordid interests and sullen prejudices ready to inflame the crowd. Consequently, Wesley was met again and again by angry mobs: pelted with mud and stones, knocked down once from behind when he was preaching, besieged in houses where the mob smashed windows and broke down doors to get at him. The amazing fact was that he was never critically injured. He had a courage and an intrepid presence that could outface and overawe violence. Once when he was preaching and a man in the center of the crowd was shouting insults, he told the people round the man to separate, so that he could see him; and when he looked him in the face, the man fell silent and slunk away. Preaching near the docks at Plymouth, Wesley was confronted by "a violence of the rabble" that "grew fiercer and fiercer, as their numbers increased." He singled out the ringleader of the mob, walked up to him, and took his hand. Instantly the man changed. "Sir," he said to Wesley, "I will see you safe home. No man shall touch you." Then to the crowd: "Stand off, I will knock the first man down that touches him"; whereupon, as Wesley noted in his *Journal*, "We walked on in great peace; my conductor every now and then stretching out his neck (he was a very tall man) to see if any behaved rudely, till we came to Mr. Hide's door. We then parted in much love." To complete the day, Wesley "stayed in the street near half an hour after he was gone, talking with the people, who had now forgot their anger."

By themselves the rabble could be dangerous enough. But the worst thing was that their emotional violence was given a cover of respectability by the cynical hostility of those who should have been on Wesley's side. Too many of the gentry had as little use as the mob for a preacher who was merciless to their own sins and to their sham religion. One of these, with his pocket full of rotten eggs which he meant to throw, joined the crowd around Wesley on one occasion, with the sardonic result, however, that someone pushed against him in the press and smashed the eggs inside his own coat. Mayors and magistrates sometimes backed the mob instead of Wesley. In Staffordshire two justices of the peace issued orders to all constables to apprehend "several disorderly persons, styling themselves Methodist Preachers [who] go about raising routs and riots to the great damage of his Majesty's liege people, and against the peace of our Sovereign Lord the King." In Ireland, the mayor of Cork, forbidding Wesley to preach, exclaimed, "Are there not churches and meeting-houses enough? I will have no more mobs or riots."

And in the Church of England, Wesley met mostly with a cold hostility. At Pensford, after he had first been given leave to preach in the parish church, Wesley was handed a note: "Sir, our minister, having been informed that you are beside yourself, does not care you should preach in any of his churches." At Epworth, once his father's own parish, Wesley was forbidden the building, by the then resident curate, whereupon he preached to a throng of people in the churchyard, standing on the flat stone of his father's grave. This same curate told his congregation that "one of the most dangerous ways of quenching the spirit was by enthusiasm; and enlarged on the character of an enthusiast, in a very florid and oratorical manner." Moreover he sent this message: "Tell Mr. Wesley, I shall not give him the sacrament; for he is not fit."

But no sort of opposition or repulse deterred John Wesley, moved as he was by "love to those souls for which Christ died." Mobs or no mobs, he went where the people were; and before he was finished on any day, immense crowds had begun to listen to him. Sometimes in a sloping meadow, standing on a rock or on a low wall, he preached to as many as twenty thousand persons, and although it seems incredible, he made himself heard. When he was fifty-six years old, he wrote, "What building except St. Paul's would contain such a congregation? And if it would, what human voice could have reached them there? By repeated observations I find I can command thrice the number in the open air, that I can under a roof."

Wesley was often impatient with the well-to-do and the comfortable, who, he thought, were so padded with the soft satisfactions of their world that the sword of the Spirit could not touch them. But he had a passion of pity for the poor and the despised.

He and the lay preachers whom he raised up as his helpers did more than any had ever done since the days of Francis of Assisi to bring the gospel to the common people. He knew that among the depraved—and all the more because of their depravity— there was a hidden hunger for the message of redemption which he brought. As he fed that hunger, human beings were transformed. "I have seen," he wrote, "(as far as a thing of this kind can be seen) very many persons changed in a moment from the spirit of fear, horror, despair, to the spirit of love, joy and peace, and from sinful desire till then reigning over them, to a pure desire of doing the will of God: him that was a drunkard and is now exemplarily sober: the whoremonger that was, who now abhors the very 'garment spotted by the flesh'. . . . This is the fact; let any judge of it as they please."

Wesley's preaching turned between two great poles. With the terrible intensity of a John the Baptist, he named and rebuked the sins of high and low, and called men to repentance. But he did not stop there. Over and above their own unworthiness, he brought to men the promise of the redeeming love of God. One of the texts on which he preached again and again was "Jesus Christ, who of God is made unto us wisdom, righteousness, sanctification and redemption." He believed that the grace of God could transform every life that received it, and inspire a daily growth in holiness. In this twentieth century a "neo-orthodoxy" has challenged and condemned a complacent humanism by its stringent and often somber emphasis upon the corruption that has gone deep into the human will. But a message which dwells too much on sin and too little on forgiveness, too much on God's judgment and too little on his mercy, is a message which at last may leave men bewildered, discouraged, and defeated. John Wesley brought to men the gospel of a shining hope. He never belittled human sinfulness; on the contrary, he made men more than ever tragically conscious of their sin. But he also made them cry, as one man mentioned in his *Journal* did, "Now I know God loveth me and hath forgiven my sins, and sin shall not have dominion over me, for Christ hath set me free."

When men seemed thus to be set free from old chains of sin

and the degradation to which these had held them down, Wesley was determined—under God—that this should prove no mere emotional illusion. With a genius as an organizer as great as his power in preaching, he formed his converts into bands and classes for instruction and for mutual examination and encouragement. Thus grew the Methodist societies; and later, because Wesley appointed lay preachers and himself ordained men to carry Methodism to America, there developed inevitably the Methodist Church. This, as a body separate from the Church of England instead of as a leavening force within it, Wesley had not intended. But too many in the Church of England were blind to the day of its visitation; and therefore the church as a whole, exaggerating precedents and conventions, and treating ecclesiastical forms as though they were articles of faith, could not make room in time for the work of its own great son whose devotion to the gospel broke through the church's inhibitions and made him say, "I look upon all the world as my parish. Whom then shall I hear, God or man?"

Wesley's *Journal* continues the record of his preaching through October, 1790, when he was nearly eighty-eight years old. On Tuesday, March 1, 1791, the day before he died, he paused a little, and then with all the remaining strength he had, cried out, "The best of all is, God is with us!"

XVIII

Frederick W. Robertson and Phillips Brooks

Sometimes the gospel has been brought to a country and to a generation like a firebrand, rousing protest and even kindling revolution. So it was with Luther and Calvin and Knox. Sometimes, on the other hand, it has come—as it did with Francis of Assisi—to be the flame of an intensely personal devotion. And sometimes it has been the quiet light, both of intellect and spirit, which has guided men along widening pathways of understanding of the truth.

It is this last which has been the contribution of some great preachers who have not lived in times of dramatic crisis. In the nineteenth century two such preachers were Frederick W. Robertson in England, and in America, Phillips Brooks.

Frederick W. Robertson

Robertson's life was very brief, and in its setting, inconspicuous. He was only thirty-seven years old when he died, and the larger part of his ministry in the Church of England was as the curate of Trinity Chapel in the relatively unimportant seacoast town of Brighton. He lived in a period which seemed outwardly serene, for it was at the beginning of the Victorian era when the British empire moved to the peak of its prosperity and power. But in the thought of the time, strong and sometimes passionate crosscurrents were running. How could the faith of the church, which hitherto had been linked with an assumption of the verbal infallibility of the Scriptures from Genesis to Revelation, be interpreted to men whose minds moved in a new world of scientific discoveries? And how could the message of the church, which had been congenial enough to the privileged and comfortable, be responsive to the cry for social justice which in that midnineteenth-century of industrial change was rising from the workingmen of England? Robertson's preaching was an answer to both needs, by a living interpretation of the Bible which made those who were hungry for religious reality—laboring people as well as the so-called intellectuals—listen to him, and which brought upon him at the same time the bitter denunciation of the reactionaries both in religion and in the social order.

Within twelve years after his death, fourteen editions of his sermons were printed in England, and others in America and in Germany. Now, after more than a century, those sermons are still readily available in the "Everyman's Library," and *The Life and Letters of Frederick W. Robertson,* as recorded and edited by Stopford A. Brooke, ranks among the religious biographies of permanent authority and power.

To sum up the message which Robertson preached, with its penetrating understanding of the Bible, its human sympathy, and its nobility of expression, would be impossible in any brief space. Fortunately, all who want to read his sermons for themselves can turn to them, and in each succeeding generation many do, with one result above all: the realization that the one supreme imperative for any interpreter of the gospel is devotion to the truth. Formulations of the truth change from age to age. The express theologies of even the greatest men—an Augustine, a Luther, a Calvin, a Knox—must be open to the reinterpretations which come with widening knowledge and enlarging experience of life. When a man believes that, and dares to speak and act in the light of it, he becomes an instrument in his time of the Holy Spirit, and one more in the long succession of torchbearers of the gospel fire.

Robertson, as his foremost biographer has written, "believed in progress. He had no fear of God's truth being overwhelmed.

To him Christianity could not be in danger. . . . It was not stir, or inquiry, or skepticism which he feared, but unrelenting conservatism and stagnation." Therefore, in all his preaching, as in all the outreach of his ministry, he was a living challenge to the timid obscurantism of those in the church who believed in "the necessity of stifling doubt; the repression of all who stir up theological discussions; the duty of keeping strictly in the old paths; the habit of shutting the eyes to difficulties, and of answering opponents without the requisite knowledge; the denial of the development of doctrine and of religious progress, and the general depreciation, as an evil to be dreaded, of active and critical inquiry."[1]

At the heart of Robertson's faith was that which has given light and power to all the great witnesses to the gospel; namely, a sense of the redeeming love of God in Christ himself, and the attempted interpretation of all life according to the mind of Christ. "He rested on a life, not on a system. He did not deny the necessity of a system of theology, but he did deny the necessary permanence of any system. Christianity was founded on a Life, the spirit of which was infinite, and capable of infinite expansion. It would, therefore, be necessarily born again and again under new forms, conditioned by the character and thought of the several countries and ages it existed in. But all this continuance, under diverse forms of Christianity, depended, in Robertson's mind, on the historical reality of Christ's person and Christ's life."[2]

In a letter to one of his friends, Robertson wrote that, as he read in the Gospels of Christ, "I think I get glimpses into His mind, and I am sure that I love Him more and more. . . . a sublime feeling of a Presence comes upon me at times, which makes inward solitariness a trifle to talk about."[3] And because this divine Presence seemed to be with him and to speak through him, it was not strange that one who listened to Robertson preach said afterward, "I never hear him without some doubt being removed, or some difficulty solved."[4]

Phillips Brooks

Akin to Frederick W. Robertson in his spirit and in his essential message was Phillips Brooks, and because of his longer life and ministry perhaps of even greater influence upon his contemporary world. What Robertson brought to England in the first half of the nineteenth century, Brooks brought to America in the second half: an interpretation of the gospel which was lifted above all narrow dogmatism and which in its immense vitality made the Christian message real to multitudes who had never been drawn to it before.

Born in Boston in 1835, Phillips Brooks was nurtured in a home where the father represented the integrity of mind and character of the best New England Unitarianism, and where the mother was a fervent evangelical. Phillips, the second of six sons, was given a religious training to which he responded with a boy's more or less routine willingness, and without any special spiritual crisis of conversion such as comes to some adolescents. When he had gone to Boston Latin School and then to Harvard College, he still had no evident religious bent. When he was a small boy his father and mother had moved from the First Parish Church, Unitarian, to St. Paul's Episcopal Church on Tremont Street; but Phillips, reserved and silent about religious matters, had not been confirmed, although his mother was constantly praying that he might be. Nor did he have any particular part in the voluntary religious organizations among the students at Harvard.

He graduated in the class of 1855 without conspicuous achievement, except for an award for an essay on "The Teaching of Tacitus regarding Fate and Destiny." But, more important, he had gained a mastery of the classics, and had developed a capacity for wide and rapid reading and for assimilating what he read. He was still only nineteen years old. He thought he would like to go abroad and study further, to fit himself some day for a possible professorship.

But first he wanted more experience and the opportunity to earn some money. He applied for a position as teacher in Boston Latin School, and was granted it. He began his work there with enthusiasm; but he had been given a class of older boys whose most lively interest was to see how they could plague this new, young teacher. Brooks proved completely unsuited for the kind of rough discipline that was called for, and which was familiar enough in the rest of the school. His classroom became a chaos; and after four months he was asked to resign. The first chapter of his postcollege life had ended in humiliation. Mr. Gardner, the headmaster, told him that in his experience a man who failed as a teacher would be good for nothing else.

The next months were a time of deep dejection. "Phillips will not see anyone now, but after he is over the feeling of mortification, he will come and see you," his father wrote to Dr. Vinton, rector of St. Paul's Church. Phillips Brooks did go to see Dr. Vinton shortly after that, and also to talk with Dr. Walker, the president of Harvard. Charles William Eliot, then a tutor in Harvard, happened to come face to face with Brooks as he was leaving Dr. Walker's office. He was startled at the look on Brooks's face, and by its extreme pallor, as though Brooks had just passed through the shock of some emotional crisis. But President Walker and Dr. Vinton were more perceptive than Mr. Gardner. Each of them recognized that the failure of a boy of nineteen to cope with a group of boys to whom he ought not to have been assigned—boys who were notorious for having frustrated three other teachers—did not indicate any essential lack in Phillips Brooks. Knowing his background, and sensing qualities in him not yet fully manifest, they advised him to study for the ministry.

Still with misgivings, and reticent, Brooks nevertheless followed their counsel. In the fall of 1856 he suddenly appeared at the Protestant Episcopal Seminary in Alexandria, Virginia, familiarly known not by its long official title, but simply as the Virginia Seminary. To one of his friends who remonstrated at his going off without anyone's knowledge, he wrote, "Please let all that matter drop. I said scarcely anything to anyone but Father and Mother. Consider me here at the seminary without debating how I got here."

At first he was uncomfortable and restless in the new surroundings. As a New Englander, he felt alien to the South where slavery still existed, and where, as he wrote in a letter, "everything seems about half a century behind the age." Also, the Seminary then was far short of the academic distinction to which it would afterward attain. As one of his classmates, Charles A. L. Richards, recognized, "There was much fervor and piety, less enthusiasm for scholarship. There was little serious thinking, little outside reading, either in theology or literature." Most of the professors seemed to be only dry-as-dust purveyors of conventional ideas. It was no wonder that Phillips Brooks grew increasingly dissatisfied, and began to consider going somewhere else if indeed he was to continue preparing for the ministry at all, of which he still was not sure.

But there were other aspects of the Seminary, and influences in it, which began to affect Brooks in ways deeper than he knew. Gradually he became intimate with Dr. William Sparrow, the dean, of whom he said, "He is a splendid man, the only real live man we have here, clear as daylight and fair and candid, without a particle of dogmatism or ecclesiastical dryrot." It was Dr. Sparrow who gave to the Seminary its motto: "Seek the truth, come whence it may, cost what it will." And from Dr. Sparrow, and from others also, Brooks took to himself the most precious gift which the Seminary had to offer: an evangelical spirit based upon a genuine devotion to Christ and a consciousness that Christ could come into a man's life as a new creation. Phillips Brooks would not be among those whom William James described as "the twice-born." When Dr. Vinton spoke to him once of being converted, he said he did not know what conversion meant. There would be no moment of identifiable crisis in his spiritual life. But capacities deep within him were at the point of flowering. As his most authoritative biographer has written: in ways beyond his immediate recognition, the Seminary was furnishing him "with the most important experience of his life. . . . By the close of his first year away from home, he had begun to take root in the new soil; the process of wilting had been survived; the sap of a new life was circulating in his veins."[5]

At the end of his first year in Virginia, Brooks was confirmed. In 1859 he graduated from the Seminary, was ordained, and was called to be the minister of the Church of the Advent in Philadelphia. In the Seminary, notwithstanding the lack of much outside stimulus, the range of his own reading was phenomenal, and he filled thick notebooks not only with summaries of what he had studied but also with his own creative imagination. Starting out to preach, he would pour into his sermons a richness of substance such as few men could possess, and with it now there was a kindled spirit. For the young man who went into the seminary hesitant and unsure, by silent processes of the soul's growth which no eye could fully measure had come out dedicated and eager for the work he was henceforth to do.

From the Church of the Advent he was called, after two years, to the more centrally located Church of the Holy Trinity in Philadelphia. In 1868 came a call from Boston to be the rector of Trinity Church. Refusing it at first, he was later moved to accept, and began there, in 1869, a ministry of twenty-two years, which ended only when he was elected bishop of the diocese of Massachusetts.

Other men have held equally distinguished posts. What made Phillips Brooks great was not the relative eminence of the pulpits from which he spoke, but the greatness of his personality, the richness of his mind, and the incandescence of his spirit.

"Preaching," he said in his Lyman Beecher Lectures at Yale Divinity School, "is the bringing of truth through personality." The truth that Phillips Brooks believed in, the eternal truth of the redeeming love of God brought near in Christ, could be spoken also by other men. But preached by him, it often had the power of a great river pouring out of the mountains as compared with the unimpressive current of the lowland stream. Back of what he said was the bigness of the man himself: in form, in intellect, in moral and spiritual conviction. Six feet four inches tall, with a massive head, strong features, and great, deep eyes, he commanded attention in any group. He could fall silent in the face of trivialities, but both in the pulpit and in conversation, his mind and spirit leaped to respond to every living interest and above all to the hunger for God which—although it might be hidden and unexpressed—he believed to be present somewhere in almost every human soul. Made in a larger mold than those about him, nevertheless he was never pompous or aloof. Companionable with his friends, alert and humorous and approachable, he knew the way also into the minds and hearts of children. William Lawrence, his successor as bishop of Massachusetts, tells that on a visitation to one of the parishes of his diocese, sitting at the rectory supper table, he was confronted with the sudden question of a small child. "Why don't you talk to *us*? Bishop Brooks always talked to us." When Helen Keller, deaf, dumb, and blind from early infancy, was a little girl, she was brought to Phillips Brooks as the one person who might make her aware of the meaning of God. And in his pulpit it was as though he heard "the still, sad music of humanity"—its hopes and its longings, its winged desires and its wistful disappointments—and it called out all his passionate desire to bring the divine answer to its needs. He used no anecdotes nor any sentimental personal reminiscences, but the throngs who listened felt that he was opening to them the ultimate profundities of his soul. A man who as a boy heard him preach only once said many years afterward that the one sentence he remembered from Phillips Brooks's sermon was expressive of the whole impact of his preaching: "Flame leaps to flame." And one of the tough drifters from the streets of Boston who chanced to hear Brooks speak in Faneuil Hall exclaimed, "By God, I believe he could make a good man of me for a week!"

Thus in what lies forever within the realm of mystery, the inner quality of a man's self, Phillips Brooks would have made an impact on any generation. Upon his own generation his impact was the greater because in a time of intellectual questioning he dared, like Dr. Sparrow, "to seek the truth," and to preach a Christian message that stood in the full light of every reality that the search for truth revealed.

In the early years of the second half of the nineteenth century, the new discoveries in science—geological discoveries concerning the age of the earth, Darwinian evidence of the evolution of man from subhuman species, together with the so-called "higher criticism" of the Bible—had thrown the ecclesiastical world into confusion. An increasing number of persons abandoned the churches because they believed them to represent ignorance and obscurantism; and within the churches angry spokesmen were answering belligerently, and insisting that what they held to be the orthodox traditions were a *sine qua non* of Christian faith. In that time when numberless people, and especially the young, were looking for some clear guidance, Phillips Brooks preached in Boston. He never descended to bitter argument. Neither did he assume that Christian interpreters had to be timid, evasive, or defensive. He believed that all truth is of God, and that every authentic new discovery does not threaten but enlarges men's knowledge of the greatness of God and the wonder of life as fulfilled in Christ.

Much of the wider understanding of the physical universe and the development of man, and of the Bible in its actual meaning as related to these, is now a part of all enlightened thinking; but the religious candor and courage which are our heritage came through the light that blazed in the creative preaching of a few men here and there, and supremely in the sermons of Phillips Brooks.

Interpretations of the Bible and of Christian faith and creeds were changing fast in those days [wrote William Lawrence, who was then a young student]. We moved along week by week, month by month, dropping opinions, prejudices and what we had thought were essentials of the Creed; questioning, and then catching a new revelation from a book or preacher. Under these conditions some of Brooks' sermons were to us epoch-making. We could recall the day and the language in which he opened door after door and let in the light. When he began with the text, "Men's hearts failing them for fear," his people were alert: *they* were the men. When he gave out the words, "One thing I know," the people who had lost much, but had held on to one or two facts of personal experience, and thereby saved their faith, listened. As the rush of words, thought and conviction

gained increasing force, one could almost hear the walls
of tradition, orthodoxy and partisanship fall down. The
atmosphere became electrified. The great Scotsman,
Principal Tulloch, after hearing him once, wrote home,
"I could have got up and shouted!"[6]

Already Phillips Brooks had become for innumerable people
another Mr. Valiant-for-truth, not now in the pages of *Pilgrim's
Progress* but in the living world; and men might have described
him then, as afterward he was to be described on the bronze
tablet to his memory at Harvard College:

A Preacher
Of Righteousness and Hope
Majestic in Stature   Impetuous in Utterance
Rejoicing in the Truth
Unhampered by Bonds of Church or State
He Brought by his Life and Doctrine
Fresh Faith to a People
Fresh Meanings to Ancient Creeds

As Phillips Brooks believed in truth, so also he believed greatly
in people, and in the presence under even the dustiest surface of
a spark of divine desire which the Word could kindle into flame.
What he preached was always the gospel, *the good news*. Passing beyond what had often been the somber emphasis of the
Calvinistic theology which belonged to his heritage and his
nurture, he preached that "man is a child of God by nature. He
is ignorant and rebellious, the prodigal child of God: but his
ignorance and rebellion never break that first relationship." Some
men, he said in his *Lectures on Preaching*, appropriate the elements of hope, while others will invariably gather up what tends
to despair. "The latter kind of man may have his uses. There are
tasks and times for which no prophet but Cassandra is appropriate. There were duties laid on some of the Old Testament
prophets which perhaps they might have done with hearts
wholly destitute of light. . . . The preacher may sometimes

denounce, rebuke, and terrify. But when he does that, he is not distinctively the preacher of Christianity."[7]

In the twentieth century, the life of which has been scorched and scarred by two world wars, there has developed a neo-orthodoxy which has emphasized the sinfulness and helplessness of man. As a corrective to all glib and shallow human self-assurance, and as a reminder of the eternal truth that man lies under the awful judgment of God's righteousness and that only by God can he be redeemed, that theology has a message which none who face reality can ignore. But it can become a paralyzing message if it brings a darkness of spirit so deep that it leaves men in despair. The words of a lecture which Phillips Brooks gave under the title "A Ministry for Our Age" has its uplifting truth for this century as surely as for his: "There is in every man's heart, if you could only trust it, a power of appreciating genuine spiritual truth, of being moved into unselfish gratitude by the love of God. The minister who succeeds is the minister who, in the midst of a sordid age, trusts the heart of man who is the child of God, and knows that it is not all sordid, and boldly speaks to it of God, his Father, as if he expected it to answer."

Phillips Brooks loved his own church, its essential faith, and forms of worship. He prized the continuity of its life and fellowship. But he had a breadth of understanding and a devotion to the spirit of Christ wherever it might be manifested which lifted him above blind partisanship. So it was inevitable that little men were afraid of the largeness of his thought, and disturbed because in his sermons they did not hear their own particular shibboleths. When he was elected bishop of Massachusetts in 1891, there were those in the church who in narrow conscientiousness tried to prevent the confirmation of his election which was required from the bishops and the Standing Committees of the other dioceses in the United States. It was ignorantly asserted that he was in some sort "a Congregationalist," that he was "an Arian" in his theology, and also "a Pelagian." Some of his friends urged him to answer, but he would not. His record, he said, was an open book; he would stand on that. Weeks of uncertainty went by. Then finally the consents to his election came. In

Boston, and all across the country, there was a great wave of rejoicing. A prominent layman of the Congregational Church wrote to him: "I am so thankful that you are elected Bishop, not of Massachusetts but of the Church Universal. All of us who share in your scholarly liberality of all denominations will call you our Bishop. May God make you Bishop of all souls and may all humble and good men love and honor you more and more." And the *Boston Daily Advertiser* wrote in its editorial: "The election of Bishop Brooks means first of all a new inspiration in every parish in the state. Next it means an upward and onward movement in living faith throughout the length and breadth of the land."

Voices like those expressed what multitudes of people recognized: that here was a man who could not be isolated within any part of the Christian church because he belonged first of all and fully to Christ. They sensed in him the fulfillment of what he himself had said ought to be the Christian's goal: "To know in one's whole nature what it is to live by Christ; to be His, not our own; to be so occupied with gratitude for what He did for us and for what He continually is to us that His will and His glory shall be the sole desires of our life." And the reality is set forth in the noble statue made by Augustus St. Gaudens, which stands by the side of Trinity Church. On the pedestal, as though in his pulpit with his face uplifted, is the great preacher. Behind him there is another figure; and that Other, whose hand is laid on Brooks's shoulder, is Jesus Christ, his Lord.

❦ XIX ❧

The Continuing Flame

The men whose names are written in the preceding chapters lived and died before the present century. What they were and what they did is now part of enduring history. Of contemporary men, the ultimate word is yet to be spoken. There must be the perspective of time before their full stature can be measured. But it can be said assuredly that in this twentieth century there have been and still are men who have made the world better because they have lived in it. Among such are these four: Wilfred Grenfell, Albert Schweitzer, Gordon Seagrave, and Thomas A. Dooley.

It is not necessary that they and their work be described at length. Numerous books by them or about them are available. But they ought to be brought to mind at the culmination of this roll of those who through all the years since Christianity began have given the spirit of Christ new expression for new times. They stand among us as evidence that the gospel fire is an ever-living fact.

Wilfred Grenfell

At the end of the nineteenth century, existence on the north Atlantic coast of Newfoundland and Labrador was harsh and grim. For the greater part of the scanty population, survival depended upon the luck of the fishing on the Newfoundland Banks and in the uncharted waters along the mainland and among the islands north and east of Labrador. Every April when the ice began to open in the harbors and straits, hundreds of fishing boats put to sea. Conditions on the banks were hard and dangerous enough, for besides the unpredictable hazards there was the continual likelihood of sudden fog in which men out in their flat-bottomed dories might stray from the schooners to which they belonged; or blizzards such as one in 1892 which caught two hundred men who started out too early in April from Trinity Bay, Newfoundland, driving their boats into the ice floes. The bodies of forty of the fishermen were found frozen to death far out to sea.

But if life for the men who went to the Banks was hard, it was worse for those who fished off Labrador. In the spring, hundreds of schooners set out toward the north from St. John's Harbor, Newfoundland, every schooner crowded indecently not only with men but with their families and their few possessions—the women and children to be put ashore in shacks along the mainland while the men went out after the cod until the fall when the ice began to form in the inlets, and the schooners took them south again. Besides this seasonal influx there were a few thousand who had come originally from Cornwall and Devon in England, who called themselves the "Liveyeres", because they "lived here" the year round in Labrador. For them, as for those who came from Newfoundland, merely to stay alive from one year to the next was a stark struggle. The fish they caught, which had no exchange value unless they were salted and shipped where they could be sold, were bought by traders who set their own price for the fish, and at the same time furnished some food, and the fishing gear, at exorbitant costs which left the isolated fishermen perpetually in debt. Through the winters all they had to eat was a little flour they had got from the traders, some molasses, tea, cheap fat, and a few dried fish. Old flour sacks were made into such makeshift clothes as the women and children had. In the ramshackle huts with their cold earthen floors, tuberculosis spread. When any fell ill, there was nothing to do but to suffer and die. Along the entire coast from the Straits of Belle Isle to the Moravian mission among the Eskimos there was not a single doctor.

That was what Labrador was like when the twentieth century began: a bleak and bitter corner of existence, with cruel poverty among forgotten people concerning whom no one seemed to care whether they might live or die.

Today Labrador is different. The name itself, which once suggested barren desolation, is linked with the transforming realities brought about all along that north Atlantic coast by the National Mission to Deep Sea Fishermen. Because of it, in the region where there was not a single doctor, there are now seven doctors, twenty-six nurses, four hospitals, a sanitarium for tubercular patients, a children's home, and two hospital ships—carrying in word and deed the gospel of Him who said, "I am come that they might have life; and have it more abundantly." All this was due mostly to the ardor and the long devotion of one man. That man was Wilfred Thomason Grenfell.

Born in 1875, he was the second son of the Rev. Algernon Grenfell, clergyman headmaster of Mostyn House School, in Parkgate, Cheshire, on the shore of the tidal estuary of the River Dee. Five miles of brimming water, or of sands when the tide was out, stretched between the shore directly in front of the school and the opposite mountains of Wales. Parkgate fishermen trawled, or seined for salmon, in the estuary, or went through the shallows with handnets to gather shrimps—always with an element of danger, because the outgoing or incoming tides were sudden and swift and powerful. The boy Wilfred, lively and talkative, made friends with the fishermen; he went out with them in their boats, and they liked him for his exuberance and his willingness to work—and also cursed him because he could be reckless in ways that to men who knew the sea were close to craziness. In his blood may have been some of the spirit of that far-off member of his family, Sir Richard Grenville, who in 1591 at the Azores defied a whole Spanish fleet, contemptuous of odds. And if Wilfred's father, absorbed in classical studies, left the control of the boys mostly to their mother, she, the descendant of a long line of soldiers, took a calm view of this son's venturesome extravagances.

When Wilfred was seventeen, his father gave up his headmastership to become chaplain of a hospital in what was called "the most foul and poverty-stricken place in England," the East End of London. About that time the son, after two not very happy years at Marlborough School, decided that he would like to be a doctor. Medical training in England of that decade was a casual and shallow business, and Wilfred Grenfell was admitted to the London Hospital School when he was only eighteen years old. At first his record had no distinction; but later he came under the influence of two brilliant and inspiring men, Dr. Frederick Treves, the surgeon, and the medical internist, Sir Andrew Clark. "From Treves," writes one of Grenfell's biographers, "he learned surgery, from Clark the art of the physician at its highest, and from both the greater lesson that in choosing this profession he was dedicating himself to the service of humanity."[1]

Meanwhile, the young student was showing outside the hospital his concern for human beings, and also following many new avenues for his outgoing energies. He rowed on the London University crew, played rugby, and went swimming in the Serpentine even when there was ice on the pond. He taught Sunday School in Bethnal Green, brought his boys to his living room on Saturdays, and started a summer camp to which they might go for a time away from the slums of London. Meanwhile, in the emergency room of the hospital or in the streets and alleys round it, he saw at first hand the drunkenness, the degradation, and the abysmal human misery which existed in what General William Booth of the Salvation Army was calling "Darkest England," and which roused at once his virile compassion for the poor and his indignation against the social indifference which let the poverty and vileness of East London continue from generation to generation as a festering sore about which nobody seemed to care.

While he was a medical student, Grenfell found himself, out of curiosity, in an evangelistic tent where Dwight L. Moody was holding a mission. Somebody was making a long and tiresome prayer; and when Moody had listened to enough of it, he called to the congregation, "While our brother is finishing his prayer, let us sing a hymn." The down-to-earth reality of that won the young Grenfell's pleased respect, and when Moody began to speak, his spirit responded to the kind of gospel which this man preached. He went out from Moody's meeting saying to himself that he would make his Christianity real, or give it up.

It happened that Dr. Frederick Treves, whom Grenfell greatly admired, was chairman of the Medical Section of a Mission which had been organized in 1882 for the fishing fleets in the North Sea. At first only an evangelistic effort, and met by many of the fishermen with jeers at the coming of the "Holy Joes," the mission had expanded into a medical service, and along with that the carrying to the men of decent reading matter and of tobacco at low price to counteract the attraction of the grog-ships that came among the fleets with tobacco, alcohol, and sometimes women. In 1888, Grenfell volunteered for a year of service. It was rough experience at the best, and this particular winter was one of the worst in weather that the fleet had known. But Grenfell took to it like a duck to water. "That it could be dangerous and hard . . . did not concern him. He was a young man being tested physically, and neither cold, wet nor weariness bothered him. This was man's work, and he loved it."[2] Dressed in oilskins like the rest of the men, he worked with them to haul in the nets, no matter if the boat might be pitching in the rough seas and the decks slick with ice. As a doctor, there was plenty for him to do. Every year as many as two hundred men were drowned or killed in the North Sea fleet, and many more were injured or fell sick: from swinging booms, falling spars, knife cuts while gutting fish, raw infections from dirty clothes, chafed skin, and salt water. Grenfell was always at hand when anybody needed him. At first "he had been shy with the fishermen, feeling an intruder among them, but he was soon at ease. The men liked him. He made it so clear that he admired them, and his eagerness to learn their craft and to serve them had a boyish quality few could resist."[3]

Within a year, Grenfell was made superintendent of the Mission; and this led to his ultimate work. As far back as 1886, a clergyman in Newfoundland had written to the Mission pleading for an extension of its work into the North Atlantic. The Mission decided that this was outside its province, and beyond its financial means. But in 1891, a member of the Mission Council who was in Canada on business sent back a report about conditions among the Newfoundland fishermen so graphic and so shocking that public opinion was stirred in England. The next year, the Mission sent a hospital ship, the *Albert*, carrying Grenfell, on an "exploratory" voyage. Landing first at St. John's, Newfoundland, the *Albert* went north along the coast of Labrador, past drifted icebergs, sailing altogether more than three thousand miles. Grenfell visited fifty settlements, saw and treated some nine hundred patients, left clothes and books and magazines where they were needed, and gathered the people for religious services on shore or on the ship. He found a depth of poverty and stark suffering such as he had not known even in the London slums. "How could any human being with a heart of flesh, after seeing such sights," he wrote to England, fail to be "haunted by these hungry pale faces of people of our own race and blood?"[4]

By the time Grenfell was sailing back to St. John's, Labrador had become to him not the bleak, empty place it seemed to many. It was a field for great adventure and for exciting service. He began to love this land of "fog, dog, and cod." Returned to England, he persuaded the North Sea Mission to extend its work across the Atlantic. In May of 1893 he set out in the *Albert* again, taking with him two doctors and two nurses—and a forty-five-foot steam launch which he had managed to buy. In that launch, he steamed north from Newfoundland along Labrador coasts and inlets where there were no lights, no charts, no channel marks, taking risks which appalled men who heard where he was going. By this time his name and his work were becoming a saga along all those subarctic shores. "Be you a real doctor?" one patient asked him with pathetic wonder, as though he were a figure come out of a fairy tale. He established a hospital at Battle Harbor and another at Indian Harbor farther north. And instead of going back to England with the *Albert* in the fall, he stayed to try to get the Newfoundland and Canadian governments to undergird the work he had begun, and to make personal appeals for it in Canada and the United States.

After that winter, he resumed his work in England, but now

his heart belonged to Labrador. From 1899, he began to give himself to the new field completely, and from that time until his death in 1940 it was his supreme devotion. The record of what he accomplished in those years—the building of new hospitals and schools, the development of co-operatives to take the people out of the power of the exploiting traders, the recruiting of workers, the provision of hospital ships that took medical help where it had never been before—would need in itself a long book to describe. Those tangible things are there as an enduring possession. And even more enduring, because of its limitless contagion, is the spirit of service which his example kindled in the hundreds of full-time workers and of eager part-time volunteers who were drawn to work beside him in Newfoundland and Labrador—the spirit which he himself expressed in *What Life Means to Me:* "I personally wish for the life of no Alexander, Caesar, or Napoleon; no Croesus or Midas, no Voltaire or Rousseau. The wealth of Herod or the learning of the Pharisees, after the lapse of centuries, I see clearly was of relatively little value, as He-who-knows counts assets. I would rather leave behind me on the sands of time the footsteps of a Judson or a Martyn or a Livingstone, of a Gordon or a Lincoln or a Lawrence, of a Lister or a Jenner or a Stevenson, than of any king, either of men of finance or of scholarship. . . . The highest reward of life to me would be to be like Jesus."[5]

Albert Schweitzer

In the Western world, wherever there is spread of general knowledge there must be few who have not heard of Albert Schweitzer. Many persons have devoted great gifts to the service of humanity; but hardly any have given so much as he, because they did not have so much to give. His life and work have been a surpassing fact, and they will become an enduring legend.

Before the Franco-Prussian War of 1870, the province of Alsace had long been a part of France. After that war it was incorporated into the new German empire. Therefore Albert Schweitzer, born in Kaysersberg of upper Alsace in 1875 was a German citizen as well as of German stock. A few weeks after his birth his father moved to the village of Gunsbach, to be the pastor of the little flock of evangelical believers in that mainly Roman Catholic place. There Albert Schweitzer, with three sisters and one brother, spent a childhood so happy that the little village and the country round it have been dear to him throughout his life. Both his father and his mother's father loved music, and the grandfather had an eager interest in organs, not only in playing them but in their construction. When Albert Schweitzer was only five years old, his father began giving him lessons on an old square piano, and when the boy was nine he played the organ at a service in the Gunsbach church.

In 1885, since there was only a primary school in Gunsbach, Albert Schweitzer was sent to live with an uncle in Mulhausen, and there for eight years he was given the wide and thorough academic training which had become the hallmark of the German "Gymnasium." After that, in 1893, he entered Strassburg University, then at the height of its reputation, with a faculty which had brought to that ancient seat of learning some of the greatest minds in the resurgent Germany.

At the end of his first session at Strassburg, Schweitzer was called up for his year of service in the German army. He took with him his Greek New Testament, and the nineteen-year-old youth began to show the creative scholarship that has marked his entire life. Studying especially the Gospel according to Matthew, he came to conclusions concerning the Messiahship of Jesus diametrically different from those of Heinrich Julius Holtzmann, his teacher at Strassburg, who stood in the top rank of German New Testament scholars; and the results of his thinking were to appear a decade later in one of the most exciting and widely influential books in the whole record of New Testament criticism, *The Quest of the Historical Jesus*. Meanwhile, at Strassburg, and then at the University of Berlin, Schweitzer completed his doctorates in philosophy and in theology, studied the organ one winter in Paris under Charles Marie Widor, and became then, even as a very young man, the leading authority in Europe on the music of Johann Sebastian Bach. All his many interests did not pull his life apart, for at his center was the same instinctive religious devotion which he had seen in his father and been imbued with at the little village church in Gunsbach. When he was twenty-four, he became deacon and curate at the Church of St. Nicholas in Strassburg, responsible for the afternoon service, the children's service, the confirmation classes and other increasing duties. "Preaching," he said, "was a necessity of my being. I felt it as something wonderful that I was allowed to address a congregation every Sunday about the deepest questions of life."[6] Every opportunity that he wanted was open to him now: scholarship, music, the ministry, in surroundings that richly fed his spirit. Presently he was made principal of the Theological College at Strassburg, "with the beautiful official quarters looking out on the sunny St. Thomas embankment, and the yearly stipend of 2000 marks."[7] What could he wish for better than to let his life go on developing where and as it was?

Then, on October 13, 1905, he dropped into a postbox letters to his parents, and to a few intimate friends, telling them that at the beginning of the winter term he would begin a course—a six-year-course—as a medical student, to go at the end of it to serve in equatorial Africa. In another letter he sent his resignation as principal of the Theological College of St. Thomas.

What had caused this almost incredible decision?

Two factors: an inner urge, unknown to others, which had been moving toward its climax; and an outer happening that in itself seemed insignificant, but yet was like the striking of a bell which announced the coming of the crucial hour.

Nine years earlier, on a brilliant summer morning at Gunsbach, when his world seemed full of happiness, "there came to me as I awoke," Schweitzer said, "the thought that I must not accept this happiness as a matter of course but must give something in return for it."[8] At that moment, he decided that until he was thirty he would be justified in pursuing his studies and his music; and that from that time on, he would give himself completely to the direct service of humanity. Now, in 1905, his thirtieth year had come.

One day on his writing table in the study at St. Thomas' College, his eye had fallen upon "one of the green-covered magazines in which the Paris missionary society reported every month on its activities."[9] He had a bond of thought with that society because as a boy in Gunsbach he had listened to letters from one of its earliest missionaries, which his father used to read aloud. In this magazine was an article on "The Needs of the Congo Mission." It was an appeal for someone to offer himself for work in Africa. For Schweitzer, that appeal gave concrete direction to the commitment he had made nine years before.

He would go to Africa. He would go not as a teacher of theology but as a doctor. Other missionaries were there already, but the desperate need was for medical help in a region full of disease and suffering. It would take him a long time to get ready, but that is what he would do. "Whenever I was inclined to feel that the years I should have to sacrifice were too long, I reminded myself that Hamilcar and Hannibal had prepared for their march on Rome by their slow and tedious conquest of Spain."[10]

Most of his friends expostulated with him on what they thought was the folly of his enterprise. That did not deter him, although it must have saddened him. "In the many verbal duels which I had to fight," he said, "as a weary opponent with people who passed for Christians, it moved me strangely to see them so far from perceiving that the love preached by Jesus may sweep a man into a new course of life."[11]

Seven years went by—six years of medical study and one year of internship—and then Schweitzer told the Paris Missionary Society that he was ready to go at his own expense to establish a clinic at the mission site in equatorial Africa which had first been established by an American missionary in 1874, but which had been taken over by the French when the Gabon province became a possession of France. It was an ironic fact that some of the directors of the Society, in the pitiful narrowness of what they believed to be their conscientious orthodoxy, were stubbornly opposed to accepting Albert Schweitzer at all. His *The Quest of the Historical Jesus* had shocked conventional ideas. What if he should pervert the sort of gospel the Negroes were supposed to listen to, and destroy the Society's reputation?

Only on the understanding that he was going out as a doctor, not as a preacher, did the majority give a final grudging approval to his going. "Not to preach any more, not to lecture any more, was for me a great sacrifice," he wrote afterward, "and till I left for Africa I avoided, as far as possible, going past either St. Nicholas' Church or the University, because the very sight of the places where I had carried on work which I could never resume was too painful."[12] But he was fortified by a purpose so simple and so deep that it could prevail over any limitation. Nearly a half century later, asked if he were glad that he had come to Africa, he answered: "Yes, very glad. Instead of trying to get acceptance for my ideas, involving painful controversy, I decided that I would make my life my argument. I would advocate the things I believed in terms of the life I lived and what I did."[13]

On March 26, 1913, Albert Schweitzer and his wife, Helen Bresslau, whom he had married the year before, embarked at Bordeaux, for the long voyage halfway down the west coast of Africa. At Cape Lopez, almost exactly on the equator, they took the river boat that went up the Ogowe River, with the dense growth of the jungle crowding both its banks, two hundred miles to Lambaréné. There the missionaries gave the Schweitzers a warm welcome, and there was no doubt that they were needed. Through the jungle paths, and by the river in canoes hollowed out of tree trunks, came an unending procession of the sick when word spread that a doctor had come to Lambaréné: medical cases and cases for surgery, malaria, sleeping sickness, dysentery, leprosy, hernias, elephantiasis tumors. What Albert Schweitzer had to work in was a chickenhouse cleaned out to be a consulting room, and one corrugated-iron building by the river, thirteen by twenty-six feet, which was an operating room and dispensary. That was the hospital at Lambaréné.

In the next eighteen months, Schweitzer managed to build some bamboo huts to shelter patients—mainly by his own labor, with the fickle native help that could be stirred to action only when he himself was there. The scattered missionaries along the Ogowe River were of a different mind from some of the officials whom Schweitzer had had to face in Paris, and he could say of them that "they soon laid aside all mistrust of me and rejoiced, as I did also, that we were united in the piety of obedience to Jesus, and in the will to simple Christian activity."[14] Regardless of the Paris prohibitions, they invited him to take part in the preaching—even though a native preacher one day waved aside an observation of Schweitzer's, "because he is not a theologian, as we are." So the field for service seemed wide open every way—and then came 1914 and the First World War.

Put under guard at first by the French authorities, the need and demand for the doctor was so great that Schweitzer was allowed to conduct the hospital; but then the cruel stupidity which is a part of war reasserted itself, and both Schweitzer and his wife were taken back to France and held for nine months in concentration camps, where he himself was gravely ill. Released at last, he seemed to have reached the end of the road. The work he had begun at Lambaréné was brought to nothing. He had no occupation, no money, no prospect for the days ahead.

Then through the dark time came a shaft of light. The Lutheran archbishop of Sweden, Nathan Söderblom, wrote to him and invited him to deliver a series of lectures at Uppsala University. Hesitant at first because he had not yet recovered from his illness, Schweitzer finally responded to the archbishop's warmhearted urging. He went to Uppsala, and his audiences received him with such overwhelming appreciation that Schweitzer was stirred emotionally to his depths, and his whole being revived. Moreover, the archbishop arranged for other lectures; for sermons in churches where Schweitzer could tell of Lambaréné; for organ recitals of the music of Bach, of which increasingly he was being recognized as the supreme interpreter. The life which he had laid down in order to go to Africa was given back to him. In place of teaching in one university he was sought now by many. His genius at the organ bench was bringing the choral splendors of Bach to great congregations not only here and there in France and Germany, as before, but in many other parts of Europe and in England. And everywhere he went, people were being moved by what he told them of the tragic needs in Africa.

Africa, and Lambaréné: unchangeably it was to these that his devotion turned. At the archbishop's prompting, he wrote *At the Edge of the Primeval Forest*. The royalties from this, and the earnings from his lectures, went to buy supplies for the hospital again. He had had to be away a long time, but he was going back. Mrs. Schweitzer was not well enough then to be in Africa. She would wait in Alsace until she could join him—which in later years she was able to do. But in 1924, he was alone as he set out for Africa, to see again at the end of the long sea voyage the mile-wide estuary of the Ogowe River, and on the shallow stern-wheeler, shabby and dirty from the years of war, make the slow progress inland, past swamps and decaying villages to the clearing between the river and the green wall of the jungle that was Lambaréné.

And the hospital: what was left of that? Almost nothing. The equatorial rains and the relentless jungle growth had wrought their devastation. Some of the buildings had collapsed; others were shells with leaking roofs. But the sick were crowding in again. They needed every hour a doctor could give; but if there was to be any place in which to treat them, the doctor had to be mason, carpenter, ditch-digger as well.

The history of the hospital at Lambaréné from that time on has been made graphic in Dr. Schweitzer's own books and in the books about him and about his work, which have caught the world's imagination. There idealism and ugliness have met in a reality the full significance of which is not instantly seen. As one visitor felt obliged to say, "Much of what you saw for the first time at the hospital seemed so primitive and inadequate as to startle."[15] Even at its fullest development, it was not much different in looks from the African villages whose people it serves and to whose comprehension Schweitzer wanted to keep it close. "But when Dr. Schweitzer walked through the grounds, everything seemed as it should be."[16] For this man represented a dedication so complete that there was nothing he would not do. He recognized that if ideals are not to be a cloudland but are to be brought down to earth, there must be foundations, and somebody must go down in the dirt to lay them. So the man who theoretically should have been able to count his working day finished when he had completed his surgery and carried his medical skill through the crowded wards had to be out unpacking and storing supplies, cutting lumber for new shelters, finding thatch to patch the roofs. There must have been times when this was a sore trial, and when it was hard to be patient with his Africans, never used to much effort or responsibility, who shirked the work which he himself then had to do. But, as Norman Cousins said, he learned when he watched Schweitzer at Lambaréné, "A man does not have to be an angel to be a saint." And Schweitzer's spirit made it true that the lamp which he caused to be lighted at night on the wharf on the Ogowe River carried into the African darkness this message: "Here at whatever hour you come, you will find light and help and human kindness."[17]

The lamp at Lambaréné has shone further than the Ogowe River. Its witness has reached out across the world, and through the years many men and women, as doctors, nurses, and varied helpers, have been inspired to join in what Albert Schweitzer began alone. His greatness is not only in what he has done, but in what he has moved others to want to do because of his example. To many whose conception of life might otherwise have been small and cheap he has brought the recognition that the truths men feel deep down in their hearts are the real truths; and as he said once to a group of boys in England, "The only ones among you who will be really happy are those who will have sought and found how to serve."[18]

Gordon S. Seagrave

While Wilfred Grenfell was carrying the flame of Christian service to the coasts of the North Atlantic; and Albert Schweitzer, to the tropical depths of Africa; another man of the twentieth century began to do the same on the continent and in the country to which Adoniram Judson had gone more than a hundred years before. Gordon Seagrave was born in Burma in 1897, where his father, grandfather, and great-grandfather, and various uncles and aunts had been evangelistic missionaries. Like the average boy, however, and notwithstanding his inheritance, he had no great taste for sermons. But when he was only five years old a great hulking Irishman stamped up the steps of the verandah of the house the boy's grandfather had built in Rangoon. He took Gordon Seagrave on his lap, and told him stories of the jungle; and of how he—this man on whose lap the boy was sitting—one day had ridden round a twist in a jungle trail almost into a wild elephant, so that the horse shied and threw him off, and how he then, with both bones broken in one of his arms, had had to walk sixty miles to a doctor. "Then he grasped the top of a heavy dining-room chair with his teeth and swung it up over his head. He asked me," the boy was afterward to tell, "for a glass of water to quench his thirst, and drank it down—standing on his head." No wonder the boy was fascinated! He asked his mother who the big man was, and she told him that he was Dr. Robert Harper, a medical missionary at Namkham, on the border between the Northern Shan States and China.

"When I grow up, I'm going to be a medical missionary in the Shan States," the boy declared.[19] And that is exactly what he did become.

In two books, *Burma Surgeon* and *Burma Surgeon Returns*, which have been read by many thousands, Gordon Seagrave has told something of his life and work. There is no fanfare, and all his descriptions are curiously laconic. It is as though he were always saying: "This is what needed to be done, and so we did it, and why make a fuss about it?" Nobody did make a fuss about it, and he had no conspicuous support. But the sort of man he was and is, and his achievements, had such inherent greatness that his name will be written in the starred records both of peace and of war.

He came to the United States and studied medicine at Johns Hopkins. "One day in the operating room there was comparative quiet, and the operating room superintendent decided to clear out all the useless broken-down surgical instruments that could no longer be repaired. I happened in as she was having the orderly take away a waste basketful of these instruments."[20] Remembering Burma and what he would find—or not find—

when he went back home, Seagrave asked for and was given that basketful. The surgical work he would do for the next five years would be done with those cast-off instruments.

In Burma again, the fledgling doctor found that he was to take over the post which had been held by the same Dr. Robert Harper who had told him stories of the jungle when he was a little boy. So he and his wife, whom he had married in America, set out from Rangoon first to Mandalay, then by river steamer three days up the Irrawaddy, and then with Chinese coolie carriers up the remaining length of Burma, through tiger and leopard country, to Namkham, at the northeast border next to China. There they inherited a hospital almost as primitive as the jungle, a rotting wooden building with twenty bare, wooden beds. The best they could say was that "if Namkham wasn't what we wanted it to be, we would get off to an early start and do something about it."[21]

Reading the pages of *Burma Surgeon* one senses always that back of the words is a man inspired by the same dedication which filled the hearts of the evangelistic preachers from whom he was descended, but a man who had no use for anything that might seem an unrelated piety. Often he must have been a trial to the more conventional minds of the American Baptist Foreign Mission, which at first gave him scanty support. Living at the edge of the jungle, he "could understand no mission work that did not care to alleviate in a really practical way the ghastly physical misery of the people. . . . If evangelistic missionaries suffered half as much at failure to 'cure' a man's 'soul' as a doctor does when he can't cure a man's body, we might get somewhere. The old-time missionaries really did."[22] And it was the unbounded devotion of "the old-time missionaries" which he repeated with his different technique. His compassion for the people, together with his down-to-earth realization of what might have to be done to help them, made him ready for whatever the next need was: whether the endless treatment of foul infections, or surgery with his wastebasket instruments, or driving in a truck two hundred and sixty miles one day—and meeting a tiger on the jungle road—to get some cement for a new building, and then building it. "Lose face?" he asked. "It is the petty person who has to fret about losing face. I can open up the manhole in our sewer system and clean it out with my bare hands in front of a crowd and not lose face thereby. In fact, the crowd will turn in and help me clean it out so they won't lose face by doing nothing when the old man is busy."[23]

Meanwhile, besides getting a new and decent hospital constructed at Namkham, Dr. Seagrave was training a body of nurses whose skill would presently become famous in the Second World War among the bitter hardships of the Burma Road. The population of Burma was a confusion of diverse and originally hostile peoples: Burmese, Kachins, Karens, Shans, and other tribes, each speaking a language not understood by the others. Seagrave began to train girls as nurses, and drew them together in a happy common loyalty to the work of the hospital and to him. He treated them "with respect and affection; affection even when an occasional nurse did not deserve affection, and respect even when it was difficult to respect many, especially in those first days when they were so dirty. A white man or woman 'respect' a native girl? Why, in the Buddhist scale, a woman is the next form of life below a male dog! Astonished at being treated with respect they tried all the harder to deserve respect. Receiving affection, they become worthy of affection. . . . The nurses did try. Bathed and bathed and bathed—until they were as clean and sweet a group of girls as you could find in any country."[24] They were quick to learn also, intelligent and efficient, and later they were to show a courage in extreme danger and a tireless endurance beyond all ordinary limits.

With the new hospital building at Namkham finished—made out of cement and cobblestones from the mountain riverbed— three smaller hospital posts, with nurses in charge, were established, thirty and forty and one hundred miles away. They were needed. In the region there were not only malignant malaria, black-water fever, and other diseases common to the jungle; an invasion of infected rats, dying in the walls, beneath the floors, dropping sometimes from the ceiling, spread bubonic plague. Then, in addition to all that, Dr. Seagrave and the few other doctors who had been drawn to him, and his nurses, had to meet the bloody backwash of the Second World War.

In a valley near Namkham there had been built an airplane factory. Shortly after the attack upon Pearl Harbor, Japanese planes poured demolition bombs upon that factory, blasting its buildings, killing and mutilating many who were caught with no escape. Other bombs fell around Namkham. Now Dr. Seagrave had to divide his work. Part of it was still continued at Namkham. But he himself and most of his nurses went out as mobile units to take care of battle casualties of the Chinese armies fighting to protect the Burma Road.

In the seven calamitous months after the attack on Pearl Harbor in December, 1941, the engulfing tide of Japanese conquests rolled on unchecked: through Malaya to Singapore, into the Netherlands East Indies and the Philippines, across the borders of Burma and over the entire country south to Rangoon. The Chinese armies on the Burma Road had been beaten and broken. Resistance now was at an end, and nothing was left but evacuation and retreat.

But under the command of General Joseph W. Stilwell, who had been sent from America to the aid of China, there began one of the epic chapters in the history of war. He led what was left of the Chinese forces and their allies, together with civilians who were imperiled by the Japanese advance, to the only way of possible escape: past the flames of bombed and burning towns and then over some of the worst terrain in the world, across the terrible mountains of North Burma, across rivers, through matted jungle trails, to Assam at the northeast corner of India. Seagrave and his Burmese nurses were in that trek, and the endurance, the cheerfulness, and the skill of these girls from Namkham gained a fame which was to increase through the years to follow.

In India, General Stilwell set himself to a task which many looked at with a supercilious skepticism, as something fantastic and impossible. What he undertook was to take what was left of the Chinese armies, beaten and partially demoralized, weakened by dysentery and malaria, and recondition them into a fighting force. Dr. Seagrave's unit, established at Ramgahr in Assam, worked under his command—waiting for the day when he and his nurses could turn their faces back to Burma and be given then what he asked for from General Stilwell—"the meanest, nastiest task of all."[25]

And that was what they got. By 1943, the disease-ridden remnants of Chinese divisions which had been brought to India had been nursed back to health, and trained by Stilwell—as many had thought they could not be trained—for effective combat. He was ready to go back. He sent his engineers to bulldoze a road—the "Lido Road"—from Northeast Assam to the Burma border and the Pansan Pass and then into Burma itself. Chinese troops were ordered forward as a screen for the engineers, and Dr. Seagrave, now commissioned a major in the United States Medical Corps, with his nurses, was sent in to follow the front line of the troops. The way led first through the wild Naga Hills, where the tribesmen until recently had been headhunters; sometimes under blazing sun and then under drenching mountain monsoonlike rains which turned the ruts of the trail where the trucks of the Chinese troops had passed into knee-deep mud; establishing casualty stations or performing operations wherever they could find or set up a bamboo shack. The Naga Hills, so-called, are mountains of incredible steepness, so that when the unit was moving, it was necessary to stop every little while to get enough breath to go on. The thick undergrowth was infested with leeches which fastened upon every human body that came near, and there was danger always of coming upon a cobra, a krait, or a Russell's viper, the deadliest three of the poisonous snakes. Along the trail there were the macabre signs of what had happened to hundreds of English and Anglo-Burmese refugees and of Chinese stragglers who had tried to find the way to India which Stilwell's group had blazed: skeletons by the tens, the twenties, the thirties where men and women and children had died of disease, or fallen exhausted on the slopes of mountains they had no strength to climb.

That was the beginning of "the way home" for the Seagrave unit. Nearly two years were to pass before they would see Namkham again. The record of what happened in that intervening time is told, at least in part, in *Burma Surgeon Returns*.[26]

"In part," because Dr. Seagrave's humorous, unruffled and self-effacing simplicity of commitment to "the meanest, nastiest task of all" never indulges in heroics; but what he and his unit did was so immense that it has needed no limelight to make it magnificent. As the fighting front went forward, the unit was always there; taking perpetual overwork and discomfort as a matter of course, ministering to the endless streams of men brought in by the litterbearers with ghastly infected wounds, or to the hundreds more who staggered from the ambulances with tropical fevers—and sometimes with cholera or smallpox. Sometimes the hospital found shelter in a half-wrecked building which had to be cleared first of its filth and foulness. By the time one place had been made decently habitable, orders would come to leave it and keep up with the front-line troops as they advanced. Operations—once one hundred ninety in a single day—might have to be performed as men still lay on the litters, under tarpaulin stretched over a broken wall and empty gasoline drums put up on top of one another. Often the hospital was within range of Japanese artillery, but everyone got used to that. At one location, "several of the men and three of the officers dug themselves trenches beside their cots, into which they flopped when the shells began to scream over. The rest of us," said Dr. Seagrave, "dug nothing. If the Japs shelled when we were not operating we crouched by the east wall of our revetment. If they shelled while we were operating, we went on operating."[27] By that kind of courage, and by his concern for all those he worked for and worked with, Dr. Seagrave communicated his spirit to the Chinese litterbearers, to the Garo porters from Assam, to his doctor associates, and above all to the tireless little nurses he had trained at Namkham, and to whom he was not only the doctor but their "Daddy." Their skill and devotion were already on the way to becoming a legend. An officer who arrived at the hospital one day announced to Dr. Seagrave: "When I was flown out to India, they asked me what famous historical sights I intended to visit and I told them there were only two famous things I wanted to see; the Taj Mahal, and Seagrave's Burmese nurses. Now let's see them!"[28]

At length they did come home, Dr. Seagrave and his nurses, to find the mission buildings mostly wrecked by the Japanese. From all the region round, the people flocked with their emotional welcome, to help him rebuild the hospital. And there through poverty, plague, and hardship, the Burma Surgeon still ministers to all who come to him, hoping—as he has written—that all Burma and countries far beyond it might "catch the spirit that seemed so beautiful to me in the girls of our unit," the girls "who had astonished not only me but a good part of the world by surmounting their racial and creedal differences for the good of their country, and had shown a spirit of selfless, untiring and loving service to the sick and wounded of all races."[29]

In a world that can so often become engrossed in its own concerns and forgetful of even the most shining facts in a far-off land, the Burma Surgeon's hospital still struggles for support. Not all that he has hoped for it has been fulfilled, but for him and in him "It was a beautiful dream—and outside the stars were shining."[30]

Thomas A. Dooley

In 1954, a young doctor, scarcely out of medical school, a lieutenant in the United States Navy, found himself in the city of Haiphong, on the Gulf of Tongking, that opens into the China Sea. The long projection of southeastern Asia, on the coast of which Haiphong is the northern port, was the French protectorate of Indochina. In the Second World War it was overrun by the armies of Japan; and after Japan's defeat, it was split into the three kingdoms of Laos, Cambodia, and Vietnam. The northern part of Vietnam was infiltrated by Communists from China, and at Dien-Bien-Phu—which to most of the Western world had previously been a meaningless name and suddenly became the focus of fascinated grim concern—a French stronghold was captured by the Communists, and the hold of France in all that region broken. By treaty, Vietnam was divided in two, the northern half to belong to a Communist regime, the southern half to establish and maintain freedom as best it could. In the treaty, it was stipulated that people in either half could migrate into the other, up to a certain deadline of time; and in 1954, refugees from the Communist north were pouring through Haiphong. The normal population of Haiphong was about one hundred thousand; but in August, 1954, that number was doubled by the refugees who swarmed through the streets and alleys and lay down in the gutters at night.

The young naval doctor who looked out on this huddled misery was Thomas A. Dooley. Vivid glimpses into what happened next come from what Dooley himself has written.[31] His commanding officer said to him, "Dooley, your job will be to build refugee camps. Get going and don't bother me with details." Not long after that the commanding officer was transferred, and the twenty-eight-year-old lieutenant was left to carry out the order that no medical-college curriculum of his had ever dealt with: to set up, organize, and run a refugee camp and hospital big enough to deal at one time with ten thousand to fifteen thousand of the ragged, half-starved people who had fled the terror in the north. What he confronted might have seemed only an impossible, dirty job in an obscure corner of the earth. What he did has become a saga of devotion of which not only Indochina but most of the Western world is now aware.

To begin with, he built the camp, with one hundred forty-nine tents sent him from Japan, set up by Moroccan soldiers lent him by the French and by two or three hundred coolies. He got machinery, a truck, water tanks, a jeep, and insecticides from ships of the American Navy—and vitamins and penicillin and band-aids and antibiotics where he could. He wrote to the great pharmaceutical companies in the United States, begging their help, and they responded. He had three medical corpsmen with him; he got as many Vietnamese nurses as he could find, and he trained some of the cleaner-looking refugees to help. Then he went to work. "Our first jobs," as he afterward wrote, "were to delouse, vaccinate, and inoculate, and to screen out all those who had communicable diseases."[32] But that was only the beginning. "So in addition we took on the job of curing the sick. We stepped up sick call and I enlarged my hospital tent for surgery."[33] By six o'clock in the morning he was in the medical tent "for the day's first assortment of tropical ailments, fractured limbs and wounds that were infected and oozed pus."[34] So it continued through the morning and the noon. At three o'clock, "when the temperature dropped to a bearable 100 degrees or so,"[35] he went to sick call, and sometimes to surgery. At five-thirty or six o'clock in the evening, he rode in a jeep to a warehouse where thousands more of refugees were quartered. "My conscience," he said, "kept driving me to do more and more . . . and . . . I could never do enough."[36] Even though he was young and strong, he had need of other resources to deal with the welter of human suffering, and the results of savage and inhuman cruelty which the refugees from the Communist side of the dividing-line brought with them; and other resources he did have. One was his religion, which was as unquestioning as a child's; another was his Irish humor. He could laugh at any glint of the ridiculous that might break through what otherwise would have been only the somber and sickening facts around him; and he could laugh at himself. One evening when he had begged an invitation to a warship because he was "in desperate need of a hot bath and a decent meal," he was flattered because the Admiral seated him at the end of the table directly facing him. But he recorded with wry amusement what the Admiral said to him: "Don't get any ideas, doctor. You just smell so bad I want you as far away as possible."[37]

The filth and misery amid which he worked did not overwhelm him. It woke in him new depths of pity and compassion. He looked at people, including the children, who "had seen death in hideous forms, had felt its shock and its terror. They had watched villages being burned and fields destroyed. But in spite of everything they still smiled, and they loved, and they made life good and complete for the rest of us."[38]

The time came when the flood of refugees, and the work with them, came to an end. Lieutenant Dooley of the Navy was back in America. What should he do next? He had wanted particularly to be a firstrate orthopedic surgeon. His professor at medical school told him that if he hoped to succeed it was time to settle down. But something more compelling would not let him go. "I could never leave behind me," he said, "the things I had seen. To me that experience had been like the white light of revelation. . . . With my own eyes I had witnessed the enormous power of medical aid in all its Christlike simplicity. Besides, I knew that the future of the world might be won—or lost—in Southeast Asia."[39]

Northern Vietnam was Communist now, and locked against him. The southern part was medically provided for. But there was Laos. He went to see the ambassador from Laos in Washington, and told him that he would volunteer for medical service among the Laotian people. Why should he be moved to do that? the ambassador wanted to know. Tom Dooley decided at that moment that the best answer he could give would be in the words of "big, hard-boiled boatswain's mate Norman Baker" who had been one of his Navy corpsmen in Haiphong: "We just want to do what we can for people who ain't got it so good!"

"My country," said the Ambassador, "would be honored to receive your mission"—his country which for nearly two million people had in it then *one* doctor recognized as trained in medicine by Western standards.[40]

Dr. Dooley went to work. He would have no government or church sponsorship or obligations. He used most of what little money he had made or saved. He begged supplies from companies which produced equipment and medicines he would need to have. He telephoned to three of his corpsmen of Haiphong: Norman Baker in San Diego, Denny Shepard in Oregon, Pete Kessey in Texas. Would they go with him to Laos?

"What! Back to Indochina? Are you crazy. You couldn't pay me to go back to that hole!"[41] But they went, all three!

In August, 1956, they were on their way to the Laotian village of Vang Vieng, at the foot of walls of rock rising three or four thousand feet into the sky, on a tributary of the Mekong River. Then began the further story of what happened, told in Dr. Dooley's books with a personal vividness which no secondhand summary can reflect: a story of abysmal human need and pathetic, patient suffering, and against it the indomitable compassion of the little group of men who had decided for themselves that "the only good reason for existence is not what you are going to get out of life but what you are going to put into it."[42]

At Vang Vieng, Dooley and his helpers found, as he admitted, a depth of misery in the midst of which they would have to work and eat and sleep and live such as even he in all his hours of planning never had foreseen. But they dealt with it, not only meeting the desperate immediate needs themselves but training some of the native personnel so that they could take over and continue. And when they could, Dr. Dooley and two volunteer replacements from America for Baker and Shepard who had finished their promised terms moved on, not out of Laos, but to the more remote village of Nam Tha; and not long thereafter Dooley went on to Muong Sing, at the extreme edge of Laos, with the border of menacing Red China only six miles away.

Then, in August, 1959, in a mud shack in Muong Sing, there was handed to Dr. Dooley a radiogram, which had been got to him through the Laos army. Recently there had been formed in the United States an organization called "Medico," inspired by what Dooley had already done, to provide medical care to the poorest of the poor, and the neediest of the needy, in threatened parts of the world. The radiogram was from Dr. Peter Comanduras, who had been made secretary-general of Medico. It read: "Dr. Dooley, urgent. Return to U. S. immediately."[43]

It was a bitter summons to receive. Why it was sent, and what it meant, Tom Dooley did not know. Must he abandon his hospital, abandon all he had done, abandon all the work of the last year? "The letters in that telegram stared up at me and stabbed my soul." [44]

There was nothing for him to do but to respond, but in a black depression because he was leaving his post when it seemed that at any hour the men he had left behind might have to face a Communist raid alone. His mind was haunted by questions he could not answer. Had Medico broken down? Would he have to stay at a New York desk to try to save it?

From Muong Sing to the Laotian capital Vientiane; to Bangkok; to Hong Kong; to London; to New York. Now he learned from Dr. Comanduras why he had been summoned home. What he had thought was an inconsequential tumor on his chest, which had been removed by surgery in Laos, had been found to be malignant cancer.

He was operated on again at Memorial Hospital in New York. Now, to his amazement, it was as though half the world had heard of him. Two or three thousand letters came to him in the hospital each day. This man who had taken upon himself so much of the tragic burden of human loneliness and pain was identified in a double way with the universal fellowship of suffering, and was to be a witness also to the gallantry of spirit which can meet and overcome disaster. Lying in his hospital bed, he remembered Muong Sing and "the night they burned the mountain." For generations every year the native people set the mountain slopes on fire before the monsoon rains, because they believed the ashes fertilized the soil for the planting of their rice. He dreamed of the burning mountain, and when the morning came, "I knew the meaning of my dream. . . . I must, into the burnt soil of my personal mountain, plant the new seedlings of my life. . . . Whatever time was left, whether it was a year or a decade, would be more than just a duration. I would continue to help the clots and clusters of withered and wretched in Asia to the utmost of my ability. The words of Camus rang through. 'In the midst of winter I suddenly found that there was in me an invincible summer.' Maybe I could now be tender in a better way."[45]

He said to himself that he would be back "home" in Laos for Christmas. He did go back; wearing round his neck a little St. Christopher's medal, on one side of which were the lines of Robert Frost which for a long time Tom Dooley had said over to himself:

> The woods are lovely, dark and deep.
> But I have promises to keep,
> And miles to go before I sleep,
> And miles to go before I sleep.[46]

He poured what strength he had into his work, with the same unlimited devotion that had been his before. "I'm not quitting," he said. "If I stop now, I'll probably die sooner."

The doctors had hoped, and even persuaded themselves to

think, that the cancer had been eliminated. But it was not so to prove. Collapsing in Laos where he had been working twenty hours a day, Tom Dooley was brought back to Memorial Hospital in New York. And there on January 18, 1961, one day after his thirty-fourth birthday, he died.

Tragically brief that eager life had seemed to be! But in the short time given to him, he had so perfected the spirit of his service that he "fulfilled a long time."

So the long succession of those who have been Men of Fire comes into the twentieth century and adds to its roll, out of contemporary life, a member of the Church of England, a German Evangelical, a Baptist, and a Roman Catholic. They, like their great forerunners, are witnesses to the eternal truth which came to them from Christ: that he who seeks his life shall lose it, and he who risks his life for the gospel saves it in the glory of his soul.

Notes

I. Peter

1. Oscar Cullman, *Peter: Disciple, Apostle, Martyr* (London: SCM Press, 1953), p. 162.
2. *Ibid.*, p. 221.
3. *Ibid.*, p. 237.
4. New York: The Century Company, 1926, p. 21.

II. Paul

1. New York: Longmans, Green and Company, 1903, p. 166.
2. Matthew Arnold, "Rugby Chapel."
3. *The Freedom of a Christian Man.* Quoted by A. C. McGiffert in *Martin Luther: The Man and His Work* (New York: The Century Company, 1911), p. 175.

III. Polycarp and Justin Martyr

1. Alexander Roberts and James Donaldson (eds.), *The Ante-Nicene Fathers* (American ed., rev. by A. Cleveland Coxe; Grand Rapids, Mich.: Wm. B. Eerdmanns Publishing Company, 1950-1951),* Vol. I, p. 33.
2. *Ibid.*, p. 35.
3. *The Encyclical Epistle of the Church at Smyrna* in *the Ante-Nicene Fathers*, Vol. I, pp. 40-42.
4. *The First Apology of Justin*, chaps. 12, 17, in *The Ante-Nicene Fathers*, Vol. I, pp. 166, 168.
5. *Ibid.*, chap. 2, in *The Ante-Nicene Fathers*, Vol I, p. 163.
6. *Dialogue with Trypho*, chap. 8, in *The Ante-Nicene Fathers*, Vol. I, p. 198.
7. *The First Apology of Justin*, chap. 66, in *The Ante-Nicene Fathers*, Vol. I, p. 185.

* This edition used throughout.

8. *Ibid.*, chap. 67, in *The Ante-Nicene Fathers*, Vol. I, p. 186.
9. *Ibid.*, chap. 46, in *The Ante-Nicene Fathers*, Vol. I, p. 178.
10. *Ibid.*, chaps. 2, 11, in *The Ante-Nicene Fathers*, Vol I, pp. 163, 166.

IV. Irenaeus

1. *The Ante-Nicene Fathers*, Vol. I, p. 568.
2. George Park Fisher, *History of Christian Doctrine* (New York: Charles Scribner's Sons, 1896).
3. Ernest F. Scott, "Gnosticism," *Encyclopedia of Religion and Ethics* (James Hastings, ed.; New York: Charles Scribner's Sons), Vol. VI (1914), p. 231.
4. *Against Heresies*, Bk. I, chap. 1, in *The Ante-Nicene Fathers*, Vol. I, p. 316.
5. *Ibid.*, Bk. II, chap. 14, in *The Ante-Nicene Fathers*, Vol. I, p. 376.
6. *The Ante-Nicene Fathers*, Vol. I, p. 574.
7. Scott, *op. cit.*, p. 241.
8. *Against Heresies*, Bk. III, chap. 4, in *The Ante-Nicene Fathers*, Vol. I, pp. 416-417.
9. *Ibid.*, Bk. III, chap. 1, in *The Ante-Nicene Fathers*, Vol. I, p. 414.
10. *Ibid.*, Bk. III, chap. 3, in *The Ante-Nicene Fathers*, Vol. I, pp. 414-415.
11. *The Ante-Nicene Fathers*, Vol. I, p. 569.
12. *Ibid.*, p. 568.

V. Tertullian

1. *History of the Christian Church* (New York: Charles Scribner's Sons, 1905), Vol. II, p. 822.
2. *Apology*, chap. 37, in *The Ante-Nicene Fathers*, Vol. III, p. 45.
3. *Ibid.*, chap. 21, in *The Ante-Nicene Fathers*, Vol. III, p. 36.
4. *Ibid.*, chap. 50, in *The Ante-Nicene Fathers*, Vol. III, p. 55.
5. *Ibid.*, chap. 45, in *The Ante-Nicene Fathers*, Vol. III, p. 50.
6. *Ibid.*, chap. 21, in *The Ante-Nicene Fathers*, Vol. III, p. 34.
7. *The Ante-Nicene Fathers*, Vol. I, p. 95.
8. *Ibid.*, p. 60.
9. *The Prescription against Heretics*, chap. 36, in *The Ante-Nicene Fathers*, Vol. III, p. 260.
10. *Ibid.*, chap. 21; *The Ante-Nicene Fathers*, Vol. III, p. 252.
11. *Apology*, chap. 39, in *The Ante-Nicene Fathers*, Vol. III, p. 46.
12. *On Fasting*, chap. 1, in *The Ante-Nicene Fathers*, Vol. IV, p. 102.
13. *Ibid.*, chap. 2, in *The Ante-Nicene Fathers*, Vol. IV, pp. 102, 103.

VI. Cyprian

1. *The Ante-Nicene Fathers,* Vol. V, pp. 267-274.
2. *Ibid.,* p. 270.
3. *Ibid.,* p. 269.
4. Philip Schaff, *History of the Christian Church* (New York: Charles Scribner's Sons, 1905), Vol. II, p. 847.
5. *Library of Christian Classics* (Philadelphia: The Westminster Press, 1956), Vol. V, pp. 124-128.
6. *Ibid.,* pp. 171-172.
7. Schaff, *op. cit.,* p. 150 n.
8. *Library of Christian Classics,* Vol. V, p. 126.
9. *The Ante-Nicene Fathers,* Vol. V, p. 263.

VII. Origen

1. *The Ante-Nicene Fathers,* Vol. IV, p. 239.
2. *A History of Christian Thought* (New York: Charles Scribner's Sons, 1932), p. 231.
3. *De Principiis,* chap. I, sections 4, 5, 6, 9.
4. *Ibid.,* chap. 2, sec. 1.
5. *The Ante-Nicene Fathers,* Vol. IV, p. 465.

VIII. Jerome

1. Edward L. Cutts (London: S.P.C.K., 1909), pp. 5, 6.
2. New York: Charles Scribner's Sons, 1905, Vol. II, p. 388.
3. *The Nicene and Post-Nicene Fathers* (Grand Rapids, Mich.: Wm. B. Eerdmans Publishing Company, 1952), Vol. VI, pp. 14, 16.
4. *Letter to Asella* in *The Nicene and Post-Nicene Fathers,* Vol. VI, p. 59.
5. *Letter to Eustochium* in *The Nicene and Post-Nicene Fathers,* Vol. VI, p. 34.
6. *Ibid.,* p. 32.
7. New York: Longmans, Green and Company, 1903, p. 368.
8. William Smith and Henry Wace (eds.), *Dictionary of Christian Biography* (London: John Murray, 1882).
9. "Jerome," *The Encyclopaedia of Religion and Ethics* (James Hastings, ed.; New York: Charles Scribner's Sons), Vol. VII, (1915), p. 500.

IX. Aurelius Augustine

1. A. A. Bevan, "Manichaeism," *Encyclopaedia of Religion and Ethics* (James Hastings, ed.; New York: Charles Scribner's Sons), Vol. VIII (1916), p. 397.
2. *Confessions*, Bk. VIII, 12.
3. *Ibid.*, 15.
4. *Ibid.*, 16, 18.
5. *Ibid.*, 29.
6. Edward L. Cutts (London: S.P.C.K., 1909), p. 67.
7. *The Varieties of Religious Experience* (New York: Longmans, Green and Company, 1903), p. 173.
8. *Confessions*, Bk. I, 1.

X. Monks and Missionaries

1. *Against Heresies*, Bk. IV, chap. 30, in *The Ante-Nicene Fathers*, Vol. I, p. 503.
2. Montalembert, *The Monks of the West* (Boston: Patrick Donahue, 1872), Vol. I, p. 166.
3. *Ibid.*, p. 164.
4. Morris L. West, *The Devil's Advocate* (New York: William Morrow and Company, 1959), p. 52.
5. Montalembert, *op. cit.*, p. 333.
6. *Ibid.*, p. 204.
7. *Ibid.*, p. 318.

XI. Francis of Assisi

1. Paul Sabatier, *Life of St. Francis of Assisi* (London: Hodder and Stoughton, 1913), Vol. I, p. xxv.
2. John R. H. Moorman, *Saint Francis of Assisi* (London: SCM Press, 1950), p. 25.
3. Sabatier, *op. cit.*, pp. 71-72.
4. Moorman, *op. cit.*, p. 34.
5. *Ibid.*, p. 87.
6. Henry Bradford Washburn, *Men of Conviction* (New York: Charles Scribner's Sons, 1931), p. 165.
7. F. R. Barry, *The Relevance of Christianity* (London: Nisbet and Company, 1931), pp. 81, 83.
8. Catherine De Hueck Doherty, *Religious Education*, Nov., 1959.

XII. Martin Luther

1. Thomas M. Lindsay, *A History of the Reformation: in Germany* (New York: Charles Scribner's Sons, 1906), pp. 2, 4.
2. *Ibid.*, p. 17.
3. Roland Bainton, *Here I Stand* (Nashville: Abingdon Press, 1950), p. 30.
4. Erik H. Erikson, *Young Man Luther* (New York: W. W. Norton and Company, 1958), p. 50.
5. *Ibid.*, pp. 164, 125.
6. Bainton, *op. cit.*, p. 65; A. C. McGiffert, *Martin Luther* (New York: The Century Company, 1911), p. 175.
7. Bainton, *op. cit.*, p. 174.
8. Lindsay, *op. cit.*, pp. 279-290.

XIII. John Wycliffe and William Tyndale

1. New York: Harper & Brothers, 1882, pp. 256-257.
2. Luther A. Weigle, *The English New Testament* (Nashville: Abingdon Press, 1949), p. 31.
3. *Ibid.*, p. 32.
4. Gordon Rupp, *Six Makers of English Religion* (New York: Harper & Brothers, 1957), pp. 13, 14.
5. J. F. Mozley, *William Tyndale* (New York: The Macmillan Company, 1937), pp. 9, 10.
6. *Ibid.*, pp. 26, 28.
7. *Ibid.*, p. 36.

XIV. John Calvin

1. Thomas M. Lindsay, *A History of the Reformation: in the Lands beyond Germany* (New York: Charles Scribner's Sons, 1907), p. 11.

XV. John Knox

1. Quoted material in this chapter comes from John Knox, *History of the Reformation of Religion in Scotland* (Glasgow: Blackie and Son, 1832).

XVI. Roger Williams, William Carey, and Adoniram Judson

1. Emily Easton, *Roger Williams: Prophet and Pioneer* (Boston: Houghton Mifflin Company, 1930), p. 136.
2. *Ibid.*, p. 153.
3. *Ibid.*, pp. 137-138.
4. *Ibid.*, pp. 173, 177.
5. *Ibid.*, p. 168.
6. *Ibid.*, p. 177.
7. *Ibid.*, p. 179.
8. *Ibid.*, p. 190.
9. *Ibid.*, p. 170.
10. *Ibid.*, pp. 258, 263, 264.
11. *Ibid.*, p. 354.
12. *Ibid.*, p. 274.
13. *Ibid.*, p. 298.
14. George Smith, *The Life of William Carey* (New York: E. P. Dutton, 1887), p. 7.
15. *Ibid.*, p. 12.
16. *Ibid.*, p. 23.
17. *Idem.*
18. *Ibid.*, pp. 25, 66.
19. *Ibid.*, pp. 37, 38.
20. *Ibid.*, p. 38.
21. *Ibid.*, p. 58.
22. *Ibid.*, p. 303.
23. Edward Judson, *The Life of Adoniram Judson* (Philadelphia: American Baptist Publication Society, 1883).
24. *Ibid.*, p. 33.
25. *Ibid.*, p. 20.
26. *Idem.*
27. *Ibid.*, p. 76.
28. *Ibid.*, p. 78.
29. *Ibid.*, p. 95.
30. *Ibid.*, p. 104.
31. *Ibid.*, p. 90.
32. *Ibid.*, p. 163.
33. *Ibid.*, p. 195.

XVII. John Wesley

1. John Beresford (ed.), *Diary of a Country Parson* (London: Oxford University Press, 1924), Vol. I, p. 38.

2. *Ibid.*
3. *Ibid.*, pp. 6, 46, 301, 302.
4. G. Elsie Harrison, *Son to Susanna* (Nashville: Abingdon Press, 1938), p. 33.

XVIII. Frederick W. Robertson and Phillips Brooks

1. Stopford A. Brooke, *Life and Letters of Frederick W. Robertson* (New York: Harper & Brothers, 1865), p. xii.
2. *Ibid.*, p. vii.
3. *Ibid.*, p. 134.
4. *Ibid.*, p. 364.
5. Alexander V. G. Allen, *Life of Phillips Brooks* (New York: E. P. Dutton and Company, 1901), Vol. I, p. 170.
6. Allen, *op. cit.*, pp. 85-86.
7. New York: E. P. Dutton and Company, 1907, p. 34.

XIX. The Continuing Flame

1. J. Lennox Kerr, *Wilfred Grenfell: His Life and Work* (New York: Dodd Mead and Company, 1959), p. 19.
2. *Ibid.*, p. 39.
3. *Ibid.*, p. 43.
4. *Ibid.*, p. 70.
5. Boston: The Pilgrim Press, 1910, pp. 27, 30.
6. Albert Schweitzer, *Out of My Life and Thought* (New York: Henry Holt and Company, 1933), p. 25.
7. *Ibid.*, p. 43.
8. *Ibid.*, p. 85.
9. *Ibid.*, p. 87.
10. *Ibid.*, p. 95.
11. *Ibid.*, p. 108.
12. *Ibid.*, p. 111.
13. Norman Cousins, *Dr. Schweitzer of Lambaréné* (New York: Harper & Brothers, 1960), p. 191.
14. Schweitzer, *op. cit.*, p. 143.
15. Cousins, *op. cit.*, p. 11.
16. *Ibid.*
17. Hermann Hagedorn, *Prophet in the Wilderness* (New York: The Macmillan Company, 1954), p. 172.
18. *Ibid.*, p. 188.
19. Gordon S. Seagrave, *Burma Surgeon* (New York: W. W. Norton and Company, 1943), pp. 11, 12.

20. *Ibid.*, p. 18.
21. *Ibid.*, p. 26.
22. *Ibid.*, p. 67.
23. *Ibid.*, p. 45.
24. *Ibid.*, p. 40.
25. Gordon S. Seagrave, *Burma Surgeon Returns* (New York: W. W. Norton and Company, 1946), p. 12.
26. *Ibid.*
27. *Ibid.*, p. 150.
28. *Ibid.*, p. 17.
29. *Ibid.*, p. 268.
30. *Idem.*
31. Thomas A. Dooley, *Dr. Tom Dooley, My Story* (New York: Ariel Books, 1960).
32. *Ibid.*, p. 15.
33. *Ibid.*, p. 16.
34. *Ibid.*, p. 18.
35. *Ibid.*, p. 19.
36. *Ibid.*, p. 20.
37. *Ibid.*, pp. 20-21.
38. *Ibid.*, p. 35.
39. *Ibid.*, pp. 59, 61.
40. *Ibid.*, p. 63.
41. *Ibid.*, p. 65.
42. *The Night They Burned the Mountain* (New York: Farrar, Straus, and Cudahy, 1960), p. 93.
43. *Ibid.*, p. 10.
44. *Ibid.*, p. 11.
45. *Ibid.*, pp. 183-184.
46. *The Collected Poems of Robert Frost* (New York: Henry Holt, 1949), p. 275.